The World's Best Bathroom Book

An Inspirational Collection
of Wit, Wisdom, Humor, and
Fascinating Facts

HONOR HB BOOKS

Inspirations and Motivation for the Seasons of Life
An Imprint of Cook Communications Ministries • Colorado Springs, CO

The World's Best Bathroom Book: An Inspirational Collection of Wit, Wisdom, Humor, and Fascinating Facts

ISBN: 1-56292-726-4
Copyright © by Bordon Books

Manuscript developed by Betsy Williams, Elece Hollis, Barbara Scott, Rebecca Currington, Christi Flagg, Patricia Lutherbeck, Shanna Gregor in association with SnapdragonGroup Editorial Services.

Contents

Introduction

What do you like to read? Something that inspires you, lifts your spirit, makes you stop and think, piques your curiosity? Maybe you like interesting facts and figures, mental challenges, or heartwarming stories. You might even be looking for some serious spiritual encouragement.

Whether you like to read in the bathroom, beside the pool, in a comfortable chair, or some other favorite place, *The World's Best Bathroom Book* is the book you'll want to have with you. Whether you prefer to read alone, to your children, or with a group of friends, it's the one you'll keep close by.

We've filled the pages of this wonderful book with a little something to suit every interest. And yet the presentation makes it easy to read just a little at a time or quite a lot. There are plenty of items to read alone and even more to share.

It's our prayer that you will enjoy this book as much as we enjoyed putting it together. God bless you as you read.

THE PUBLISHERS

YOU CAN SAY THAT AGAIN!

Humorous Quotations

I have enough money to last me the rest of my life,
unless I buy something.

JACKIE MASON

✳

The trouble with life in the fast lane is that
you get to the other end in an awful hurry.

JOHN JENSEN

✳

Groundhog Day has been observed only once
in Los Angeles, because when the groundhog came out of
its hole, it was killed by a mudslide.

JOHNNY CARSON

✳

I just got wonderful news from my real-estate agent in
Florida. They found land on my property.

MILTON BERLE

✳

The cost of living is going up,
and the chance of living is going down.

FLIP WILSON

✳

Somewhere on this globe, every ten seconds,
there is a woman giving birth to a child.
She must be found and stopped.

SAM LEVENSON

✳

Tell the truth and run.

YUGOSLAVIAN PROVERB

✳

Gravity isn't easy, but it's the law.

AUTHOR UNKNOWN

✳

Oh well, half of one, six dozen of the other.

JOE GARAGIOLA

✳

I locked my keys in the car and had to
break the windshield to get my wife out.

RED SKELTON

✳

The two biggest sellers in any bookstore are
the cookbooks and the diet books. The cookbooks tell you
how to prepare the food, and the diet books tell you how
not to eat any of it.

ANDY ROONEY

✳

The most remarkable thing about my mother is that for
thirty years she served the family nothing but
leftovers. The original meal has never been found.

CALVIN TRILLIN

✳

Always go to other people's funerals.
Otherwise, they won't come to yours.

YOGI BERRA

✳

Philosophical Quotations

The happiness of life is made up of minute fractions—the little, soon forgotten charities of a kiss or smile, a kind look, a heartfelt compliment, and the countless infinitesimals of pleasurable and genial feeling.

COLERIDGE

*

The difficulties, hardships, and trials of life, the obstacles one encounters on the road to fortune are positive blessings. They knit the muscles more firmly and teach self-reliance. Peril is the element in which power is developed.

W. MATHEWS

*

The world is full of cactus,
but we don't have to sit on it.

WILL FOLEY

*

An acre of performance is worth
a whole world of promise.

W. D. HOWELLS

*

The shortest and surest way to live with honor
in the world is to be in reality what we would appear to be;
and if we observe, we shall find that all human virtues
increase and strengthen themselves by the practice
and experience of them.

ARISTOTLE

✳

There are joys which long to be ours.
God sends ten thousand truths, which come about us like
birds seeking inlet; but we are shut up to them,
and so they bring us nothing, but sit and sing
awhile upon the roof, and then fly away.

HENRY WARD BEECHER

✳

From the little spark may burst a mighty flame.

DANTE

✳

In actual life, every great enterprise begins with and takes
its first forward step in faith.

SCHLEGEL

✳

Each day of your life, as soon as you open your eyes in the
morning, you can square away for a happy and successful
day. It's the mood and the purpose at the inception of each
day that are the important facts in charting your course for
the day. We can always square away for a fresh start, no
matter what the past has been. It's today that is the
paramount problem always. Yesterday is but history.

GEORGE MATTHEW ADAMS

✳

It's great to be great, but it's greater to be human.

WILL ROGERS

✳

Do not waste a minute—not a second—in trying to demonstrate to others the merits of your performance. If your work does not vindicate itself, you cannot vindicate it.

THOMAS W. HIGGINSON

✳

We live in deeds, not years; in thoughts, not figures on a dial. We should count time by heart throbs. He most lives who thinks most, feels the noblest, acts the best.

PHILIP JAMES BAILEY

✳

No matter how small and unimportant what we are doing may seem, if we do it well, it may soon become the step that will lead us to better things.

CHANNING POLLOCK

✳

Good men are not cheap.
Capital can do nothing without brains to direct it.
No general can fight his battles alone. He must depend upon his lieutenants, and his success depends upon his ability to secure the right man for the right place.
There is no such thing as luck.
Most men talk too much. Much of my success has been due to keeping my mouth shut.
The young man who wants to marry happily should pick out a good mother and marry one of her daughters—any one will do.

J. OGDEN ARMOUR

✳

Inspirational Quotations

When we are wrong, make us willing to change.
And when we are right, make us easy to live with.

PETER MARSHALL

✳

Never be afraid to trust an unknown future
to a known God.

CORRIE TEN BOOM

✳

Everything that is done in this world is done by hope.

MARTIN LUTHER

✳

The most beautiful thing we can experience is the
mysterious. It is the source of all true art and science. He to
whom the emotion is a stranger, who can no longer pause
to wonder and stand wrapped in awe, is as good as dead;
his eyes are closed. The insight into the mystery of life,
coupled though it be with fear, has also given rise to
religion. To know what is impenetrable to us really exists,
manifesting itself as the highest wisdom and the most
radiant beauty, which our dull faculties can comprehend
only in their most primitive forms—this knowledge, this
feeling is at the center of true religiousness.

ALBERT EINSTEIN

✳

Faith is positive, enriching life in the here and now.
Doubt is negative, robbing life of glow and meaning.
So though I do not understand immortality,
I choose to believe.

WEBB B. GARRISON

✳

Talent is God-given; be thankful.
Conceit is self-given; be careful.

THOMAS LA MANCE

✳

God's promises are sealed to us, but not dated.

SUSANNA WESLEY

✳

God: All other beings are distinguished by their shadow,
but he is distinguished by his light.

JOSEPH JOUBERT

✳

We must wait for God, long, meekly, in the wind and wet,
in the thunder and lightning, in the cold and the dark.
Wait, and he will come. He never comes to those
who do not wait.

FREDERICK WILLIAM FABER

✳

The greatest word is God. The deepest word is soul.
The longest word is eternity. The swiftest word is time.
The nearest word is now. The darkest word is sin.
The meanest word is hypocrisy. The broadest word is truth.
The strongest word is right. The tenderest word is love.
The sweetest word is home. The dearest word is mother.

JAMES L. GORDON

*

Man is born broken. He lives by mending.
The grace of God is glue.

EUGENE GLADSTONE O'NEILL

*

Many live in dread of what is coming. Why should we?
The unknown puts adventure into life. It gives us something
to sharpen our souls on. The unexpected around the corner
gives us a sense of anticipation and surprise. Thank God for
the unknown future. If we saw all good things which are
coming to us, we would sit down and degenerate.
If we saw all the evil things, we would be paralyzed.
How merciful God is to lift the curtain on today;
and as we get strength today to meet tomorrow,
then to lift the curtain on the morrow.
He is a considerate God.

E. STANLEY JONES

*

Our concepts of measurement embrace mountains and men,
atoms and stars, gravity, energy, numbers, speed, but never
God. We cannot speak of measure or amount or size or
weight and at the same time be speaking of God,
for these tell of degrees and there are no degrees in God.
All that he is he is without growth or
addition or development.

A. W. TOZER

*

INSPIRATIONAL PROFILES

Neil Armstrong
(1930—)

From the time he was a boy, Neil Armstrong wanted to fly. He took his first airplane ride when he was six years old and began to build model airplanes at age nine. As a teenager, he got a job after school to earn money for flying lessons, and on his sixteenth birthday, two years after he began taking lessons, he passed his flying test and became a pilot.

In an attempt to study aeronautical engineering, Armstrong enrolled in Purdue University; but the Korean War began about the same time. Armstrong became a fighter pilot in the United States Navy and flew seventy-eight flights in his three years in Korea. He was shot down behind enemy lines on one flight; and on another, he flew a damaged plane to safe landing on an aircraft carrier. He was awarded three Air Medals.

As a result of his well-known piloting skills, he was asked to become a test pilot after he left the Navy and had finished his degree at Purdue. As a test pilot, many of the planes he flew had never been flown before. One such plane was the X-15—part airplane and part rocket. In flying the X-15, Armstrong flew 3,989 miles an hour and as high as thirty-eight miles above the earth's surface. No other airplane had ever flown as fast or as high.

Armstrong became part of NASA in the 1960s with the start of the Gemini program. In 1966, he was launched into space for the first time in Gemini 8. The mission was intended to connect the Gemini 8 craft with another spacecraft; but during a test hookup, the two spacecraft began to tumble out of control. Armstrong made quick decisions that allowed the craft to return safely to earth.

While testing a Lunar Landing Research Vehicle (LLRV) at an air base in Houston in 1968, Armstrong nearly lost his life. He was able to pull the eject handle and parachute to safety just moments before the LLRV crashed into the ground. He later said, "The only damage to me was that I bit my tongue."

In 1969, Armstrong was aboard Apollo 11 with astronauts Edwin "Buzz" Aldrin Jr. and Michael Collins as it was launched at Cape Canaveral, Florida. Three days later, the men found themselves in an orbit around the moon, 240,000 miles from earth.

On July 20, 1969, Armstrong and Aldrin flew the landing craft Eagle away from the Apollo 11 command module. After navigating his way around an area covered with large rocks, Armstrong found a safe place for the lunar module to land. As he brought the craft to rest on the moon's surface, he radioed back a simple message, "Tranquility Base here. The Eagle has landed."

After several hours of preparation, Armstrong opened the Eagle door, climbed slowly down a ladder, and set foot on the moon. Millions around the world applauded. Armstrong's statement upon touching the moon's surface has been echoed through the decades: "That's one small step for man, one giant leap for mankind." He and Aldrin left a message on the moon that was signed by the three astronauts and President Richard Nixon. It read, "Here men from the planet earth first set foot upon the moon July 1969, A.D. We came in peace for all mankind."

Clara Barton
(1821-1912)

I don't know how long it has been since my ear has been free from the roll of the drum," Clara wrote to her father. "It is the music I sleep by, and I love it."

Although she was timid, Clara Barton seemed to have two passions from the time she was a child—a desire to enlist in the military, which was impossible for her as a woman, and a desire to help others. Her first experience in "helping" came when she was eleven. For two years, she nursed her brother David, who was injured in a fall. Later, during a smallpox epidemic she nursed her neighbors. Clara, however, did not pursue a career in nursing. Rather, she became a teacher at age fifteen and taught for eighteen years. She began a school for poor children of sawmill workers in Massachusetts and later founded a public school in Bordentown, New Jersey. Her school grew to sixty students in two years, at which time the board selected a man to run it, saying "The job was too important for a woman to hold." Clara promptly resigned and, in anger, moved to Washington, D.C., where she took a job in the Patent Office.

From childhood, Clara idolized her father, a soldier who taught her to be a superb horsewoman and a dead shot with a revolver. She was strong physically and could handle a saw and a hammer, as well as a wagon team. When the Civil War broke out, it seemed only natural for her to get involved. She advertised for food and medical supplies for the wounded and then organized their distribution. Her efforts took her and her mule trains of supplies to the front lines. She refused to allow the Army to have any control over her activities, thus sidestepping bureaucratic delays. She received no government financial backing, but rather she raised virtually all of her operational funds from private donors. In addition to her supply-line work, she was the supervisor of nurses at a field hospital. Her efforts opened the way for other women to serve in battlefield hospitals.

After the war ended, Barton organized a search for missing soldiers and was able to locate more than 22,000 missing men in four years. Four years later, she went to Europe and became involved there with the International Red Cross. In 1881, she and several friends founded the American National Red Cross Society, and Barton served as president. Her goal differed slightly from that of the international group—Barton believed the Red Cross should help not only wounded soldiers but also victims of natural disasters. Only months after the Society was established, it sent volunteers and more than $80,000 in supplies to an area of Michigan devastated by a forest fire.

Barton worked for twelve years to convince the United States to officially join the International Red Cross, but she eventually succeeded. Her efforts at marshaling forces to aid in disasters were so effective in the United States that the International Red Cross eventually adopted a similar stance, expanding its purpose to the meeting of needs that were not related to the battlefield.

In spite of her own frail health, Clara Barton worked tirelessly in her Red Cross role until she was in her nineties.

Ludwig van Beethoven
(1770-1827)

What word do you use to describe a musician who is an accomplished pianist by the age of ten and whose compositions are published by age thirteen? What word befits a musician who is a paid professional organist at eleven and a member of the court musical staff at thirteen? Virtuoso! It is a word often associated with Ludwig van Beethoven.

What few do not know is the tragic side of Beethoven's early years. As a black-haired, swarthy-complexioned, pockmarked youngster, Beethoven was taunted by name-callers in his hometown along the Rhine River, an area of blond children. When his alcoholic father discovered his talent, he determined that the young Ludwig become his financial support, and he insisted that Ludwig become a slave to the keyboard. Herr Pfeiffer, a talented musician who was also an alcoholic, became Ludwig's live-in teacher, and thus, at age nine Ludwig had two difficult taskmasters to please. Beethoven later said that he could recall no moments of childhood happiness. His life had been one of work, tears, beatings, lessons, and angry tirades from his father. Although she was gentle and understanding, his mother was overworked and afraid of life—her greatest encouragement to Beethoven was this advice: "Be strong, my son. Be strong. Someday you will be great."

As a young man, Beethoven's brilliance at the keyboard won him the applause of Vienna, praise from Mozart, and Haydn as a teacher. His compositions were not as well received since they broke the "rules" of music in his day. His impatience with high society was not forgiven. And all the while, Beethoven struggled against yet another unseen enemy: deafness.

Beethoven first began to lose his hearing in his twenties, and by his late forties, he was totally deaf. He declared, however, "I will grapple with Fate; it shall never drag me down." When he could no longer play in public because of his deafness, he threw all of his energies into composing. He withdrew to a great extent from society, and in spite of illness—near constant gout and growing rheumatism—he continued to say to himself, "Courage! My spirit shall rule." His years of deafness became his most prolific.

In all, Beethoven composed nine symphonies, thirty-two piano sonatas, five piano concertos, ten sonatas for the piano and violin, a series of string quartets, vocal music, theater music, and much more. His compositions greatly influenced later composers such as Brahms, Wagner, Schubert, and Tchaikovsky. He is credited with expanding the size of orchestras, lengthening symphonies, placing increasing value on piano, and marking the transition from the classical to romantic style of music.

Near death, Beethoven knew that the world had not understood him or his music, but with a happy smile on his face, he whispered, "I shall hear in Heaven."

Corrie ten Boom
(1892-1983)

Corrie ten Boom's early life seemed normal and average in every way. She grew up as one of four children born to a devout Dutch Reformed family that had been watchmakers for generations. The family's business contacts with Jewish suppliers in Germany first alerted the ten Booms to the dangers of Nazism. Willem, Corrie's brother, joined the Dutch underground to help provide escape routes for Jews seeking to leave Germany. Word spread quickly among the Jews that the ten Boom family— which by the time World War II arrived consisted of the father and two unmarried daughters—could be trusted. The hidden passages and attic nooks of their three-story house became a sanctuary for hunted Jews.

In 1944, exactly a hundred years after her grandfather began a Christian prayer meeting for the purpose of praying for the Jewish people, Corrie ten Boom, her sister, and her father were arrested by the Gestapo after they were betrayed by a fellow Dutchman who suspected them of being Jewish sympathizers. Amazingly, the Jewish fugitives hidden in their home escaped detection.

Corrie and her sister, Betsy, were imprisoned at Ravensbruck, a notorious women's death camp, and their father languished in a prison cell until he died a few months later. At Ravensbruck, Corrie and Betsy encouraged the women around them to trust God, and at night, they huddled together and read the Bible and prayed aloud to inspire faith in the prisoners. Betsy died on Christmas Day, and Corrie was released soon afterwards through a "clerical error." The remaining women in her age group were exterminated a week after her release.

Calling herself an "old maid in her mid-fifties," Corrie devoted the next thirty-three years of her life to telling the story of God's faithfulness in her time of pain and misery. She traveled to sixty-four nations, telling her story and speaking against the injustices and anti-Semitism that had caused the Holocaust. Her book, *Tramp for the Lord*, and her autobiography that became a movie, *The Hiding Place*, brought her international notoriety.

One of the most difficult moments of her life was her return to Ravensbruck in 1947. She traveled to Germany to share the gospel with the German people, telling them that God's love and forgiveness extended to all people, even to those who had actively participated in exterminating the Jews. At the close of the meeting, she found herself face-to-face with one of the most cruel and despicable guards from Ravensbruck. She later reflected: "It could not have been many seconds that he stood there—hand held out—but to me it seemed hours as I wrestled with the most difficult thing I ever had to do." Then, recognizing that she had to forgive even as Christ had forgiven her, she extended her hand to this man. The experience led her to proclaim to audiences around the world, "Jesus is Victor," and that in Christ, "we can be more than conquerors." She had validated her message of God's mercy and love in her own life.

George Washington Carver
(1864-1943)

George Washington Carver was born during the Civil War in Missouri, and since his mother was a slave of Moses Carver, he was known in his early years simply as "Carver's George." Moses Carver was a hard-working farmer who did not approve of slavery but had no other way of acquiring farmhands. The Carvers raised George as they would have raised a son, giving him a few chores to do and allowing him to explore the woods after his chores were finished. He became fascinated with the natural world.

With their blessing, George left the Carvers to search for a Negro school when he was just a boy. He earned a living as a cook, house-worker, laundryman, and seamster. It was when he enrolled at school that he adopted the name "George Washington Carver." When he felt he was ready, he applied to colleges and was eventually accepted at Simpson College in Iowa. Then in 1894, he transferred from there to Iowa State College. Upon graduation, he was offered a faculty post teaching systematic botany.

In 1896, the administrators at Tuskegee Institute in Alabama offered Professor Carver the opportunity to head its newly formed department of agriculture, and he jumped at the opportunity, even though the department was largely "on paper only." Carver put together a laboratory and began the work that would become his life. He began a campaign of education for every farmer he met. He taught farmers to rotate their crops and single-handedly launched and promoted the peanut industry as an alternative to cotton. He identified one hundred and forty-five useful products made from peanuts and lobbied hard for a tariff on peanuts so the peanut industry might develop.

He also developed a number of medicines from barks and herbs, discovered unusual dyes and pigments, and found countless new uses for old products—and he never took out a patent or sought to commercialize his findings. He was interested only in helping other human beings. Above all, he valued a simple life of research and teaching. He received numerous awards and honors in agricultural chemistry, both in the United States and England, and in later years he poured his life's savings into the Carver Foundation for agricultural research. He and President Franklin Delano Roosevelt spoke often of their joint desire to see people everywhere "better fed, better housed, and better clothed."

Also an artist, Carver never thought it unusual that he enjoyed embroidery, knitting, crochet, and painting. He enjoyed designing unusual patterns and working with different textures. Painting, creating, and collecting delicate handicrafts were his lifelong hobbies.

Carver was never ashamed of his faith. When a reporter once asked him about his philosophy of life, he replied, "I go into the woods, and there I gather specimens and study the great lessons that Nature is eager to teach us. Alone in the woods each morning I best hear and understand God's plan for me."

Christopher Columbus
(1451-1506)

Although some argue as to whether Christopher Columbus was the first European to "discover" America, few debate his role as the first to open up a way for exploring and settling a "new world."

In his lifetime, however, Columbus was not regarded as a hero. He was scorned and ridiculed during his long years of preparation as being a half-insane fanatic, and he was often neglected or abused after his voyages. In actuality, he was a clear-thinking man of great faith, who faced an opposition that would have left a less-committed person completely overwhelmed.

"Christoforo Columbo" was an Italian who grew up with a love for the sea. He went to sea as a teenager and made possible voyages to England and Iceland. He became an excellent mapmaker in the process. It was after marrying a woman in Lisbon that he came into possession of her family's navigational charts. Those charts, along with his own experience and his reading of the adventures of Marco Polo, made him determined to find a direct route to the East.

The idea of a "round" earth was proposed by Aristotle, but even in Columbus's time, few believed it. Columbus was willing to risk his life to find out. He began immediately to seek funding for a voyage. After being turned down in Genoa and Portugal, he went to Spain and spent years presenting his case to Queen Isabella and King Ferdinand. From time to time he retreated to monasteries to rest, and while at a convent at La Rahiba, he met Juan Perez, Queen Isabella's former confessor. Perez wrote a letter to the queen on Columbus's behalf, and the queen subsequently sold some of her personal jewels to outfit three vessels for the voyage, the largest of which was only 163 feet long.

On August 3, 1492, Columbus set sail from Palos—sailing straight into the "Sea of Darkness." They sailed for weeks without any sign of land. Even when the crew threatened mutiny, Columbus remained firm and refused to turn back. Signs of land eventually appeared, and early in the morning on October 12, the ships landed. Columbus named the landing site San Salvador (now a Bahamian Island). In December he landed at "Espanola" (now Haiti).

Columbus made three more voyages to the Western Hemisphere. During the third voyage he was greatly discouraged to find his "colonies" in disarray and tried in vain to restore order. A governor sent from Spain placed him in chains and had him sent back to Spain. In 1502, he made his fourth voyage but again encountered difficulties as well as personal illness. He died in disappointment in 1506, never knowing the lands he had discovered were not Japan.

Throughout his life, Columbus had a strong sense of spiritual vision regarding his voyages. His first act upon landing at San Salvador was to plant a cross and to commission his sailors to preach the gospel to those they might encounter. He spoke often of being under the illumination of the Holy Spirit. In 1502, he wrote to Ferdinand and Isabella: "In the carrying out of this enterprise of the Indies, neither reason nor mathematics nor maps were any use to me: fully accomplished were the words of Isaiah" (regarding the gathering of the remnant of Israel in the last day).

Jacques-Ives Cousteau
(1910-1997)

Jacques Cousteau once said, "When I was four or five years old, I loved touching water. Water fascinated me—first floating ships, then me floating and stones not floating." Cousteau developed two other great loves in his life: gadgets and filmmaking. He spent his life combining his three passions.

His father was an international business manager, and the family traveled a great deal. Cousteau was born in a village near Bordeaux, France. The young Cousteau made his first underwater dive at a summer camp in Vermont when he was ten years old, helping clear a lake of dead twigs and branches.

At age eleven, he built a model of a machine for loading cargo onto ships. Two years later, he wrote and published on a mimeograph machine his own book, *An Adventure in Mexico*. Next, he bought a secondhand movie camera and printed stationery: "FILMS ZIX—Jack Cousteau producer, director, and chief camera man." His father confiscated the stationery, however, until his schoolwork improved!

At age nineteen, Cousteau entered the French Naval Academy because, in his words, "I thought it was a good way to go places." Four years later, he was a naval officer. Then, tragedy struck. He was seriously injured in an automobile accident and for months could not move either arm. Much of his effort to regain the use and strength of his arms involved swimming in the sea. His first underwater dive with goggles gave his life a new direction.

In 1937, he married Simone Melchior, who also had a great love for the sea, and they, along with their two sons, began a lifetime pursuit of experiments and the invention of devices to make underwater exploration easier. Cousteau and French engineer Emile Gagnan developed a Self-Contained Underwater Breathing Apparatus—scuba for short—that was patented under the name "Aqua-Lung." The world that Cousteau discovered on his Aqua-Lung dives was one he wanted to share. He developed a watertight case for his old movie camera and began to take the world's first underwater pictures. During World War II, the French military assigned him to full-time underwater research, which included locating and dismantling underwater mines, finding shipwrecks, and filming torpedoes launched from submarines. Two of his films won prizes at the new Cannes Film Festival.

In 1950, Cousteau began a new chapter in ocean research with the outfitting of a ship he named *Calypso*. His motto became, "We must go and see for ourselves." In Calypso, he and his crew of scientists traveled from the Amazon to the Red Sea, Alaska to Antarctica. The French government, along with family and friends, financed his early expeditions. His wife even sold her jewelry to help pay the bills. Later, earnings from books, films, and American television networks provided the funding he needed. In all, he wrote more than fifty books and made more than sixty television documentaries about life under the sea. In 1973, he formed the Cousteau Society to help combat the pollution of the world's oceans and waterways.

Marie Curie
(1867-1934)

Little Marie had no idea why her beautiful and loving mother never kissed her. It was only after her mother died when Marie was eleven that she learned her mother had tuberculosis. Her mother's death only compounded the sorrow Marie had felt at the death of her older sister. Their deaths were the first of many hardships and sorrows she would face in her life.

At age nineteen, Marie left her poverty-stricken home to take a position as a governess. For three years, she taught in an environment that left her feeling lonely and unhappy. She sent every extra penny she earned to help her brother get an education. When her brother finished his schooling, Marie saved her money to buy a one-way, fourth-class ticket to Paris. There, she began her own university studies. She found that her scientific studies, especially, were more exciting than any fairy tale she had ever read.

As a student, Marie lived as simply and cheaply as possible, traveling to the university on foot in all kinds of weather and spending her evenings at the library so she didn't have to heat her small rented room. She continued this way through a master's degree and then two more degrees—one in physics, one in mathematics. She did not seem to mind her poverty. She was enthralled with her studies and her friends, one of whom was Pierre Curie, a fellow scientist devoted to research. They were married without fanfare. In fact, when a friend insisted on buying her wedding dress, Marie said, "If you are going to be kind enough to give me one, please let it be practical and dark, so that I can put it on afterward to go into the laboratory."

Marie was relentless in her determination to isolate radium, scorning fatigue and financial problems, not to mention a damp, icy-cold shed that was the Curies' laboratory. She often forgot to eat or sleep. In the end, they succeeded—she and Pierre won the Nobel Prize in 1903 for their discovery of radium. No woman had ever achieved such acclaim in science. The Curies might have profited greatly from their research and fame, but they decided neither to take out patents nor to profit materially from their discovery.

Only three years later, Pierre was killed in a street accident in Paris. At age thirty-eight, Marie entered a new realm of loneliness and sadness. She continued her work, however, without giving in to her anguish. In 1911, she was awarded the Nobel Prize in chemistry, becoming the first person to receive the Nobel Prize twice.

When World War I began, Marie gave all she had to assist the French. She installed her X-ray apparatus wherever it was most needed and helped surgeons in their operations. She is estimated to have installed more than two hundred radiological rooms, which were used to help more than a million soldiers.

In her later years, Madame Curie suffered ill health and experienced degenerating eyesight. A professor noted, "Madame Curie can be counted among the eventual victims of the radioactive bodies which she and her husband discovered." Nonetheless, her discovery of radiation led to treatments that have saved the lives of millions through the years.

Thomas Edison
(1847-1931)

What would a logical person expect from a man who was branded by a schoolmaster as "retarded" and who finished only three months of formal education? Certainly not the versatile and inventive life of Thomas A. Edison!

Edison produced his first invention, an electric vote-recorder, when he was only twenty-one years old. It did not sell as Edison had hoped. He refused, however, to be discouraged and moved on to invent an improved stock ticker system. It did sell—for $40,000, a tremendous sum in the late nineteenth century. A series of other inventions followed, and Edison was soon both wealthy and famous. He didn't seem to notice, however. He was too busy inventing. He patented the phonograph in 1877 and the practical incandescent light in 1879.

He was not the first to invent an electric lighting system, but he was the first to develop a system of distributing electric power, which made electricity available for ordinary home use. In 1882, his company began producing electricity for homes in New York City, and the home use of electricity spread rapidly throughout the world thereafter. He later organized several industrial companies, including General Electric Company.

Among Edison's achievements, he contributed greatly to the development of motion-picture cameras and projectors; made significant improvements to the telephone, telegraph, and typewriter; and invented a dictating machine, a mimeograph machine, and a storage battery. In all, he patented more than a thousand separate inventions.

Early in his career, Edison set up a research lab at Menlo Park, New Jersey, where he employed a group of assistants to help him in his research. This became the prototype of large research laboratories that many industrial firms established later. He is credited with developing the concept of "corporate R&D"—in-house research and development divisions that employ scientific research teams to develop practical products.

What few people know about Edison is that for most of his life he suffered from seriously impaired hearing. He chose to compensate for this impairment in two ways: hard work and a focus on inventions that would either enhance his ability to hear or give him ample means of communicating apart from the spoken word.

Many of Edison's inventions were not "firsts" in a particular field, but rather, important enhancements that made creative inventions more usable. Edison sought to make the genius of others accessible and practical. In that, he succeeded as no other American has.

He continued to work with dogged persistence until his death at age eighty-four, well liked by those who knew him and an inspiration to other inventors and entrepreneurs who followed him.

Albert Einstein
(1879-1955)

From childhood, Albert Einstein found himself curious about the "riddle of the huge world." He turned his curiosity toward the study of physics. After completing university studies, he worked as an office clerk by day and worked on his own ideas at night. In 1905, at age twenty-six, he began publishing scientific papers explaining his new theories. Some scoffed, especially when they learned he was not a university professor. Others were intrigued and began to test his hypotheses. Their observations confirmed his theories, and within sixteen years, he was a scientific superstar and winner of the Nobel Prize for science.

From the time Einstein's theories first gained notoriety, he found himself swept into world politics. He openly opposed World War I, and when the Nazi party rose to power in Germany in the 1930s, he moved to the United States of America to become a professor at Princeton University. As a Jew, he used his influence to help thousands of Jews flee Europe and to work for the establishment of a Jewish homeland. David Ben-Gurion, first prime minister of Israel, asked him to be Israel's first president. And while Einstein felt honored, he refused, saying, "I am a scientist, not a politician."

Although Einstein is considered a genius, he was so slow in learning to talk that his parents were alarmed. In school, he was labeled a "misfit," his classmates avoided him, and he earned poor grades. He failed his first college entrance exam. Rather than complete routine assignments, he preferred to daydream about riding on a beam of light and, indeed, these daydreams led to the theory of relativity and his most famous formula: $E=mc^2$ (energy equals mass multiplied by the speed of light squared).

Einstein's theories about energy and mass were used by other scientists to create nuclear power. During World War II, when Einstein heard that the Nazis were developing atomic weapons based on his theories, he wrote to the president of the United States to warn him. Einstein had intended for his discoveries related to atomic power to be used for peaceful purposes, and he later voiced regret at their use for war. He said after World War II, "We have won the war, but we have not won the peace."

Throughout his life, Einstein was noted for quiet humility. When *Scientific American* magazine offered a $5,000 prize for the best explanation of relativity in 3,000 words, Einstein said, "I am the only one in my entire circle of friends who is not entering. I don't believe I could do it." He once gave this as his formula for success: If a is success . . . I should say the formula is a equals x plus y plus z, x being work and y being play." And z? "Keeping your mouth shut."

A ten-year-old girl once visited Einstein regularly to receive help with her math homework. She explained, "People said that at No. 112 there lives a very big mathematician, who is also a very good man. I asked him to help me. He was very willing and explained everything very well. He said I should come whenever I find a problem too difficult." When the mother apologized for her daughter's intrusion, Einstein said, "I have learned more from the conversations with the child than she has from me."

Father Flanagan
(1886-1948)

Edward Joseph Flanagan was born in Ireland, but at age eighteen he moved to the United States and began to prepare for priesthood in the Roman Catholic Church. After training in Emmitsburg, Maryland; Rome; and Innsbruck; he was ordained in 1912 as a priest for the archdiocese of Omaha, Nebraska.

One main problem in Omaha that Father Flanagan found and chose to address personally: derelict boys. Many of these boys had no mothers, no fathers, and no homes. They had no one to love them or teach them right from wrong. Virtually all had dropped out of public school. They became known in the city for breaking store windows, being petty thieves (often stealing food), and starting street fights.

One day a grocer noted to Flanagan, "These boys should be arrested. They need to be taken away."

Looking beyond their vandalism Father Flanagan saw hungry faces and ragged clothes. He responded, "What they need is a home. They need someone to love them."

The grocer asked, "But who would take them in?"

He replied, "Maybe I will." And he did.

Father Flanagan borrowed a few dollars to rent an old house and then asked those in the immediate neighborhood to give him furniture, dishes, and bedding to furnish it and help fix it up. He invited five boys to move in with him, offering them a place to eat, sleep, play, and pray. Soon these boys were laughing, learning, and attending church regularly. The neighbors were impressed. More and more boys began coming to his door, eager for the normalcy of life he offered them. Father Flanagan finally concluded, "The boys need a town of their own."

In 1922, Father Flanagan found a farm for sale eleven miles outside Omaha, and again he asked friends and neighbors to help with the purchase price and then to help build a town. They built streets, sidewalks, houses, shops, a church, and a post office. One large dining room was built as a place for the boys to eat, and a pool was constructed to give them a place to swim. Boys from across the nation began to arrive. One day a boy who could not walk arrived in Boys' Town, and Father Flanagan asked one of the older boys to carry him to his room. The big boy hoisted the newcomer onto his back as Father Flanagan asked, "He's not too heavy, is he?"

The older boy smiled and said, "He ain't heavy, Father. He's my brother!" The statement became the hallmark of Boys' Town. The action was immortalized in bronze, and the statement became a well-known quote across the nation.

Father Flanagan insisted that the entire "town" be devoted to developing character in homeless boys by giving them religious and social education, as well as vocational training. The institution was such a success that Father Flanagan became a sought-out authority on the training and reclamation of boys who had become juvenile delinquents. After World War II he served as a consultant to the United States government in setting up youth programs in Japan and Korea. He died while on a similar mission to Europe.

Benjamin Franklin
(1706-1790)

Most people might not give a runaway with only two years of formal education much chance of succeeding in life, but that was the start of life for Benjamin Franklin.

One of seventeen children, Ben was largely self-educated, and after running away from an apprenticeship in the printing business, he worked in England and then moved to Philadelphia, where he founded his own printing business and newspaper. He often wrote under pseudonyms, including a character named "Silence Dogood" in Boston. "Poor Richard" was Ben's voice for expressing his thoughts on freedom, justice, and public spirit. *Poor Richard's Almanack*, which Ben not only wrote but also published, became the most widely read book after the Bible in the American colonies.

Franklin was a prolific writer, inventor, and student. Among his inventions were a stove that emitted more heat than a conventional fireplace, the lightning rod, bifocals, the gliding rocking chair, and a musical instrument he called the "armonica." Franklin never patented his inventions—he intended them for everyone's use.

Franklin was equally known as a leader and public-service innovator. He helped establish the first public library in North America, a police force, a volunteer fire department, a hospital, the first garbage-collection service, and an academy that became the University of Pennsylvania.

He retired from his printing business at age forty-two to pursue his "hobbies." During this time, he learned French, Spanish, Italian, German, and Latin; continued to invent; became interested in electricity; and worked for the colonial government. He was sent by the colonies to England in 1757 in an attempt to convince England to uphold colonial rights. When he finally realized that England would not listen to colonial complaints, he returned home in 1775 to help draft the Declaration of Independence. At the end of the Revolution, he helped negotiate peace with England and became the first United States ambassador to France.

In the 1780s, he was called upon to help draft the U.S. Constitution. And it was in 1787 at the Constitutional Convention that Ben took one of his most courageous stands. The convention was on the verge of failure over the issue of whether small states should have the same representation as large states. The deadlock seemed hopeless. At age eighty-one, Franklin rose with a suggestion. He was convinced that the Bible is right in saying, "Unless the Lord builds the house, its builders labor in vain" (Psalm 127:1), and he said: "Gentlemen, I have lived a long time and am convinced that God governs in the affairs of men. If a sparrow cannot fall to the ground without His notice, is it probable that an empire can rise without His aid? I move that prayer imploring the assistance of Heaven be held every morning before we proceed to business." The motion carried. And from then on prayer was offered each morning until a compromise was reached.

Galileo Galilei
(1564-1642)

An inventor, scholar, and researcher, Galileo is credited by historians as being the person who ushered in the scientific revolution. It was a revolution, however, that caused him great personal pain.

From his earliest years in Pisa and Florence, Italy, Galileo was interested in the natural world. The more he studied, the more he concluded that the inner workings of the universe could be revealed through patient study and research. In a work titled *On Motion*, he challenged the ideas of Aristotle. The book was not published, but it was circulated among his friends at the University of Pisa, where he was a professor of mathematics. What he wrote alarmed university officials as being too radical, and he was dismissed.

Galileo left Pisa so poor that he had to walk the final hundred miles to Padua to take a university position there. During his career, he invented the hydrostatic valance, the first practical thermometer, the geometric and military compass, the compound microscope, the "pulsilogia" (an instrument to measure the pulse), and the astronomical telescope. He became the first person to see the mountains on the moon, to discover the rings of Saturn, and to discover that the sun revolved and that the earth and planets revolved around the sun.

With opinions as revolutionary as his discoveries, Galileo's critics began to spread rumors that he was a heretic. He believed science had an important role in determining the truth—an opinion that the Roman Catholic Church took as a direct challenge. Galileo traveled to Rome three times to win the pope's support for his work. The pope gave conditional approval, forcing Galileo to agree never to support Copernicus, who was the first to say the planets revolved around the sun.

In 1632, Galileo published *Dialogue Concerning the Two Chief World Systems*. The book challenged common teachings that two sets of unrelated natural laws governed heaven and earth. Galileo argued that humans and all things on earth were subject to natural laws, which physics and mathematics could describe. The book was published in Italian rather than Latin because Galileo wanted everyone to be able to read his work. The Dialogue was initially approved by Church authorities and was highly regarded by scientists and philosophers. The pope, however, had Galileo tried by the Inquisition for failing to keep their agreement. Galileo's books were banned, and he was placed under house arrest for the rest of his life. While under house arrest, he continued to write and to conduct research with pendulums. He died four years later.

In response to those who accused him of heresy, Galileo said, "I do not think it necessary to believe that the same God who gave us our sense, our speech, our intellect, would have us put aside the use of these, to teach us instead such things as with their help we could find out for ourselves, particularly in the case of these sciences." He believed strongly that his ideas did not challenge the Church or the Bible, but rather that the truth could be found both in the Bible and nature. He wrote, "The Holy Bible and the phenomena of nature proceed alike from the Divine Word."

Jesus of Nazareth
(3 BCE-30 CE estimated)

Jesus Christ, to the Christian, is the Hero of all people who make a difference. Only Jesus lived a sinless life. Only Jesus was fully God and fully Man. Only Jesus died a sacrificial death so that those who believe in Him and accept His death as being on their behalf will receive forgiveness of sins, be reconciled to God, and be given eternal life.

No other person has changed history as much as Jesus of Nazareth did. Ralph Waldo Emerson once said, "The name of Jesus is not so much written as plowed into the history of the world." More books have been written about Him than any other person.

His life impacted all sectors of human existence. He wrote no poetry; but Milton, Dante, and scores of the world's finest poets were inspired by Him. He composed no music; but Handel, Haydn, Beethoven, Bach, and Mendelssohn reached their highest perfection when composing hymns, symphonies, and oratorios to His praise. He painted no pictures; but Raphael, Michelangelo, and Leonardo da Vinci were inspired to greatness in painting His life and ministry.

Jesus taught, preached, and healed the sick in active ministry for only three years, whereas many of the world's most noted "philosophers" taught much longer—Socrates for forty years, Plato for fifty, Aristotle for forty. Yet Jesus' teachings transcend the impact left by the combined 130 years of teaching by these three men of antiquity. The calendar of the Roman (Western) world was changed to reflect His death, with B.C. meaning "Before Christ" and A.D. referring to "Anno Domini," in the year of the Lord.

His impact on the world is not based upon what He said nearly as much as on who He was and what He did. The divinity of His life is clearly expressed in the "Nicene Creed," perhaps the foremost statement of belief in Jesus as the Savior:

> We believe in one Lord, Jesus Christ, the only Son of God, eternally begotten of the Father, God from God, Light from Light, true God from true God, begotten, not made, of one Being with the Father.
>
> Through him all things were made.
>
> For us and for our salvation he came down from heaven: by the power of the Holy Spirit he became incarnate from the Virgin Mary, and was made man.
>
> For our sake he was crucified under Pontius Pilate; he suffered death and was buried.
>
> On the third day he rose again in accordance with the Scriptures; he ascended into heaven and is seated at the right hand of the Father.
>
> He will come again in glory to judge the living and the dead, and his kingdom will have no end.

In Jesus' own words, "He who believes in Me has everlasting life" (John 6:47 NKJV).

Martin Luther King Jr.
(1929-1968)

Martin Luther King Jr. was born the son of a prominent Baptist minister and grew up in a thirteen-room house in the best black neighborhood of Atlanta without experiencing many of the indignities that poorer blacks suffered. He also grew up in a home that was active in resisting anti-black biases, and he was raised to believe that quality of character, not race, should be the basis on which a person is judged.

As a boy, he enjoyed sports, jitterbugging, nice clothes, and girls. He was also an excellent student, skipping two grades in high school. At age fifteen, he entered Morehouse College. He considered becoming a doctor or lawyer, but in the end he chose the family tradition of ministry. He was ordained immediately after graduation from college and was elected co-pastor of his father's church. He later enrolled at Crozer Theological Seminary in Chester, Pennsylvania, where he was only one of six blacks in a class of one hundred students. He graduated as president and valedictorian of his class and went on to Boston University to earn a Ph.D. in systematic theology in 1955. He also took courses in philosophy at Harvard, and while in Boston, he met and married Coretta Scott.

After Boston, King took a position as pastor of the Dexter Avenue Baptist Church in Montgomery, Alabama. Shortly after his arrival, Rosa Parks took a seat in the "white" section of a city bus and refused the driver's orders to move to the "black" section. Her arrest and the subsequent bus boycott that lasted for 381 days brought Martin Luther King into the national limelight. He was active in urging blacks to "protest courageously, and yet with dignity and love." He was arrested in Birmingham after leading a civil rights march, and while in jail, he wrote a nine thousand-word statement about racial justice that truly marked him as the recognized leader of the Civil Rights Movement. His famous "I Have a Dream" speech was delivered in front of the Lincoln Memorial during the Freedom March in Washington, D.C., on August 28, 1963. In 1964, President Lyndon Johnson signed the Civil Rights Bill, which opened public facilities to black people and desegregated public accommodations. In October 1964, King received the Nobel Peace Prize.

In areas of the South where blacks were denied the right to vote, King continued to lead marches. In 1965, Congress passed the Voting Rights Act. King then turned his attention to poverty. He began plans for a Poor People's March on Washington, D.C. While planning this event, King went to Memphis, Tennessee, where predominantly black sanitation workers were on strike for higher wages. There, while standing on his motel room's balcony, he was assassinated by a sniper's bullet. He was only thirty-nine years old.

Throughout his life, King advocated a course of nonviolent protest. He said as part of his final speech in Memphis, "We've got some difficult days ahead. But it really doesn't matter with me now. Because I've been to the mountaintop. . . . Like anybody I would like to live a long life . . . but I'm not concerned with that now; I just want to do God's will. I may not get there with you, but I want you to know tonight that we as a people will get to the Promised Land."

C. S. Lewis
(1898-1963)

Clive Staples Lewis was born in a small Irish town near Belfast in 1898. After serving in the military and being wounded in France during World War I, he returned to Oxford University to complete his education. He was elected Fellow of Magdalen College in 1925, and he spent the rest of his working life, from 1925 to 1962, at the universities of Oxford and Cambridge, tutoring two generations of students in medieval and Renaissance literature. He wrote numerous books during those years, including theological writings, children's books, science fiction, and scholarly works.

A long-standing bachelor, Lewis nonetheless acquired two "families." While training for World War I, he befriended Paddy Moore and volunteered to take care of Paddy's mother if he did not return from the war. Paddy was killed in action, and Lewis looked after Mrs. Moore and her daughter, Maureen, until Mrs. Moore died in 1949. In 1957, he acquired another family, this time marrying a dying divorcee from New York, Joy Davidsman Gresham. She and her two sons joined Lewis and his brother, Warren, at his home, "The Kilns," until her death in 1960.

With friend and colleague on Oxford's English faculty, J. R. R. Tolkien, Lewis added writing to his teaching. He desired to be a poet but failed to gain popularity in that genre. He then wrote children's stories, collectively called *The Chronicles of Narnia*. Among his spiritual works, he is perhaps best know for *The Screwtape Letters, Mere Christianity,* and *The Problem of Pain.*

As a young man, Lewis thought of himself as an atheist, but while reading in his university room at the age of twenty-eight, he had a conversation with colleague Thomas Dewar Weldon that set him on a spiritual search that ended three years later. Lewis wrote, "I gave in, and admitted that God was God, and knelt and prayed: perhaps, that night, the most dejected and reluctant convert in all England." Several months later, he wrote to a friend, 'I have just passed on from believing in God to definitely believing in Christ—in Christianity." By the end of 1931, Lewis was going to church, praying regularly, and taking communion regularly. He shortly thereafter began to give sermons, a number of which were broadcast nationally in England and later collected into books.

His reputation as a teacher and writer continued to grow in the years after his death. Lewis's stories, including his life stories, were translated to film and video. His writings became the subject of literature courses and were woven into church curriculum. He gained a reputation as the "scholar pilgrim"—a man who did not perceive that logic and faith were enemies, but rather, that logic was a legitimate path toward faith. He was willing to admit when a long-held philosophy did not stand up to soundly reasoned Christian apologetics.

C. S. Lewis died on the same day John F. Kennedy was assassinated and Aldous Huxley died. His death received little notice on the world stage, but in the years since, his life has been remembered with increasing respect and admiration.

Abraham Lincoln
(1809-1865)

Abraham Lincoln knew a great deal about loss. His mother died when he was nine; he lost an election to the Illinois state legislature (1832), failed to obtain a desired appointment as Commissioner of the General Land Office in Illinois (1849), lost Senate races (1855, 1858), lost a vice presidential nomination (1856); and in 1864, he seemed on the verge of losing a bid for a second term as president. In 1850, his four-year-old son died; in 1851, his father died; and in 1862, his twelve-year-old son died. Few people, however, remember Lincoln's losses because his victories were so important.

Born in a log cabin in Kentucky, Lincoln attended only a few months of "blab school"—a school with no books at which the students repeated the teachers' words aloud. He moved with his family to southwest Indiana and then later to Illinois. He became a captain in the Black Hawk War and was elected to the Illinois state legislature in 1834. Along the way, he taught himself mathematics, read classical literature, and worked on his writing style. He took the Bible as his model for writing and speaking, and he disciplined himself to produce crisp, clear, simple sentences. He once said, "I will study and prepare myself, and one day when the time comes, I will be ready." He wrote to a friend, "Always bear in mind that your own resolution to succeed is more important than any other one thing."

Lincoln worked as a general store shopkeeper for a while, a venture that went bankrupt and left Lincoln owing $1,100, a tremendous sum in those days. He promised to pay it all. It took him fifteen years, but he kept his word. Lincoln began his law practice in 1836; when his clients overpaid him, he sent refunds. People in the area began to call him "Honest Abe."

As a state legislator, Lincoln took his first stand against slavery. His stand was not popular—only five lawmakers sided with him, and seventy-seven sided with the slave owners in a key vote about slavery. He became the first president ever elected without an electoral vote from a slave state. By the time Lincoln took office, the Confederacy had declared its existence, and the Civil War began during his first year in office.

A major turning point of the Civil War came with victories at Gettysburg and Vicksburg. Lincoln was asked by his generals on the eve of the Gettsyburg battle why he was so calm. He answered, "I spent last night in prayer before the Lord. He has given to me the assurance that our cause will triumph and that the nation will be preserved." Lincoln's "Gettysburg Address" is considered one of the most outstanding political speeches in American history. It was only five days after General Lee surrendered—on the evening of Good Friday 1865—that Lincoln was shot while attending a performance at Ford's Theater.

Throughout his life, Lincoln was unwavering in his desire to do what was right and to do his best. He once said during the Civil War, "I do the very best I know how; the very best I can; and I mean to keep on doing it to the end. If the end brings me out all right, what is said against me will not amount to anything. If the end brings me out all wrong, then a legion of angels swearing I was right will make no difference."

Juliette Gordon Low

(1860-1927)

Everybody called her Daisy. And nobody ever expected her to do what she did.

As a young woman, Georgia-born Daisy spent much of her time giving or attending parties and flitting from one pet project to another. She was charming and entertaining, but those who weren't her friends often thought of her as odd and undependable. She had health problems, could barely hear, and had no children.

But then, at age forty-six, Daisy found herself a restless, lonely widow. She longed to do something worthwhile, even as she slowly returned to her life of parties and travel. Then in May 1911, six years after her husband died, Daisy met the famous British war hero General Sir Robert Baden-Powell at a luncheon.

He was the founder of the Boy Scouts, and what Sir Robert told Daisy about his work fascinated her. In March of the next year, she formed two "Girl Guide" patrols. Each girl was given a notebook, pencil, and a yard of cord to practice knot tying. The first name to ever appear under the "Promise" was Daisy's niece and namesake, Margaret "Daisy Doots" Gordon.

By the time the first handbook was published in 1913, the organization's name had officially become "Girl Scouts." Two years later, the first national convention was held, and the following year, the Brownies began. Daisy was off to a fast start with her organization.

From the beginning, Daisy sought to give girls more value in their lives, and in turn, she valued the girls in her life. Her first troop outside her home in Scotland consisted mostly of poor girls who were facing the prospect of leaving home at an early age to work as maids in the city. Daisy developed troop projects to help them earn money raising chickens and spinning wool, which enabled them to stay home with their families. Whenever a problem arose in the Girl Scouts, Daisy's first response was, "Ask the girls. They'll know what's best." This was a radical approach at the time, when few thought children had the ability to make choices.

The Girl Guides took over all Daisy's thoughts and energy. She paid the organization's expenses the first four years and traveled widely to help interested persons organize new troops. She called on Mrs. Woodrow Wilson, the president's wife, to be the honorary president of the Girl Scouts. Mrs. Wilson accepted, and each subsequent First Lady has been the honorary president of the Girl Scouts. With increasing numbers of troops, and thus increasing costs, Daisy became the organization's principal fund-raiser. One of her favorite ploys was to wear a hat trimmed with parsley and carrots to fashionable luncheons. When asked about her hat, she would say, "I can't afford to have this hat done over. I have to save my money for my Girl Scouts. You know about the Girl Scouts, don't you?" At the time of her death, there were nearly 168,000 members of the Girl Scouts. Today, there are more than 3.4 million.

Will and Charles Mayo
(1861-1939 and 1865-1939)

When Will returned home after completing medical school, a family friend assumed he would work in his father's practice awhile and then move on. "St. Paul or Chicago?" he asked.

Will replied, "To neither one, sir. I intend to remain right here in Rochester and become the greatest surgeon in the world."

A physician and surgeon, Will's father pioneered ovariotomies (the removal of ovarian tumors). Will and his brother Charles had grown up mixing salves and helping apply bandages and splints. It seemed only natural to them to follow in their father's footsteps. Will went to medical school at age nineteen and Charles at age twenty. They purposefully chose different schools so they might get different viewpoints on medicine. Will specialized in eye surgery.

Then in 1883, Mother Alfred, mother superior of the Sisters of St. Francis, decided to build St. Mary's Hospital in Rochester. It opened in 1889, with forty-five beds, and the Mayos were the primary physicians, not only responsible for medical practice and policy, but also for equipping the operating room. Charles, who came to be called Dr. Charlie, built the operating table and made some of the surgical instruments.

Dr. Charlie soon took over the eye surgeries, and Dr. Will specialized in appendectomies. Any time the brothers heard about a new surgical technique, they would travel to see it firsthand—one brother traveling in the spring and the other in the fall to engage in what they termed "brain busting" by studying with outstanding surgeons. Their singular purpose was to acquire new knowledge, better techniques, and more skill. Along the way, Dr. Charlie continued to invent or improve equipment and instruments to improve surgical treatments of bones, joints, veins, and nerves. Dr. Will added stomach surgery to his expertise and Dr. Charlie, thyroid surgery.

The brothers eventually formed a group they called the Surgeons Club. They invited surgeons to come to Rochester to watch their surgeries, during which they talked nonstop about what they were doing and why. Their reputation began to spread among referring physicians and surgeons, and patients began to travel to Rochester from across the nation. As other surgeons began to move to Rochester to work with them, the Mayos innovated methods for joint consultation about patients, a sharing of patient files, and even in-house conference phone calls—all of which used techniques not seen before in clinics or hospitals. As physicians joined them, they became full "partners" and were given autonomy to travel and study, just as the Mayo brothers continued to do. The Mayo Clinic became the first of its kind: a private-practice cooperative group clinic. They also funded the Mayo Foundation for Medical Education and Research to help ensure that Minnesota would be able to provide graduate training in medical specialties long after their deaths. The Mayo brothers literally changed not only the way surgeons shared skills and information, but also the way private medical practice was run—and in the process, they created one of the most highly respected medical centers.

Moses
(About 1500 BCE)

M oses was hardly a novice young shepherd boy. He had been tending sheep in the deserts of Moab for nearly forty years. And he was nearly eighty years old when he saw a burning bush in the desert that captured his attention because it was not consumed.

Not only was the burning bush not consumed, but Moses also heard the voice of God speaking from it. And what God said did not bring Moses joy. When God told Moses that He was going to send him back to Egypt to free the children of Israel, Moses argued, "Who am I that I should go to Pharaoh?" Moses knew that although he had been rescued from the river by Pharaoh's daughter and had been raised in Pharaoh's court, a new Pharaoh was on the throne, and he, Moses, was a fugitive wanted for murder. Moses also knew that he had little association with the Israelites and that he was slow of speech.

Continuing to argue his inadequacy for the task ahead, Moses was assured of God's presence and His miracle-working power. He promised Moses that Aaron would be his spokesman. Moses asked his father-in-law for permission to return to Egypt with his wife, Zipporah, and their son, and he granted it. And thus, Moses began the third chapter of his life. Repeatedly, Moses went to Pharaoh's court to speak the words of the Lord, "Let My people go."

Amazingly, Moses himself was not killed by the Egyptians as plague after plague erupted in Egypt in the aftermath of Pharaoh's refusals to let the Israelites leave. Amazingly, he was not killed by the Israelites, who experienced an increase in their workload as a result of Pharaoh's anger. The final plague, which brought the death of firstborn children and animals throughout Egypt, moved Pharaoh to grant permission for their exodus. By that time, the Israelites were also convinced of their need to leave Egypt.

Moses and the people fled, only to reach an impasse several days later between the advancing chariots of Pharaoh and the Red Sea. Miraculously, the waters of the sea parted when Moses obeyed the Lord by stretching out his rod over the sea. All of the Israelites walked across the dry sea bottom to safety, but Pharaoh's army and chariots were consumed by the waters of the sea as they attempted to pursue the Israelites.

For forty years, Moses led the Israelites through the wilderness. During those years, Moses interceded often for the Israelites, provided food and water for them as he followed God's directives regarding provision, developed a judicial system for the people, and received from the Lord the commandments that were to provide both the religious laws and social customs for the Israelites.

Throughout Jewish history, Moses has been regarded with high honor as the premier lawgiver and prophet of the Jewish people. The "law" which he gave to the Jewish people at God's command is not only the basis for Jewish law, but it is also at the heart of the judicial systems in England and the United States. The "Ten Commandments" are regarded by millions of people as being the core of morality for more than four thousand years.

John Muir

(1838-1914)

John Muir, often called the "Guardian of the Wilderness," immigrated to the United States with his family when he was ten years old and spent his teen years on the family's farm in Wisconsin, enjoying every hour he could escape to the nearby woods. In the winters, he spent his time inventing a saw mill, waterwheels, thermometers, clocks, and other devices.

His inventions led him to enroll in a university, where he became fascinated with botany and began to keep a journal of his travels and nature studies. He hiked and camped extensively throughout Wisconsin, Indiana, and Ontario, Canada, and he completed a thousand-mile walk across the southeastern United States. At age thirty, he traveled to San Francisco in search of "anywhere that is wild."

His search ended in Yosemite Valley, which became his home, classroom, and laboratory. It was while climbing and studying the mountains and glaciers of Yosemite—his "University of the Wilderness"—that Muir learned about the damage the grazing sheep were doing to the mountain environment. He also became alarmed that the huge, ancient sequoia trees were being cut for lumber.

In the winter months, Muir worked as a sawyer, sawing down trees, and in the springs and summers, he guided tourists through Yosemite. He also tramped the wildernesses of Nevada, Utah, California, the Pacific Northwest, and Alaska. At age forty-two, he married Louise Stentzel, and for eight years he spent much of his time running the Stentzel fruit ranch, with periodic excursions to Alaska, and especially to Glacier Bay.

As the result of articles he wrote about his travels and wilderness studies, he gained a reputation as the "guardian of the wilderness." He combined scientific information with narratives of his outdoor adventures, including several brushes with death. His fame grew, and he spent increasing amounts of time in the San Francisco area to be near research libraries. He noted, "They will see what I meant in time. There must be places for human beings to satisfy their souls. Food and drink is not all. There is the spiritual."

Muir's family leased or sold part of the Stentzel ranch so he could work full-time writing and defending wilderness areas. In the early 1880s, he began work on national legislation to enlarge the government-protected areas in Yosemite Valley and nearby Mariposa Big Tree Grove, and to set aside land in the Sierra Nevada Mountains as a public park. He spoke often about the forests being "God's first temples." His work led to the creation of Yosemite, Sequoia, and Kings Canyon National Parks in California.

In 1892, friends of Muir formed the Sierra Club and elected Muir its president. He later joined the national Forestry Commission in Chicago, which recommended to President Cleveland that thirteen new nature preserves be established in eight states, that timber and mining laws be changed to eliminate "fraud and robbery," and that the Grand Canyon and Mount Rainier be named national parks. He later urged President Theodore Roosevelt to establish the Forest Service. He was considered the strongest voice of the "conservation movement" and has been called the "father of our national parks."

Jesse Owens
(1913-1980)

No stranger to racial prejudice, Jesse Owens grew up in a small town in the South, the son of a sharecropper, at a time when African Americans had no rights, no legal protection, and few educational opportunities. By the time he moved to Cleveland, Ohio, he was so conciliatory to the white majority around him that he allowed a teacher to rename him Jesse—she had mistakenly thought he was saying "Jesse" when he was actually saying "J. C." (the initials of his name, James Cleveland, and the name he went by in the South).

As a child, Jesse Owens was frail, shy, and sickly. It was a teacher who speculated that sports might help improve his health.

Running became his favorite activity, in part because Owens later noted, "We couldn't afford any kind of equipment, and we had nothing to do but run." And so Jesse, in his own words, "Ran and ran and ran." He later said, "I loved [running] because it was something you could do all by yourself, and under your own power."

Owens' first official race was a losing effort in a 40-yard dash. He said, "I got left in the holes," referring to the holes that sprinters dug in an era before starting blocks. The loss only made Owens more determined to run faster. By the time he was a senior in high school, he was setting high-school world records. He attended Ohio State University at a time before college scholarships were given to track-and-field athletes, and he operated a night elevator at the State Office Building so that he could run by day.

In a fall in 1935, just days before the Big Ten meet, Owens was seriously injured. On the day of the meet, he was in such pain that he was unable to warm up. He chose to concentrate on the one thing that mattered to him more than pain: competing. He hurdled, dashed, and broad jumped his way to five world records and tied for a sixth in less than an hour. His one jump in the long jump established a world record that stood for a quarter of a century, longer than any other track-and-field mark has ever stood.

The 1936 Olympics were held in Berlin and were intended to be used by Nazi leader Adolph Hitler as a demonstration of the supremacy of the white race. His intended demonstration of an Aryan-supremacy theory was demolished by the stunning performances of a number of African Americans, whom Hitler had ridiculed as "black auxiliaries." The most notable performance was that of Owens, who won four gold medals. In just six days, Owens broke Olympic records nine times and tied them twice. He won gold in the 100-meter race, broad jump, 200-meter race, and as part of the 400-meter relay team. The one hundred thousand fans who saw him perform were at first struck to silence by his performance but then hailed him as the supreme athlete in the world. A street in Berlin was named for him.

A long-time stutterer, Owens overcame his speech difficulties to give as many as two hundred inspirational speeches during the last twenty years of his life. His hometown engraved a monument in his honor: "He inspired a world enslaved in tyranny and brought hope to his fellow man."

Rosa Parks
(1913—)

Rosa Louise Parks is someone few would have marked to become a hero. Born in Tuskegee, Alabama, she was educated in a rural schoolhouse and completed her education at age eleven. Her mother then enrolled her in Montgomery Industrial School for Girls (also known as Miss White's School for Girls), and several years later she went to Alabama State Teachers' College for Negroes for tenth and eleventh grade. She was unable to graduate with her class, however, because of illness and the death of her grandmother. As she prepared to return to school, her mother became ill, and Rosa remained at home to care for her. It wasn't until 1934, at the age of twenty-one, that she received her high school diploma.

Serving as secretary and later as youth leader of the Montgomery branch National Association for the Advancement of Colored People (NAACP), Rosa worked with her husband, Raymond. She was preparing for a major NAACP youth conference at the time she took a bold action that changed not only her life, but also the life of the nation.

Rosa has said, "As a child, I learned from the Bible to trust in God and not be afraid. I have always felt comforted by reading the Psalms, especially Psalms 23 and 27. . . . I felt the Lord would give me the strength to endure whatever I had to face. God did away with all my fear. It was time for someone to stand up—or in my case, sit down. I refused to move."

While riding a city bus on December 1, 1955, Rosa refused to surrender her seat to a white male passenger. Her quiet act of protest resulted in her arrest and a fine of ten dollars plus court costs. Her arrest also sparked a boycott of the city bus line by the black people of Montgomery and sympathizers of civil rights for blacks. For 381 days, blacks who had used the city buses either walked or arranged other transportation in the city. The events in Montgomery set in motion a chain of events that included nonviolent sit-ins, eat-ins, swim-ins, and walkouts in other parts of the nation. The bus boycott in Montgomery ended on December 21, 1956, after the United States Supreme Court declared bus segregation unconstitutional. The day after the boycott ended, Rosa rode a nonsegregated bus for the first time. She later said, "It is funny to me how people came to believe that the reason that I did not move from my seat was that my feet were tired. . . . My feet were not tired, but I was tired—tired of unfair treatment."

Rosa and her husband moved to Detroit in 1957, but they remained active in the Civil Rights Movement, traveling, speaking, and participating in peaceful demonstrations. From 1965 to 1988, Rosa worked in the office of Congressman John Conyers of Michigan. In 1987, she began the Rosa and Raymond Parks Institute for Self-Development, an organization designed to motivate and direct youth to achieve their highest potential. She has spoken extensively at schools, colleges, and national organizations on the theme of human potential and the freedom necessary to pursue potential. Says Rosa, "As long as people use tactics to oppress or restrict other people from being free, there is work to be done."

Saint Patrick
(about 385-461)

The first time Patrick went to Ireland, it was not by choice. When he was only sixteen, he and a number of other youth were kidnapped and sold into slavery in pagan Ireland.

Patrick spent six years pasturing flocks, enduring extreme hardships. He later wrote in his book, *Confession*, that at sixteen, he "knew not the true God," but in Ireland, Patrick began to pray. He wrote, "The love and fear of God more and more inflamed my heart; my faith enlarged, my spirit grew. . . . I said a hundred prayers by day and almost as many by night. I arose before day in the snow, in the frost, and the rain, yet I received no harm . . . for then the spirit of God was within me."

In a dream, Patrick heard a voice saying he was soon to be free. He took that as a sign to make an escape, and he ran two hundred miles to the sea. After gaining passage on a ship and sailing three days, Patrick and the others on board traveled for twenty-eight days more on foot through unknown countryside until their provisions ran out. Patrick encouraged the sailors to trust God to provide for them, and almost immediately, a herd of wild pigs crossed their path. They killed a number of them, ate their fill, offered thanks to God, and at length, reached habitation. At age twenty-three, Patrick was restored to his family.

And then came the call. One night he heard Irish voices calling him back to Ireland, saying, "We beg you, holy youth, to come and walk among us again." Patrick answered this call, leaving his family voluntarily this time and resuming his education. He studied for the priesthood and was ordained in 417. He worked as a priest in Auxerre, France, for about fifteen years, always with a desire to minister in Ireland, and in 432, St. Germanus consecrated him bishop and sent him to Ireland.

Soon after his arrival, Patrick lit a bonfire on the eve of Easter. The local king had ordered that no fires be lit that night until the court druids had lit their fires for a sacred druid festival. Seeing Patrick's blaze in the distance, the High King Laoghaire ordered Patrick to his court for punishment. The king, queen, and courtiers were so struck by the nobility of Patrick's bearing that they gave him an opportunity to speak. He said of the druids, "They can bring darkness, but they cannot bring Light." He preached Christ to the court and made converts of the queen and her two daughters, as well as some of the druids present. He was released unharmed.

For the next twenty-five years, Patrick worked tirelessly in Ireland, facing great perils and hardships. He fasted often, prayed nearly continuously, built churches and monasteries, ordained priests and bishops, baptized and confirmed new believers, and gave Ireland a new faith. When he died, Ireland as a nation mourned him for twelve days.

He said of his work in Ireland, "I am ready to give my life most willingly; to spend myself even to death in this country. . . . Among this people I want to wait for the promise made by Christ in the Gospel, 'They shall come from the east and the west, and sit down with Abraham, Isaac, and Jacob.'" (See Matthew 8:11-12.)

J. C. Penney
(1875-1971)

When James Cash Penney's father told him that he would have to start buying his own clothing, the eight-year-old boy acted quickly. He ran errands, sold junk, and invested in a pig. He soon had purchased a dozen pigs . . . but then the neighbors began to complain. His father called a halt to the enterprise, saying, "We can't take advantage of our neighbors." His words became part of Penney's lifelong business philosophy.

After high school Penney clerked in a store and then moved to Colorado, where he opened a butcher shop. That venture failed when he refused to supply a bottle of bourbon each week to the chef of a local hotel. The owner of a Wyoming dry-goods store gave Penney his next chance by helping him open his own store in Kemmerer. Penney called it "The Golden Rule Store." Five years later, he added two more stores and introduced profit-sharing for his employees.

By 1912, he owned thirty-four stores. Two years later, he incorporated and moved his headquarters to New York City. By 1917, at age thirty-nine, he resigned as president and became Chairman of the Board. During the next twelve years, the chain grew to 1,400 stores nationwide.

Along the way Penney's personal life was marked by tragedy. His first wife died in 1910, and then his second wife died in childbirth in 1923. He said later that he experienced an intense desire to drink after his first wife's death—a desire that was "persistent and terrible, lasting not only through weeks and months, but even years. Many a night I walked the streets battling with this temptation and the darkness that had settled upon me." He had similar feelings after the stock market crash in 1929, when J. C. Penney stock plunged from 120 points per share to only thirteen. He was virtually broke by 1932, and he had to drop many of his Christian philanthropies, among them the *Christian Herald* magazine for which he wrote a popular column for many years. He eventually wound up in a Battle Creek, Michigan, sanitarium. While there, he regained his faith and hope. His health and spirit renewed, he began the long climb back to the financial top at the age of fifty-six.

By 1951, there was a J. C. Penney store in every state, and for the first time sales surpassed $1 billion. During the 1950s, Penney expanded the merchandise lines to include major appliances, home electronics, furniture, and sporting goods. The chain added J. C. Penney Financial Services in 1967 and purchased the Thrift Drug Company in 1969. Penney remained the company's premier goodwill ambassador long after retirement. He attended fifty-one store openings, participated in twenty-seven TV and radio programs, gave 105 speeches, and traveled sixty-two thousand miles at the age of eighty-four!

The Penney Idea, or code of ethics, was adopted in 1913 and asked the consumer for "a fair remuneration and not all the profit the traffic will bear." The company promised "to test our every policy, method and act in this wise: 'Does it square with what is right and just?'" Penney stuck by his "Golden Rule" ethic even in hard financial times and even when mocked by peers.

Ronald Reagan
(1911-2004)

Ronald Reagan, 40th president of the United States, is known for his buoyant optimism. It is a trait he appears to have had from childhood, in spite of the difficulties of growing up in a very modest home and with an alcoholic father, an early bout with viral pneumonia, and numerous accidents and injuries.

At the height of the Great Depression, Reagan graduated from Eureka College, having worked his way through school with a sports scholarship and a job in the kitchen of his fraternity house. After college, he became a radio sportscaster in Davenport, Iowa, providing commentary on more than sixty baseball games. He took up horseback riding and joined a U.S. Army special cavalry unit. In 1937, while in California reporting on a spring training camp, he approached a Hollywood studio for a screen test. He won a contract with Warner Brothers, and soon after, he appeared in his first of fifty-three films.

During World War II, Reagan was called into active duty in the U.S. Army and was assigned to narrate Army Air Corps training films. He began to take interest in organizations set up to benefit screen actors who testified in Washington during the McCarthy investigations on behalf of entertainers who were not communists. He became president of the Screen Actors Guild in 1947. In 1954, he became the spokesperson for the *General Electric Theater*, a weekly television program. He also gave speeches on behalf of G.E. across the nation.

Although he was a Democrat in his early years, Reagan found himself aligning more and more with conservative politics; and in 1962, he voted as a Republican. He actively campaigned and raised funds for the Republican Party in the 1964 presidential campaign; and in 1966 he scored a stunning victory in his bid to be governor of California. During his two terms as governor, he led a move to reform the state's tax, welfare, and education systems, and to turn the state's budget from a deficit to a surplus. In 1975, he "retired" to his ranch and devoted his time to speaking engagements and writing a weekly newspaper column.

Elected president in 1980 with a landslide victory, Reagan immediately moved to enact a major tax cut that turned a sluggish U.S. economy toward prosperity. He led an effort to create a network of weapon-interception devices known as "Star Wars" (Strategic Defense Initiative) and held meetings with the leader of the Soviet Union to bring an end to the "Cold War" and to initiate the first arms-reduction acts. He developed a strong policy against terrorism and selected the first woman to the Supreme Court.

Reagan survived an assassination attempt and continued for years after his presidency to be one of the nation's most popular and highly paid speakers and authors, primarily because his message was upbeat, inspirational, and rooted in enduring values.

Many people don't know that Ronald Reagan worked as a lifeguard for seven summers and is credited with saving seventy-seven people from drowning. In addition to his many political accomplishments, Ronald Reagan is most certainly a hero to those he rescued.

Paul Revere
(1735-1818)

Paul Revere was born to Apollos Rivoire, who had immigrated to the New World alone at age thirteen. Rivoire apprenticed to a Boston metalsmith who was a quiet, religious man. By the time he was twenty-eight, he had opened his own silver shop. He changed his name to Revere, married, and his son Paul was born in 1735. Paul grew up in comfort, and after finishing his formal schooling at age thirteen, he became an apprentice in his father's shop. In his spare time, he and friends formed a society to ring the bells of Christ Church, and he also listened to the sermons of Jonathan Mayhew, who spoke boldly against the tyranny of kings.

After his father died in 1754, Paul took over responsibility for the silver shop. Two years later, he answered a call to arms to fight French soldiers who were raiding the colonies, and he spent a year as a soldier. He married, fathered six children, and became a master silversmith. When England passed the Stamp Act, he began to meet with others in Boston who took the name Sons of Liberty and had as their rallying cry, "Taxation without representation is tyranny." He gained a reputation as a man who could get things done. Silver was a luxury in the colonies, and Revere expanded his trade: he engraved copper plates, became a political cartoonist, and learned to make false teeth. His drawing of a Liberty Tree became a well-known symbol in the colonies. Revere's wife died giving birth to their seventh child, and he remarried; he and his second wife had eight children. In 1773, he did something unusual for a silversmith: he bought a horse and taught himself to ride well.

When the Boston Tea Party took place in December 1773, Revere rode his horse 350 miles in eleven days to New York and Philadelphia to tell what had happened. He made the trip a second time when England blocked the Boston harbor and a third time to deliver the Suffolk Resolves to the First Continental Congress. When not traveling or working, he spied on the British in their taverns. The spying network was effective in discovering the British plans to attack Concord. Paul was one of two riders appointed to spread word of the attack. Since he was well-known, he was chosen to go a secret route across the Charles River in a rowboat and then make the rest of the journey on horseback. It was April 18, 1775, when he made his famous midnight ride. Even though he was pursued by the British, he made his way safely to Lexington to inform Hancock and Adams of the attack. About halfway to Concord, he was captured by the British but was quickly released.

During the Revolutionary War, Revere learned to make cannons and gunpowder, and he supervised a powder mill. He engraved copper plates for the printing of paper money and the official colonial seal. He rode as an express rider, and for a while, he was commander of the fort at Castle Island. After the war, he made copper sheathing for the Constitution ship and for the dome of the Boston statehouse and other buildings. He also became an expert bell maker, producing more than four hundred bells for churches throughout New England. It seemed fitting that he died on a Sunday because church bells he had made rang all over Boston.

Jackie Robinson
(1919-1972)

I never cared about acceptance as much as I cared about respect." That was the way Jackie Robinson summed up his baseball career in his autobiography, *I Never Had it Made.*

Initially, baseball in America was integrated. But by 1892, as segregation grew deep roots in the South, African Americans were no longer welcome in organized baseball. They formed separate leagues . . . until 1947, when Jackie Robinson, the grandson of a slave, battered at that barrier.

Robinson's early years didn't give any indication of his later greatness. He became associated with a gang as a teenager, and although he finished high school and attended Pasadena Junior College, he dropped out of UCLA just months before graduation. He was inducted into the United States Army but was honorably discharged after being court-martialed in a race-related incident.

Nevertheless, Robinson also had a reputation for being an outstanding all-around athlete and an intelligent person who came from a fine family. His record at the Kansas City Monarchs, a Negro League team, was excellent. Very few realized that one reason for the difference was Jackie Robinson's newfound faith in Jesus Christ.

Baseball scout Clyde Sukeforth took the chance of bringing him to the attention of Dodger leader Branch Rickey, a man who was not only willing, but also eager to see the color barrier removed from baseball. Rickey outlined the troubles that were likely to erupt if he signed Robinson. Jackie said, "Mr. Rickey, do you want a Negro who's afraid to fight back?"

Rickey replied, "I want a ballplayer with guts enough not to fight back." Rickey also loaned Robinson *The Life of Christ* by Giovanni Papini and reminded him that Jesus called us to turn the other cheek.

Robinson agreed, "If you want to take this gamble, I will promise you there will be no incident."

And there wasn't. Even though he was rejected by some of his teammates and was the target of hate letters, death threats, and unsportsmanlike conduct from opposing team members, Robinson let his bat and glove do the talking. He remained silent through his first two seasons in the minor leagues. In 1947, at the end of his first two seasons in the minor leagues, he was selected National League Rookie of the Year. Two years later, he won the National League's Most Valuable Player Award.

Robinson not only opened the way for other African

American baseball players, but he also became an inspiration to African Americans nationwide. They saw him as a symbol that other racial barriers might be removed. In 1949, Rickey said to him, "Jackie, you're on your own now. You can be yourself now." And with that release from his promise to Rickey, Robinson did begin to speak. He testified before the House Un-American Activities Committee on racial matters, and in 1953, he took a personally bold step in integrating the dining rooms of major hotels in Cincinnati and St. Louis. His public statements became noted for intelligence, humor, and a willingness to understand and forgive, as Jesus did.

In his career, Robinson played in six World Series and was inducted into baseball's Hall of Fame in 1962. Throughout his career, he openly maintained "the most luxurious possession, the richest treasure anybody has—his personal dignity."

Will Rogers
(1879-1935)

Will Rogers seemed to have been roping and riding all of his life. Not long after he learned to walk, he was riding a pony. When he was a toddler, a ranch hand showed Will how to throw a rope, and Will was soon roping everything in sight, even his mother.

After his mother died when he was only ten years old, Will was given a beautiful buckskin pony named Comanche to help him deal with his grief. His father encouraged him to ride hard and help with the ranch work. The harder Will worked, the better he felt, and the better he became at riding and roping. After finishing his education at Kemper Military School in Missouri, Will took a job in Texas as a horse wrangler, worked the family ranch in Oklahoma for a while, and eventually worked on ranches in Argentina and South Africa.

While he was in South Africa, he became part of Texas Jack's Wild West Show and was billed as "The Cherokee Kid" because of his part-Indian background. When he heard about an

American circus touring through Australia and New Zealand, he traveled to New Zealand to become part of the troupe, riding and roping, and eventually he earned enough money to pay for a ticket back to the United States. For a while, he ran the family ranch, but on weekends, he entered roping contests. He left the ranch again to perform at the 1904 World's Fair in St. Louis in a wild west show and never returned home. After the fair, he performed daily in a Chicago theater and then was given the opportunity to go to New York City with Colonel Mulhall's Wild West Show.

When Will roped a wild runaway steer at the opening night of the show in Madison Square Garden, he became an overnight celebrity with a front-page headline, "Indian Cowboy's Quickness Prevents Harm." He soon was in demand in theaters all over the city, where he charmed audiences with his rope tricks and the stories and jokes he told in a slow cowboy drawl. In 1919, he was given the lead role in a silent movie, and audiences loved him on the movie screen as much as they did in the theater. Will and his wife, Betty, moved to California with their children, and Will bought a ranch north of Hollywood, continued to make movies, and added a weekly newspaper column to his workload. By 1928, he was arguably the best-liked person in America. For his part, he said, "I never met a man I didn't like." He seemed to thrive on a busy schedule. As he once told his wife, "Years crammed full of living—that's what I like."

During the drought years of the 1930s, Will organized benefit performances to help many of the farm families who were in need. He raised more than $225,000 in eighteen days while visiting fifty cities and towns in Texas, Arkansas, and Oklahoma. He asked that part of the money he raised be set aside for the Cherokee people in Oklahoma who were also victims of the "dust bowl."

Will Rogers was killed in a plane crash while traveling with famous pilot Wiley Post on a trip to Alaska in 1935. Always known for his modesty, Rogers once said, "Shucks, I was just an old cowhand that had a little luck. Why all this here fuss about me?"

Wilma Rudolph
(1940-1994)

Few people would argue that the most popular person at the 1960 Olympics in Rome was Wilma Rudolph, a shy twenty-year-old who was overwhelmed by the crowds that lined the streets shouting, "Vil-ma! Vil-ma!" Even to think that Wilma Rudolph ever made it to Rome was astonishing.

Born the twentieth of twenty-two children to a tobacco plant worker in Tennessee, Wilma found life as a poor Southern African American girl was not enough of a challenge. She also had a multitude of childhood illnesses including pneumonia, scarlet fever, and polio. Her left leg was paralyzed when she was four years old. Wilma later said, "The doctors told me I would never walk, but my mother told me I would, so I believed my mother." Wilma's mother made countless sacrifices to get Wilma the medical treatment she needed, and for two years family members took turns massaging her leg four times daily. By age six, Wilma could walk with a brace, and soon after, she graduated to an orthopedic high-top shoe. At age eleven she was able to walk unaided, and at thirteen she tried out for the school's basketball team. At fifteen she was All-State.

Wilma always considered running to be "pure enjoyment." Her ability on the track—undefeated in three years of competition—resulted in her breaking several state high school records. She tried out for the United States Olympic team, and when she made it, local merchants banded together to give her new clothes and luggage for her first trip by airplane . . . to Australia. She brought home a bronze medal for her part in the 4x100 relay and that same year, enrolled at Tennessee A&I to run full-time for the "Tigerbelles." Illness and injury struck again, and for two years Wilma missed most of her track dates. She was determined, however, to make the 1960 Olympics. Even though she had the flu during the trials, she set a world record in the 200-meter races and was part of a relay team that won both 100- and 200-meter relays.

Once in Rome, Wilma won her first race, the 100-meter dash,

and set a world record. Her second gold was in the 200-meter run. The 400-meter race was more difficult. A mistake was made as the baton was passed to Wilma, and the poor pass allowed the German team to move into first place. Wilma ran with long graceful strides and overtook her German opponent and crossed the finish line a full three yards in the lead. Her run electrified the crowd, and overnight she was heralded around the world as the fastest woman in history.

Olympic victories brought invitations to speak around the world, a thought that scared her far more than any track competition. She rose to the challenge and whenever possible, she used her fame to help advance the cause of civil rights.

After being named the most outstanding female athlete in the world, Wilma retired from running. She generously signed her last pair of track shoes and gave them to a boy who asked for an autograph. She then pursued a career as a second-grade teacher and high-school track coach. She established a foundation to help young athletes, and until her death she was a role model for millions of young African-American women.

Charles Schulz
(1922-2000)

Charles Schulz found a different kind of pulpit for preaching about God's love, exposing the foibles of human nature, and pointing people toward the absolutes of God's righteousness: the comic strip. His *Peanuts* strip, which debuted in 1950, ran in 2,600 newspapers in seventy-five nations. He often used the strip to quote Bible verses or to reinforce the spiritual meaning of Christian holidays, all with a tone of gentle humor and a child's-eye view of the weaknesses of human nature.

After he saw a "Do you like to draw?" ad, Schulz studied art. He served in the Army during World War II, and after the war, he began lettering for a church comic book. He taught art and sold his cartoons to *Saturday Evening Post* magazine. He developed the *Li'l Folks* strip for the *St. Paul Pioneer Press* in 1947. The strip was sold to a syndicate in 1950, and the name was changed to *Peanuts*, a title he never liked. Over the years, a host of spin-off products were developed and licensed, including a series of television programs, numerous books, and a musical, *You're a Good Man, Charlie Brown.*

The *Peanuts* strip was Schulz's lifetime work for nearly fifty years. The characters changed little during that time. Charlie Brown was always looking for a winning ball game from the pitcher's mound and saw many reasons to give a "Good Grief!" Lucy still gave sharp-tongued advice for a nickel at a lemonade stand. Linus still looked for the Great Pumpkin and carried a blanket for comfort. Snoopy, the typewriting beagle, still took World War I flights of fantasy as the archenemy of the Red Baron.

An intensely private man, Schulz nevertheless had international fame. He was devoted to his wife, Jeanne, and children Amy, Jill, and Craig. In later years, he enjoyed playing ice hockey at the Redwood Empire Ice Arena in his home city of Santa Rosa, California, and sipping coffee with friends and fellow players at the Warm Puppy snack bar at the rink. He opted to retire his well-loved comic strip as he battled colon cancer so he could focus his energy on family and friends without the pressures of a daily deadline. Those who knew him well recalled that he worked every day and "never ran out of ideas."

Schulz won comic art's highest award, the Reuben Award, in both 1955 and 1964. In 1978, he was named Cartoonist of the Year, an award voted on by his comic-artist peers around the world. He was also selected for a Lifetime Achievement Award by the National Cartoonists Society before his death. In 1986 Schulz was inducted into the Cartoonist Hall of Fame by the Museum of Cartoon Art.

Schulz died the evening before his final strip was to run. His "Dear Friends" strip showing all of the *Peanuts'* characters became not only a message of thanks to his friends for their support, but also his epitaph. He once said of his work, "Why do musicians compose symphonies and poets write poems? They do it because life wouldn't have any meaning for them if they didn't. That's why I draw cartoons. It's my life."

A fellow cartoonist said after Schulz's death, "In a couple of centuries when people talk of American artists, he'll be one of the few remembered. And when they talk about comic strips, probably his will be the only one ever mentioned."

Amanda Smith

(1837-1915)

Amanda Smith's life was largely one of overcoming. Her father, Samuel Berry, was a slave who worked for years at night, after long days of field labor, to make brooms and husk mats to pay for freedom for himself, his wife, and his five children.

She taught herself to read by cutting out large letters from newspapers and asking her mother to make them into words. At age thirteen, with only three and a half months of formal schooling, she went to work near York, Pennsylvania, where she was employed as the servant of a widow with five children. While there, she attended a revival service at the Methodist Episcopal Church and resolved she would "be the Lord's and live for Him."

As a cook and a washerwoman, she worked hard to support herself and her daughter after her husband was killed in the Civil War. Prayer became a way of life for her as she trusted God for shoes, the money to buy her sister's freedom, and food for her family. She also became well-known for her beautiful voice, and as a result, opportunities to evangelize in the South and West began to open up for her. Everywhere she traveled, she wore a plain poke bonnet and a brown or black Quaker wrapper, and she carried her own carpetbag suitcase.

In 1876, she was invited to speak and sing in England, and although she was afraid of going to England and afraid of the ocean, she went, her way provided by friends who had given gifts so generous she was able to travel in a first-class cabin. The captain invited her to conduct religious services onboard, and she later said modestly, "The Lord helped me to speak, sing, and pray." The passengers quickly spread word of her, and she received invitations to speak that kept her in meetings for a year and a half in England and Scotland.

During her stay in England, she accepted an invitation to visit India, and again she prayed and received not only adequate financing, but also sufficient money to pay for her daughter's schooling in America. She spent nineteen months evangelizing in several cities in India. After a two-month return to England, she traveled to Liberia and remained there for eight years. She organized women's and men's prayer groups, gospel temperance societies, and children's meetings. While in Africa, she adopted two African children, whom she sent to England for education.

In 1890, she returned to the United States and eventually founded the Amanda Smith Orphans' Home for African-American children in a suburb of Chicago. She continued to travel on short mission trips to various nations and gained a reputation as "God's image carved in ebony."

Amanda Smith's motto throughout her life was "without holiness, no man shall see the Lord." She had a practical under-standing of holiness and of reliance upon the Lord to supply every need in her life.

Her example—as a former slave who rose to worldwide leadership in Christian circles—became an inspiration to thousands of women during the early 1900s.

Joni Eareckson Tada
(1950—)

One July day in 1967, Joni Eareckson dove into the murky waters of Chesapeake Bay, and in less than a second, she felt her head strike something hard and her body sprawl out of control. Her life was changed forever. Miraculously rescued from the water, she was rushed to a hospital, and after surgery she awoke to find herself in a Stryker frame with a broken neck—a diagonal fracture between the fourth and fifth cervical bones of the spine. She was a total quadriplegic.

Joni remained three and a half months in the hospital and was released to what she regarded as an unknown life. She didn't know any paralyzed people, was told she would not be able to go to college, and faced great physical pain. Her first response was to ask a friend to give her an overdose of pills to end her suffering. Her second response was to live—and living prevailed.

During rehab, Joni began to paint ceramic discs using a paintbrush held in her mouth. Her father, an artist, had encouraged her to draw during her childhood, and she recalled later that it was a simple sketch of a cowboy and horse that was a turning point in her life. Joni also became strong enough in physical rehab to sit in a wheelchair. A little over a year after her accident, she began to attend classes at a university. She took a course in public speaking and focused her speeches on things she knew: how to relate to people with handicaps, what it meant to accept life in a wheelchair, and her experience as a Christian. Deep inside, she sensed God was preparing her for a meaningful life.

Over the years, Joni experimented with different art mediums and techniques. She gave her artwork to friends and family members as presents. Then, in the early 1970s, a Christian businessman arranged for an exhibit of her work, and her commercial success as an artist began. A book and film were released about her story, television and radio talk programs sought her as a guest, and she became a partner in a Christian bookstore as an outlet for selling her artwork. With each piece of art, she included a brief testimony about her relationship with Christ Jesus.

Joni made a list of those things that were her "heart's desire." They included: "I feel it is time to step out on my own. To step into a new dream. To be a 'doer' of God's Word, I must help others—disabled people with dreams of their own." Out of this desire, Joni founded Joni & Friends, a ministry to bring together Christians and disabled people around the world. The ministry sponsors workshops, publishes counseling letters, and gives financial aid. Joni also served on the president's National Council on Disability. She now hosts her own radio program on more than nine hundred broadcast outlets worldwide, is married, and is a sought-after speaker. She has written eighteen books, including children's books and books dealing with such diverse issues as euthanasia and Heaven.

She has written, "I don't know what lies ahead. But I do know who I am. I have a dream, and I know where I am going."

Mother Teresa
(1910-1997)

A s a little girl, Agnes Gonxha Bojaxhiu grew up in an Albanian family in Macedonia. She loved to sing in the church choir, read, and write poems about her love of God. By the time she was twelve, she firmly believed she was called to a religious life, and at age fourteen, she joined a church society for young girls. It was there she first heard about Catholic missionaries. As a senior in high school, she felt drawn to the Loreto Order in Bengal, India. She later said, "I decided to leave my home and become a nun, and since then I've never doubted that I've done the right thing. It was the will of God. It was His choice."

After a training period in Loreto Abbey outside Dublin, she sailed to Calcutta, India, where she lived for a while before going to the convent in Darjeeling. In addition to studying English, she learned Hindi and Bengali, and she was given instruction in teaching. She took her vows and the name Teresa, patron saint of missionaries, in 1931. Her first work was as a teacher at a convent school in Calcutta. She took her final vows in 1937. Although she enjoyed teaching, she longed to help the suffering outside the convent, something forbidden in the Loreto Order.

Mother Teresa was the school's principal in 1946, when a massive riot erupted. She literally had to roam Calcutta's streets in search of food for her students. There, she saw many of the twenty thousand Calcuttans who were injured or dead. The next month, aboard a train for a retreat in Darjeeling, she experienced what she called "the call within a call" to "leave the convent and help the poor while living among them." The next year, Rome granted her permission to work with the poor in the slums and to start her own order.

Before embarking on her work in 1948, she received basic medical training. As an independent nun, she literally walked the streets of Calcutta looking for ways to give of herself and spent the nights at St. Joseph's. She wrote, "I picked up a man from the street, and he was eaten up alive from worms. Nobody could stand him, and he was smelling so badly. I went to him to clean him, and he asked, 'Why do you do this?' I said, 'Because I love you.'"

Eventually Mother Teresa was joined by other nuns who worked alongside her in the streets and went from house to house asking for donations. The order she established in 1950, The Missionaries of Charity, grew quickly, and in 1965, it was granted papal recognition, which meant she could expand her work outside India. She also established a self-supporting leper community in India, an order for male missionaries, and two associations of "Co-Workers" who vowed to live simply, pray for the suffering, and provide financial support. By 1990, Missionaries of Charity houses numbered 450 in ninety-five nations. In 1979, Mother Teresa received the Nobel Peace Prize and the Bharat Ratna—India's highest civilian honor.

She routinely taught those who joined her order to treat each person, no matter how ill, as God's child. She wrote, "Speak tenderly to them. Let there be kindness in your face, in your eyes, in your smile, in the warmth of your greeting. . . . Don't only give your care, but give your heart as well."

Margaret Thatcher
(1925—)

As an eleven-year-old, Margaret gave her speech in clear and measured tones in a competition of music and arts at the Finkin Street Methodist Church. A few minutes later, she took the stage a second time to play a piano solo and a piano duet with her friend Eileen. When the prizes were announced, Margaret stepped forward to receive the silver medal in the junior speech class and the gold medal for her piano duet. A teacher told her how lucky she was to win. Margaret looked her in the eye and replied, "I deserved it."

Success and prizes appeared to come easily to her, but Margaret Thatcher worked hard to get what she wanted, including her place in England's political arena. When she was asked why she thought she had defeated Edward Heath to become the first woman leader of the Conservative Party, she replied, "Merit." It was her answer after winning the prime ministership of Great Britain for three successive terms.

Margaret Roberts grew up in an apartment above the grocery store in an agricultural village. She and her family attended the Methodist Church four times on Sunday. She worked two to three hours on homework each night, and her grades in school were superior. On Friday evenings and Saturdays she worked in a shop. She was an avid reader of biographies and books about history and politics. She was the star of the debate team in school.

When she was seventeen Margaret enrolled at Oxford University, and there she divided her time between her chemistry major and conservative campus politics. She eventually became president of Oxford University Conservative Association. In that role, she met all the visiting politicians who went to Oxford—and they, in turn, met her. After graduation, she worked as a chemist in a factory that made celluloid and plastic tubing, but her life on weekends was devoted to Conservative Party functions.

After Thatcher lost her first two bids for a seat in Parliament, she concentrated on a law degree and became a wife and the mother of twins. She passed the bar exam when her twins were only four months old. In 1959, a Conservative seat opened in the wealthy Finchley district outside London. She was one of two hundred politicians who sought to win the seat—and she did. Just days before her thirty-fourth birthday, she became a member of Parliament. She held a number of cabinet posts throughout the following years, serving in social security, housing and land, treasury, fuel and power, and education departments. In 1975, she became leader of the Conservative Party, and in 1979, when her party gained control of Parliament, she became the first woman prime minister in England's history.

As prime minister, she became known as the "Iron Lady" for her tough economic policies, her military defense of the Falkland Islands, and her negotiations with the leader of the Soviet Union.

As a child, Thatcher's father said to her, "Margaret, never do things just because other people do them. Make up your own mind about what you are going to do and persuade people to go your way." She made that statement the guiding principal of her life.

Harriet Tubman

(about 1820-1913)

When Harriet was fifteen years old, she was shucking corn with other slaves on the plantation when one of the slaves bolted to escape, and the overseer chased him. Harriet followed. As the overseer caught up with the runaway slave and prepared to whip him, he saw Harriet and asked her help in tying down the slave. She refused. The slave again fled, and Harriet blocked the overseer's path. Angered, he threw a two-pound lead weight at the slave, and it hit Harriet, wounding her on the head. She was in a coma for weeks, lying on a bed of rags in her family's small cabin. She could not walk for months. It was an experience that gave purpose to her life—she was determined to be free.

Harriet married John Tubman, a free Negro, in 1844, and she was determined to escape from the South. She later wrote, "There was one of two things I had a right to, liberty or death; if I could not have one, I would have the other; for no man should take me alive; I should fight for my liberty as long as my strength lasted, and when the time came for me to go, the Lord would let them take me." Harriet finally made her escape in 1849. From her safe position in Philadelphia, working in a hotel washing dishes, she later said, "To this solemn resolution I came. I was free, and [my parents, brothers, and sister] should be free also."

Along the Underground Railroad to Philadelphia, Harriet began to conduct her "family." She said, "I never ran my train off the track, and I never lost a passenger." During her lifetime, she made at least nineteen trips to the South, personally helping more than three hundred slaves escape along the "railroad." If slaves became reluctant and desired to return to slavery, she was known to point her revolver at the slave and say, "Move or die!" None of her passengers ever turned back.

By 1854, the woman who was called "the Moses of her people" had a twelve thousand dollar bounty on her head. An antislavery colleague noted, "Great fears were entertained for her safety, but she seemed wholly devoid of personal fear. The idea of being captured by slave-hunters or slave-holders seemed never to enter her mind." When her identity became more widely circulated and she no longer was able to work safely in Philadelphia, she moved to St. Catharines, Canada, near Niagara Falls. Her trek to freedom, once a ninety-mile journey, became a five hundred-mile trip. She continued her work in spite of the extra difficulty.

The Union Army in South Carolina employed Tubman in military hospitals and also organized a very successful scouting service at the request of the army. Armed with a rifle, she led one 1863 raid with Colonel Montgomery to free more than seven hundred slaves on the banks of the Combakee River. She worked for the army without pay or thanks.

Leonardo da Vinci
(1452-1519)

Many consider Leonardo da Vinci to be the greatest genius in history. He embodied an entire era—the Italian Renaissance—as an artist, scientist, engineer, architect, inventor, and musician. His ideas were often scorned by those who knew him, however, because they were so far ahead of their time.

Leonardo was recognized as a genius during his childhood and was apprenticed to a leading artist in Florence to study painting, sculpture, music, science, and mathematics. While still a young man, he moved to Milan and worked there for the city's ruler as an artist, musician, engineer, inventor, and producer of parades and pageants. For him, there was no line between art and science. His notebooks were filled with ideas and illustrations that showed plants and animals in realistic detail. He studied the flight of birds and observed patterns of water and wind, light and shadow, and the movement of stars. He drew sketches of airplanes, armored tanks, paddleboats, and many other mechanical devices that were not "invented" until many, many years later. He was a mapmaker, bridge designer, and medical theorist (predicting a prime cause for the spread of epidemics). To keep his notes private, he wrote backwards: to read his ideas, a person had to hold his notes in front of a mirror.

As diligent as he was in science and math, he also placed great value upon reflection. He often sat for days without moving as he waited for inspiration for a new idea or image to fill his mind. For days he waited for the moment when he felt the face of Christ was revealed to him for his painting of *The Last Supper*. When the image came to him, he painted it quickly and with an air of certainty.

In spite of his great imagination and skill, many of his projects were never completed. Others were lost or damaged. *The Last Supper* began to disintegrate shortly after its completion because of a new paint formula he had tried. When Milan was invaded by France in 1499, he went from one Italian city-state to another, never able to settle down and concentrate on any one project for very long. While he was often commissioned to design weapons and defense systems, he found it to be "a bestial madness."

As an old man, he worked for King Francis I in France. He filled thousands of pages with ideas, hoping they would be published after his death to help humanity. Instead, they were hidden in collections across Europe for nearly three hundred years. Most of his paintings were lost, but those that survived have been highly praised. His portrait *Mona Lisa* is perhaps the most famous painting in history.

As a young man, Leonardo da Vinci was popular—strong, handsome, witty, a practical joker, and a sought-out conversationalist. As he grew older and became more accomplished, people stated that while they admired him, they did not understand him. While other Renaissance philosophers believed the earth was for people's use, Leonardo saw humans as just small players on a huge stage of existence. He became increasingly isolated. It was only many years after his death that his ideas regained popularity.

George Washington
(1732-1799)

George Washington was a man of varied experiences, many born of crisis. When he was eleven, his father died, and George sought training as a surveyor to help support his family. From age sixteen to nineteen, he traveled the western frontier and managed to save enough of his earnings to purchase several plots of land. His brother secured a position for him in the Virginia militia when he was nineteen. Various conflicts with the French not only gave him battle experience, but also a growing reputation as an able officer. In 1755, under General Braddock, he fought in the battle of Fort Duquesne. He had two horses shot from under him, and his coat showed four bullet holes after the battle, but Washington was not wounded. For three years he commanded all of Virginia's forces.

Through the death of his half brother, he inherited Mount Vernon. He added to his estate with his marriage to Martha Dandridge Curtis, a wealthy widow. At age twenty-seven, Washington appeared to be set for a leisurely life as a distinguished landowner who enjoyed hunting, entertaining guests, and serving on his church vestry and in the House of Burgesses.

He was appointed to represent Virginia at the First Continental Congress, and while he took part in no debates, Patrick Henry said of him, "If you speak of solid information and sound judgment, Colonel Washington is unquestionably the greatest man on the floor." During the Second Congress, he was unanimously voted as Commander-in-Chief of the Continental Forces. He thus became the leader of fourteen thousand men who had no discipline, no arms, no commissary, and no morale. Through personal perseverance and expert motivational skills, he welded together a loyal army and proved himself a brilliant military tactician. Ironically, Washington would have been denied military service by a modern draft board because he had suffered smallpox, influenza, tubercular pleurisy, dysentery, and malaria. Yet he was never ill during the Revolutionary War.

After the war, Washington returned to Mount Vernon. He was

sent by Virginia to the Constitutional Convention in 1787 and later was unanimously elected president. He served two terms. Among his final remarks to the nation in 1796, he said, "Of all the habits that lead to political prosperity, religion and morality are indispensable supports. In vain would men claim the tributes of patriotism who would work to destroy these great pillars of human happiness." He also said, "It is impossible to rightly govern the world without God and the Bible."

Few American presidents have advocated prayer more openly than Washington. He routinely went to his library early each morning for devotions. During his presidency, his secretary found him several times at "work" on his knees with his Bible before him. He gave orders relieving troops as far as possible from duty on Sundays and gave them opportunity to attend worship services. He strongly denounced vulgarity and profanity. He was the first to declare a national day of thanksgiving, noting "it is the duty of all nations to acknowledge the providence of Almighty God, to obey His will, to be grateful for His benefits."

Wilbur and Orville Wright
(1867-1912 and 1871-1948)

In 1903, a famous scientist published an article proving "conclusively" the impossibility of controlled human flight. The vast majority of the world agreed. However, three months after this opinion was voiced, the impossible was achieved by two bicycle makers name Wilbur and Orville Wright. The sons of a preacher, with ancestors who had been pioneer settlers, Wilbur and Orville grew up with adventurous spirits, believing in the impossible. Their mother, Susan Koerner Wright, passed on to her sons her mechanical mind—she was ingenious in her ability to invent household devices. The two brothers read voraciously and attended high school, although they did not graduate. In 1892, when the fad for bicycles was at its peak, they opened a bicycle sales-and-repair shop. In the winter, they worked at manufacturing their own models of bicycles. The "Wright Special" sold at a bargain price of eighteen dollars!

An article about German Otto Lilienthal's experiments in gliding and his fatal crash turned the brothers' curiosity to aeronautics. They began to read all they could on the subject and focused primarily on the problem of balance. They developed plans for a "passenger kite" that might enable a person to manipulate an airship. Before long, they had built a prototype glider that incorporated their ideas. Their first aircraft, with a wingspan of seventeen and one-half feet, was floated as an unmanned kite at Kitty Hawk in 1900. In 1901, they experimented with a twenty-two-foot-wingspan glider with a weight of ninety-eight pounds, and they surpassed all earlier achievements in gliding.

Back at the Wright Cycle Company that winter, the brothers built a "wind tunnel." They tested more than two hundred types of wing surfaces, at various angles, to determine the best ratios between wing curvature, angle, and air pressure or "lift." From these experiments, they revised their craft, and the following year, they added a movable rudder to counteract possible tailspins. They applied for a patent in 1903. In September 1903, they built a plane with a propeller, a forty-foot wingspan, and flexible wingtips. It weighed 750 pounds, including the pilot. On December 17, 1903, they made the first generally recognized powered flight known to man—their longest flight was 852 feet in fifty-nine seconds.

News of their flights was regarded with great skepticism, even when documentation was supplied. The brothers ignored the pessimism of the critics and turned their attention to making their invention "practical." It wasn't until 1908 at air shows in LeMans, France, and Fort Myers, Virginia, that they convinced the general public of their success. Their work was well-funded the next year, and the Wright Company was founded. Both brothers continued to work in aeronautical research until their deaths.

Why were the Wright brothers successful when others weren't? Those who have studied their lives have concluded that their success was rooted in their extraordinary teamwork, in their commitment to careful and well-documented experimentation, and in their willingness to use parts already tested and manufactured by others (including their first engines). They were team players focused on a singular goal.

THE POETS' CORNER

A Legacy

JOHN GREENLEAF WHITTIER

John Greenleaf Whittier (1807-1892) was an
American-Quaker poet and reformer.

Friend of my many years!
When the great silence falls, at last, on me,
Let me not leave, to pain and sadden thee,
A memory of tears.

But pleasant thoughts alone
Of one who was thy friendship's honored guest
And drank the wine of consolation pressed
From sorrows of thy own.

I leave with thee a sense
of hands upheld and trials rendered less—
The unselfish joy which is to helpfulness
Its own great recompense;

The knowledge that from thine,
As from the garments of the Master, stole
Calmness and strength, the virtue which makes whole
And heals without a sign;

Yea more, the assurance strong
That love, which fails of perfect utterance here,
Lives on to fill the heavenly atmosphere
With its immortal song.

Roadside Flowers

Bliss Carman

*Bliss Carman (1861-1929) was known as the
"unofficial poet laureate of Canada." His verse praises
the beauty and power he saw in nature.*

We are the roadside flowers,
Straying from garden ground;
Lovers of idle hours,
Breakers of ordered bounds.

If only the earth will feed us,
If only the wind be kind.
We blossom for those who need us,
The stragglers left behind.

And lo, the Lord of the Garden,
He makes His sun to rise,
And His rain to fall like pardon
On our dusty paradise.

On us He has laid the duty—
The task of the wandering breed—
To better the world with beauty,
Wherever the way may lead.

Who shall inquire of the season,
Or question the wind where it blows?
We blossom and ask no reason,
The Lord of the Garden knows.

Heaven

ISAAC WATTS

Isaac Watts (1674-1748) was an English pastor,
preacher, poet, and hymn writer.

There is a land of pure delight,
 Where saints immortal reign;
Infinite day excludes the night,
 And pleasures banish pain.

There everlasting spring abides,
 And never-withering flowers;
Death like a narrow sea divides
 This heavenly land from ours.

Sweet fields beyond the swelling flood
 Stand dressed in living green;
So to the Jews old Canaan stood,
 While Jordan rolled between.

But timorous mortals start and shrink
 To cross this narrow sea,
And linger shivering on the brink,
 And fear to launch away.

Oh! Could we make our doubts remove,
 These gloomy thoughts that rise,
And see that Canaan that we love
 With unbeclouded eyes—

Could we but climb where Moses stood,
 And view the landscape o'er,
Not Jordan's stream, nor death's cold flood,
 Could fright us from the shore.

He Prayeth Well

SAMUEL TAYLOR COLERIDGE

Samuel Taylor Coleridge (1772-1834) was a lyrical poet, critic, and philosopher in England. His Lyrical Ballads, written with William Wordsworth in 1798, launched the English Romantic movement.

He prayeth well who loveth well
Both man and bird and beast.
He prayeth best who loveth best
All things both great and small;
For the dear God, who loveth us,
He made and loveth all.

Formula for Achievement

AUTHOR UNKOWN

Plan more work than you can do;
Then do it.
Bite off more than you can chew;
Then chew it.
Hitch your wagon to a star;
Keep your seat
And there you are!

Sonnet 18

WILLIAM SHAKESPEARE

*William Shakespeare (1564-1616) was one of England's most
prolific playwrights and poets of all time.*

Shall I compare thee to a summer's day?
Thou art more lovely and more temperate:
Rough winds do shake the darling buds of May,
And summer's lease hath all too short a date:
Sometime too hot the eye of heaven shines,
And often is his gold complexion dimm'd,
And every fair from fair sometime declines,
By chance, or nature's changing course untrimm'd:
But thy eternal summer shall not fade,
Nor lose possession of that fair thou ow'st,
Nor shall death brag thou wander'st in his shade,
When in eternal lines to time thou grow'st,
So long as men can breathe, or eyes can see,
So long lives this, and this gives life to thee.

An English Prayer

AUTHOR UNKNOWN

Give us, Lord,
A bit of sun,
A bit of work,
And a bit of fun.

She Walks in Beauty

LORD GEORGE BYRON

Lord George Byron (1788-1824) was a well-known English poet of the Romantic Period.

She walks in beauty, like the night
Of cloudless climes and starry skies;
And all that's best of dark and bright
Meet in her aspect and her eyes:
Thus mellowed to that tender light
Which heaven to gaudy day denies.

One shade the more, one ray the less,
Had half impaired the nameless grace
Which waves in every raven tress,
Or softly lightens o'er her face;
Where thoughts serenely sweet express
How pure, how dear their dwelling place.

And on that cheek, and o'er that brow,
So soft, so calm, yet eloquent,
The smiles that win, the tints that glow,
But tell of days in goodness spent,
A mind at peace with all below.
A heart whose love is innocent!

The Man Who Quits

AUTHOR UNKNOWN

The man who quits has a brain and hand
As good as the next, but lacks the sand
That would make him stick, with a courage stout,
To whatever he tackles, and fight it out.

He starts with a rush, and a solemn vow
That he'll soon be showing the other how;
Then something new strikes his roving eye,
And his task is left for the bye-and-bye.

It's up to each man what becomes of him;
He must find in himself the grit and vim
That brings success; he can get the skill
If he brings to the task a steadfast will.

No man is beaten till he gives in;
Hard luck can't stand for a cheerful grin;
The man who fails needs a better excuse,
Than the quitter's whining, "What's the use?"

For the man who quits lets his chances slip,
Just because he's too lazy to keep his grip.
The man who sticks goes ahead with a shout,
While the man who quits joins the "Down and out."

A Tiny Little Minute

AUTHOR UNKNOWN

Just a tiny little minute.
Sixty seconds in it.
Forced upon me;
Didn't ask it, didn't choose it.
Yet, it's up to me to use it;
Must give account if I abuse it.
Just a little minute.

As We Rush,
As We Rush in the Train

JAMES THOMSON

James Thomson (1834-1882) was an English poet.

As we rush, as we rush in the train,
The trees and the houses go wheeling back,
But the starry heavens above the plain
Come flying on our track.

All the beautiful stars of the sky,
The silver doves of the forest of Night,
Over the dull earth swarm and fly,
Companions of our flight.

We will rush ever on without fear;
Let the goal be far, the flight be fleet!
For we carry the Heavens with us, Dear,
While the Earth slips from our feet!

My Quest

JOHN GREENLEAF WHITTIER

We search the world for truth, we cull
The good, the pure, the beautiful,
From graven stone and written scroll,
From the old flower-fields of the soul,
And weary seekers for the best,
We come back laden from our quest,
To find that all the sages said
Is in the Book our mothers read.

The Happiest Man

WILLIAM COWPER

William Cowper (1731-1800), a friend of the Rev. John Newton, achieved great literary success as a poet, hymn writer, letter writer, and translator.

Happy is he who by love's sweet song
Is cheered today as he goes along.
Happier is he who believes that tomorrow
Will ease all pain and take away all sorrow.
Happiest he who on earthly sod
Has faith in himself, his friends, and God.
Happiness depends, as Nature shows,
Less on exterior things than most suppose.

Age

ALFRED LORD TENNYSON

Alfred Lord Tennyson (1809-1892) was regarded as the chief representative of the Victorian Age of poetry. He succeeded Wordsworth as Poet Laureate of England in 1850.

Old age hath yet his honour and his toil;
Death comes all: but something ere the end,
Some work of noble note may yet be done . . .
Though much is taken, much abides; and though
We are not now that strength which in old days
Moved earth and heaven, that which we are, we are;
One equal temper of heroic hearts,
Made weak by time and fate, but strong in will
To strive, to seek, to find, and not to yield.

Sonnet XLIII, From the Portuguese

ELIZABETH BARRETT BROWNING

Elizabeth Barrett Browning (1806-1861) was an English poet who published Sonnets from the Portuguese *in 1850. The forty-four sonnets celebrate her love for her husband, Robert.*

How do I love thee? Let me count the ways.
I love thee to the depth and breadth and height
My soul can reach, when feeling out of sight
For the ends of Being and ideal Grace.
I love thee to the level of every day's
Most quiet need, by sun and candlelight.
I love thee freely, as men strive for Right;

I love thee purely, as they turn from Praise.
I love thee with the passion put to use
In my old griefs, and with my childhood's faith.
I love thee with a love I seemed to lose
With my lost saints,—I love thee with the breath,
Smiles, tears, of all my life!—and, if God choose,
I shall but love thee better after death.

Meeting at Night

ROBERT BROWNING

Robert Browning (1812-1889) was an English poet, who achieved recognition for his work only after the death of his beloved wife, Elizabeth.

I

The grey sea and the long black land;
And the yellow half-moon large and low;
And the startled little waves that leap
In fiery ringlets from their sleep,
As I gain the cove with pushing prow,
And quench its speed i' the slushy sand.

II

Then a mile of warm sea-scented beach;
Three fields to cross till a farm appears;
A tap at the pane, the quick sharp scratch
And blue spurt of a lighted match,
And a voice less loud, through its joys and fears,
Than the two hearts beating each to each!

It Is Too Late!

HENRY WADSWORTH LONGFELLOW

*Henry Wadsworth Longfellow (1807-1882) was one of
the most popular American poets of the nineteenth century.*

It is too late! Ah, nothing is too late
Till the tired heart shall cease to palpitate.
Cato learned Greek at eighty; Sophocles
Wrote his grand Oedipus, and Simonides
Bore off the prize of verse from his compeers,
When each had numbered more than fourscore years . . .
Chaucer, at Woodstock with the nightingales,
At sixty wrote the *Canterbury Tales*;
Goethe at Weimar, toiling to the last,
Completed *Faust* when eighty years were past.
These are indeed exceptions, but they show
How far the gulf-stream of our youth may flow
Into the Arctic regions of our lives. . . .
For age is opportunity no less
Than youth itself, though in another dress;
And as the evening twilight fades away
The sky is filled with stars invisible by day.

The Pillar of the Cloud

John Henry Newman, Cardinal

*Cardinal John Henry Newman (1801-1890) was considered to be
one of the most illustrious English converts to the Catholic Church,
a philosopher, and man of letters.*

Lead, Kindly Light, amid the encircling gloom,
Lead Thou me on!
The night is dark, and I am far from home—
Lead Thou me on!
Keep Thou my feet; I do not ask to see
The distant scene—one step enough for me.

I was not ever thus, nor prayed that Thou
Shouldst lead me on.
I loved to choose and see my path; but now
Lead Thou me on!
I loved the garish day, and, spite of fears,
Pride ruled my will; remembered no past years.

So long Thy power hath blessed me, sure it still
Will lead me on,
O'er moor and fen, o'er crag and torrent, till
The night is gone;
And with the morn those angel faces smile
Which I have loved long since, and lost awhile.

Jabberwocky

LEWIS CARROLL

Lewis Carroll (1832-1898) was the pseudonym of English author and mathematician Charles Lutwidge Dodgson, who is best-known for his children's book Alice's Adventures in Wonderland.

'Twas brillig, and the slithy toves
Did gyre and gimble in the wabe:
All mimsy were the borogoves,
And the mome raths outgrabe.

"Beware the Jabberwock, my son!
The jaws that bite, the claws that catch!
Beware the Jubjub bird, and shun
The frumious Bandersnatch!"

He took his vorpal sword in hand:
Long time the manxome foe he sought—
So rested he by the Tumtum tree,
And stood awhile in thought.

And, as in uffish thought he stood,
The Jabberwock, with eyes of flame,
Came whiffling through the tulgey wood,
And burbled as it came!

One, two! One, two! And through and through
The vorpal blade went snicker-snack!
He left it dead, and with its head
He went galumphing back.

"And has thou slain the Jabberwock?
Come to my arms, my beamish boy!

O frabjous day! Callooh! Callay!"
He chortled in his joy.

'Twas brillig, and the slithy toves
Did gyre and gimble in the wabe:
All mimsy were the borogoves,
And the mome raths outgrabe.

Trees

ALFRED JOYCE KILMER

*Alfred Joyce Kilmer (1886-1918), an American poet,
was killed in action on July 30, 1918, near the French town of Seringes
during World War I at the age of thirty-one.*

I think that I shall never see
A poem lovely as a tree.

A tree whose hungry mouth is prest
Against the sweet earth's flowing breast;

A tree that looks at God all day,
And lifts her leafy arms to pray;

A tree that may in summer wear
A nest of robins in her hair;

Upon whose bosom snow has lain;
Who intimately lives with rain.

Poems are made by fools like me,
But only God can make a tree.

The Wind

ROBERT LOUIS STEVENSON

Robert Louis Stevenson (1850-1894) was a Scottish essayist,
poet, and author of travel books and novels, including the
beloved children's classic Treasure Island.

I saw you toss the kites on high
And blow the birds about the sky;
And all around I heard you pass,
Like ladies' skirts across the grass—
O wind, a-blowing all day long,
O wind, that sings so loud a song!

I saw the different things you did,
But always you yourself you hid.
I felt you push, I heard you call,
I could not see yourself at all—
O wind, a-blowing all day long,
O wind, that sings so loud a song!

O you that are so strong and cold,
O blower, are you young or old?
Are you a beast of field and tree,
Or just a stronger child than me?
O wind, a-blowing all day long,
O wind, that sings so loud a song!

Send Forth, O God, Thy Light and Truth

JOHN QUINCY ADAMS

John Quincy Adams (1767-1848) was better known as the sixth president of the United States, rather than as a poet. His father, John Adams, was the second president and helped draft the Declaration of Independence.

Send forth, O God, Thy light and truth,
And let them lead me still,
Undaunted, in the paths of right,
Up to Thy holy hill.
Then to Thy altar will I spring,
And in my God rejoice;
And praise shall tune the trembling string,
And gratitude my voice.
O why, my soul, art thou cast down?
Within me why distressed?
Thy hopes the God of grace shall crown;
He yet shall make thee blessed.
To Him, my never failing Friend,
I bow, and kiss the rod;
To Him shall thanks and praise ascend,
My Savior and my God.

Count Your Blessings

JOHNSON OATMAN JR.

*Johnson Oatman Jr. (1856-1922) was ordained as a
American Methodist Episcopal minister and wrote the lyrics
for more than five thousand gospel songs.*

When upon life's billows you are tempest tossed,
When you are discouraged thinking all is lost,
Count your many blessings, name them one by one,
And it will surprise you what the Lord has done.

Are you ever burdened with a load of care?
Does the cross seem heavy you are called to bear?
Count your many blessings, ev'ry doubt will fly,
And you will be singing as the days go by.

Count your blessings, Name them one by one;
Count your blessings, See what God has done.
Count your blessings, Name them one by one;
Count your many blessings, See what God has done.

When you look at others with their lands and gold,
Think that Christ has promised you His wealth untold;
Count your many blessings, money cannot buy
Your reward in heaven, nor your home on high.

So, amid the conflict, whether great or small,
Do not be discouraged, God is over all;
Count your many blessings, angels will attend,
Help and comfort give you to your journey's end.

The Weaver

AUTHOR UNKNOWN

My life is but a weaving
Between my Lord and me;
I cannot choose the colors
He worketh steadily.

Ofttimes He weaveth sorrow
And I in foolish pride,
Forget that He seeth the upper,
And I the under side.

Not till the loom is silent
And the shuttles cease to fly,
Shall God unroll the canvas
And explain the reason why.

The dark threads are as needful
In the Weaver's skillful hand,
As the threads of gold and silver
In the pattern He has planned.

When God Inclines
the Heart to Pray

AUTHOR UNKNOWN

When God inclines the heart to pray,
He hath an ear to hear;
To him there's music in a groan,
And beauty in a tear.

A Birthday

CHRISTINA ROSSETTI

Christina Rossetti (1830-1894) was one of the most important of English women poets.

My heart is like a singing bird
Whose heart is in a watered shoot:
My heart is like an apple-tree
Whose boughs are bent with thickset fruit;
My heart is like a rainbow shell
That Paddles in a halcyon sea;
My heart is gladder than all these
Because my love is come to me.

Raise me dais of silk and down;
Hang it with vair and purple dyes;
Carve it in doves and pomegranates,
And peacocks with a hundred eyes;
Work it in gold and silver grapes,
In leaves and silver fleurs-de-lys;
Because the birthday of my life
Is come, my love is come to me.

Hope Is the Thing with Feathers

EMILY DICKINSON

*Emily Dickinson (1830-1886) was an American lyrical poet.
An extremely private person, only seven of her 1,800 poems were
published during her lifetime.*

Hope is the thing with feathers
That perches in the soul,
And sings the tune without the words,
And never stops at all,

And sweetest in the gale is heard;
And sore must be the storm
That could abash the little bird
That kept so many warm.

I've heard it in the chilliest land
And on the strangest sea;
Yet, never, in extremity,
It asked a crumb of me.

I Am My Neighbor's Bible
Author Unknown

I am my neighbor's Bible:
He reads me when we meet,
Today he reads me in my house,
Tomorrow in the street;
He may be relative or friend,
Or slight acquaintance be;
He may not even know my name,
Yet he is reading me.

On the Morning of Christ's Nativity

JOHN MILTON

*John Milton (1608-1674), an English poet,
was most famous for his epic* Paradise Lost.

This is the month, and this the happy morn,
Wherein the Son of Heav'n's Eternal King,
Of wedded Maid and Virgin Mother born,
Our great redemption from above did bring;
For so the holy sages once did sing
That He our deadly forfeit should release,
And with His Father work us a perpetual peace.

That glorious Form, that Light unsufferable,
And that far-beaming blaze of Majesty,
Wherewith He wont at Heav'n's high council-table
To sit the midst of Trinal Unity,
He laid aside; and, here with us to be,
Forsook the courts of everlasting day,
And chose with us a darksome house of mortal clay.

Say, Heavenly Muse, shall not thy sacred vein
Afford a present to the Infant God?
Hast thou no verse, no hymn, or solemn strain,
To welcome Him to this His new abode,
Now while the Heaven, by the sun's team untrod,
Hath took no print of the approaching light,
And all the spangled host keep watch in squadrons bright?

See how from far upon the eastern road
The star-led wizards haste with odours sweet:
O run, prevent them with thy humble ode,

And lay it lowly at His blessed feet;
Have thou the honour first thy Lord to greet,
And join thy voice unto the Angel choir,
From out his secret altar touched with hallowed fire.

The Lamb

WILLIAM BLAKE

*William Blake (1757-1827) was a British poet, painter, and engraver,
who illustrated and printed his own books.*

Little lamb, who made thee?
Dost thou know who made thee?
Gave thee life, and bid thee feed
By the stream and o'er the mead;
Gave thee clothing of delight,
Softest clothing, woolly, bright;
Gave thee such a tender voice,
Making all the vales rejoice?
Little lamb, who made thee?
Dost thou know who made thee?

Little lamb, I'll tell thee,
Little lamb, I'll tell thee:
He is called by thy name,
For He calls Himself a Lamb.
He is meek, and He is mild;
He became a little child.
I a child, and thou a lamb,
We are called by His name.
Little lamb, God bless thee!
Little lamb, God bless thee!

Ah, Be Not False

RICHARD WATSON GILDER

Richard Walton Gilder (1844-1909) was an American editor-in-chief of
the Century Monthly Magazine *and a poet.*

Ah, be not false, sweet Splendor!
Be true, be good;
Be wise as thou art tender;
Be all that Beauty should.
Not lightly be thy citadel subdued;
Not ignobly, not untimely.
Take praise in solemn mood;
Take love sublimely.

TRUTH IS STRANGER
THAN FICTION

MANNA—the mysterious bread that God sent to feed the starving Israelites—can be found today in several valleys of the mid-Sinai. It is a resinous gum exuding from the fragile twigs of the tamarisk, an evergreen shrub. The honey-like drops appear usually during June and July just before sunup, while the air is cold and dewy. They are said to taste sweet and gummy.

SEVEN—the holy number—beats out all others when it comes to the Bible, especially in terms of creation. Consider this: There are 7 days in creation, 7 days in the week, 7 phases of the moon, every 70 years was the sabbatical, and 7 times 7 years was the Jubilee. There are 7 divisions in the Lord's Prayer, and 7 deacons chosen by the apostles. Enoch, who was translated, was 7th from Adam; Jesus Christ was the 77th in a direct line. Our Lord spoke 7 times on the cross, on which He suffered for 7 hours. He appeared 7 times after His death, and after 7 times 7 days, He sent the Holy Spirit to the believers in Jerusalem.

There appeared 7 golden candlesticks and 7 stars in the hand of Him who was in the midst; 7 lambs before the 7 spirits of God; the book with the 7 seals; the lamb with 7 horns and 7 eyes; 7 angels bearing 7 plagues, and 7 vials of wrath. The vision of Daniel was 70 weeks; and the elders of Israel were 70.

There are 7 heavens, 7 planets, 7 wise men, 7 champions of Christendom, 7 notes in music, 7 primary colors, and 7 wonders of the world.

THE "BUTTERFLY" was originally called a "flutterby."

THE BACKBONE of a camel is perfectly straight.

THE CASHEW NUT is a member of the poison ivy family.

Think Again!

A SILKWORM is not a worm. It's a caterpillar.

THE MEXICAN JUMPING BEAN is not a bean. It's a hollow shell containing worms or larvae.

CARAWAY SEED is not a seed. It's a dried ripe fruit.

SCHOOL CHALK is not chalk. It's plaster of Paris.

PANAMA HATS are not made in Panama. They are made in Colombia and Ecuador.

DRY CLEANING is not dry. All articles are placed in a washer containing a wet solution and thoroughly saturated.

A FIREFLY is not a fly, and a glowworm is not a worm. They are both beetles.

CASSIQUIARE CANAL—the river that runs both ways—is a natural waterway in South America. Depending on the rainfall, the stream flows into the Orinoco Basin or into the Amazon. At flood tide of the Amazon it flows into the Orinoco, while at the flood tide of the Orinoco it flows into the Amazon.

BABE RUTH—arguably the greatest baseball player of all time—hit 125 home runs in one hour. This feat took place at an exhibition game on Wrigley Field in 1927. Several pitchers threw balls to Babe as he stood at the plate. After an hour, 125 of those balls had been walloped over the fence.

A POUND OF FEATHERS weighs more than a pound of gold because feathers are weighed by "avoirdupois" weight, which has sixteen ounces to a pound, while gold is always weighed by "troy" weight, which contains only twelve ounces to the pound.

METHUSELAH—the oldest man in the Bible—died before his father. Methuselah was the son of Enoch, who was taken to heaven by God and, according to Hebrews 11:5, never saw death.

You Must Be Mistaken!

THE IRISH POTATO is not a potato, and it did not come from Ireland. (It's a tuber plant, and it came from Peru.)

MUSTARD GAS is not gas, and it isn't mustard. (It's a volatile liquid.)

PEANUTS are not nuts. (They're beans.)

A JUNE BUG is not a bug. (It's a May beetle.)

THE EGYPTIAN SPHINX is not a sphinx. (It's the statue of the god Armachis.)

SEALING WAX contains no wax. (It's made of shellac, Venice turpentine, and cinnabar.)

TURKISH BATHS are not Turkish, and they aren't baths. (They're hot-air rooms of Roman origin.)

THE WHITE ANT is not an ant, and it's not white. (It belongs to the order of Orthoptera, and it's brown in color.)

THE ENGLISH HORN is not English, and it's not a horn. (It's French, and it's a wood-wind.)

THE BELGIAN HARE is not a hare. (It's a rabbit.)

AN AMERICAN RABBIT is not a rabbit. (It's a hare.)

A PINEAPPLE is not an apple, and it isn't a pine. (It's a berry.)

THE PULMONARY VEIN is not a vein. (It's an artery.)

RICE PAPER is not made from rice. (It's made from a pithy plant called "tung-tsar.")

MOVING PICTURES do not move. (They're a series of still pictures.)

WESTMINSTER ABBEY is not an abbey. (It's the Collegiate Church of St. Peter's.)

CATGUT does not come from cats. (It comes from sheep.)

THE SILVERFISH is not a fish. (It's an insect.)

BANANA OIL is not made from bananas. (It's a by-product of petroleum.)

A DEER FOREST is not a forest, and it doesn't necessarily contain deer. (It's a fenced enclosure for wild game.)

THE MULBERRY is not a berry. (It's a multiple-stone fruit.)

TIN CANS are not made of tin. (They are rolled iron, thinly coated with tin.)

THE STEEL GUITAR is not made of steel. (It's made of wood and played with a steel bar.)

A SEAT ON THE STOCK EXCHANGE is not a seat. (The word seat merely implies a membership.)

THE HORNED TOAD is not a toad. (It's a lizard.)

OXTAIL SOUP is not made with ox tails. (It's made with the tails of cows and steers.)

AN ALLIGATOR PEAR is not a pear, and it's not an alligator. (It's a berry.)

THE DACHSHUND is not German. (It was known in Egypt four thousand years ago.)

A FEW DROPS OF BLACK PAINT will make a can of white paint whiter. By adding four or five drops of black paint to a pail of white paint, the black drops act as a bleaching agent, making the white paint more purely white.

IN NUUANU VALLEY, a short distance from Honolulu, Hawaii, and visible from the highway, can be seen a waterfall that "falls" uphill. The water starts to fall down the cliff, but the wind currents there are so strong that they catch the water as it bursts into spray and blows it back over the precipice again, where it condenses into rain, forming a river that runs off in another direction.

MADAME DE LA BRESSE, of Paris, in a testament executed in 1976, left 125,000 francs for the benefit of snowmen—yes, snowmen—to provide them with clothing for the sake of "la decence." Her will was contested in court on the grounds that the testator had been mentally unbalanced, but the judge decided to rule in favor of the snowmen.

A SNAKE in the London Zoo was fitted with a glass eye.

SOUND WILL TRAVEL through granite eleven times as fast as through the air.

A LAKE THAT BLOWS BUBBLES is situated on the island of Java. Steam and gases rising from the surface condense into bubbles six feet in diameter. After sailing high into the air like balloons, they explode with a loud report.

YAMANA WOMEN OF FIRELAND, South America, learn to swim from infancy. Yamana men, however, cannot swim a stroke, although they spend most of their lives in boats.

THE EXPERIENCE OF THE CLIPPER SHIP "Crusader," with a full crew and 214 passengers aboard, tops any sailor's yarn ever heard.

The immigrant ship, en route from England to New Zealand, was only five days out of the Bay of Biscay in 1874 when it sprang a leak. The crew manned the pumps, but the harder they worked the faster the sea seemed to flow in. To make matters worse, two of the pumps broke down.

The hold filled so rapidly that all hope for saving the ship was abandoned. The captain prepared to transfer the passengers to the lifeboats and ordered all hands on deck. Suddenly a shout of exultation went up from the weary pump hands in the hold. The water was no longer rising. They kept up their efforts and the danger soon passed.

The remainder of the voyage was comparatively uneventful. When the captain put the ship in Chalmers Dock for overhauling, an astounding discovery was made. The ship had been saved by a fish's tail. Tightly wedged in a hole in the ship's bottom was the caudal appendage of a gigantic fish. The inrush of water had carried the fish with it and plugged up the hole.

The survivors of this trip formed a commemorative society called "The Crusader's Passenger Association." The membership was restricted to actual survivors and their next of kin. They met periodically at Littleton and Christchurch to keep alive the memory of the miracle that saved the "Crusader" from a watery grave.

INSECTS comprise four-fifths of the whole animal kingdom.

THE GAZELLE AND LLAMA never drink water.

DAVID, KING OF ISRAEL, was twice as rich as the richest country in the world. According to 1 Chronicles 22:14 and 29:4, David possessed 103,000 talents of gold and

1,007,000 talents of silver. The intrinsic value of this is $6,041,070,000. In terms of present-day purchasing power, it would equal $120 billion

UNTIL 1766 EATING PLACES were always part of a hotel or an inn. In that year, a chef named Boulanger opened the first public dining place in Paris. The owner placed a sign in front of his establishment. The sign bore an adaptation of the scripture from Matthew 11:28: "Come unto me, all ye that are hungry and I shall restore you." From the word restore (in French restaurerai) the establishment became known as a "restaurant," and this name has since been applied to eateries the world over.

JOHN TYLER literally "cried" himself into the presidency! At the convention in 1840, when William Harrison was nominated over Henry Clay, John Tyler (one of Clay's friends) was so disappointed that he burst into tears. This prompted the convention to nominate him for vice president. When Harrison died after one month in office— Tyler became president.

THE HISTORY OF THE INDIES is a book that has neither been written nor printed. Instead, each letter was cut by hand into a page of the finest parchment. The pages are interlined with blue silk and the incised text is as easily read as the best modern print. The labor that went into this masterpiece must have been prodigious. There are 1,200,000 letters on its three hundred pages, each letter carved by hand. In 1640, the German emperor, Rudolph II, offered to buy it for the equivalent of $1,100,000. The princely DeLigne family of Belgium, owners of the volume, turned down his offer. They still own the book.

WHAT DOES THE BIBLE SAY ABOUT THAT?

Assurance
ROMANS 8:38–39

I am convinced that neither death nor life, neither angels nor demons, neither the present nor the future, nor any powers, neither height nor depth, nor anything else in all creation, will be able to separate us from the love of God that is in Christ Jesus our Lord.

Atonement
HEBREWS 9:28

Christ was sacrificed once to take away the sins of many people; and he will appear a second time, not to bear sin, but to bring salvation to those who are waiting for him.

Blessings
JOHN 1:16

From the fullness of his grace we have all received one blessing after another.

Boldness
Joshua 1:9
Be strong and courageous. Do not be terrified; do not be discouraged, for the Lord your God will be with you wherever you go.

Character
PROVERBS 5:21 NRSV

Human ways are under the eyes of the Lord,
and he examines all their paths.

Commitment
PSALM 37:5

Commit your way to the LORD; trust in him and he will do this.

Communication
PROVERBS 13:3

He who guards his lips guards his life.

Compassion
PSALM 145:9

The LORD is good to all;
he has compassion on all he has made.

Contentment
1 TIMOTHY 6:6

Godliness with contentment is great gain.

Decision Making

Psalm 37:5–6

Commit your way to the LORD; trust in him and he will do this: He will make your righteousness shine like the dawn, the justice of your cause like the noonday sun.

Devotion to God

1 Chronicles 28:9

Acknowledge the God of your father, and serve him with wholehearted devotion and with a willing mind, for the LORD searches every heart and understands every motive behind the thoughts. If you seek him, he will be found by you; but if you forsake him, he will reject you forever.

Eternal Life

John 17:3

[Jesus said,] "This is eternal life: that they may know you the only true God, and Jesus Christ, whom you have sent."

Faith

Ephesians 6:16

Take up the shield of faith, with which you can extinguish all the flaming arrows of the evil one.

Family

Deuteronomy 5:16

Honor your father and your mother, as the LORD your God has commanded you, so that you may live long and that it may go well with you in the land the LORD your God is giving you.

Forgiveness

Matthew 6:14–15

[Jesus said,] "If you forgive men when they sin against you, your heavenly Father will also forgive you. But if you do not forgive men their sins, your Father will not forgive your sins."

Friendship

Proverbs 27:6

Wounds from a friend can be trusted.

Giving

2 Corinthians 9:7 NRSV

Each of you must give as you have made up your mind, not reluctantly or under compulsion, for God loves a cheerful giver.

God's Love
ROMANS 5:8

God demonstrates his own love for us in this: While we were still sinners, Christ died for us.

God's Will
1 JOHN 2:17 NRSV

The world and its desire are passing away, but those who do the will of God live forever.

God's Word
2 TIMOTHY 3:16–17 NRSV

All scripture is inspired by God and is useful for teaching, for reproof, for correction, and for training in righteousness, so that everyone who belongs to God may be proficient, equipped for every good work.

Grace
JAMES 4:6

[God] gives us more grace. That is why Scripture says: "God opposes the proud but gives grace to the humble."

Heaven
REVELATION 21:4

[God] will wipe every tear from their eyes. There will be no more death or mourning or crying or pain, for the old order of things has passed away.

Holiness
2 PETER 3:11–12

You ought to live holy and godly lives as you look forward to the day of God and speed its coming.

Hospitality
1 PETER 4:9

Offer hospitality to one another without grumbling.

Humility
1 PETER 5:5

Clothe yourselves with humility toward one another, because, "God opposes the proud but gives grace to the humble."

Integrity
PSALM 84:11

The LORD God is a sun and shield; the LORD bestows favor and honor; no good thing does he withhold from those whose walk is blameless.

Jesus
LUKE 1:32

He will be great and will be called the Son of the Most High. The Lord God will give him the throne of his father David.

Kindness
PROVERBS 14:31

Whoever is kind to the needy honors God.

Life
JOB 33:4

The Spirit of God has made me; the breath of the Almighty gives me life.

Love
1 CORINTHIANS 13:13–14:1

These three remain: faith, hope and love. But the greatest of these is love. Follow the way of love.

Money
LUKE 12:15

[Jesus said to them,] "Watch out! Be on your guard against all kinds of greed; a man's life does not consist in the abundance of his possessions."

Patience
ROMANS 12:12

Be joyful in hope, patient in affliction, faithful in prayer.

Perseverance
2 CORINTHIANS 4:17

Our light and momentary troubles are achieving for us an eternal glory that far outweighs them all.

Prayer
JEREMIAH 29:12

[The Lord said,] "You will call upon me and come and pray to me, and I will listen to you."

Priorities
MATTHEW 6:33

[Jesus said,] "Seek first his kingdom and his righteousness, and all these things will be given to you as well."

Purpose
PSALM 138:8

*The LORD will fulfill his purpose for me;
your love, O LORD, endures forever—do not abandon the works of your hands.*

Relationships
GALATIANS 6:2, 10

*Carry each other's burdens, and in this way you will fulfill the law of Christ. . . .
Therefore, as we have opportunity, let us do good to all people, especially to those who belong to the family of believers.*

Reputation
PROVERBS 22:1

A good name is more desirable than great riches; to be esteemed is better than silver or gold.

Self-Control
1 PETER 5:8

Be self-controlled and alert. Your enemy the devil prowls around like a roaring lion looking for someone to devour.

Self-Image
MATTHEW 10:29–31

[Jesus said,] "Are not two sparrows sold for a penny? Yet not one of them will fall to the ground apart from the will of your Father. And even the very hairs of your head are all numbered. So don't be afraid; you are worth more than many sparrows."

Service
COLOSSIANS 3:23–24

Whatever you do, work at it with all your heart, as working for the Lord, not for men, since you know that you will receive an inheritance from the Lord as a reward. It is the Lord Christ you are serving.

Strength
PHILIPPIANS 4:13

I can do everything through . . . [Christ] who gives me strength.

Talents and Gifts
1 CORINTHIANS 7:7 NRSV

Each has a particular gift from God, one having one kind and another a different kind.

Thankfulness
1 CHRONICLES 16:34

*Give thanks to the LORD, for he is good;
his love endures forever.*

Truth
JOHN 14:6

Jesus answered, "I am the way and the truth and the life. No one comes to the Father except through me."

Wisdom
PSALM 111:10

*The fear of the LORD is the beginning of wisdom;
all who follow his precepts have good understanding.
To him belongs eternal praise.*

THE MOST ABSORBING QUESTION OF OUR GENERATION

What's Up with Toilet Paper?

What did people use before toilet paper? Well . . . different strokes for different folks—Romans used wool and rosewater and sponges soaked in saltwater at the end of a stick; "well-to-do" Frenchmen used lace, wool, and hemp; Vikings used lamb's wool; Eskimos used snow and Tundra moss; sailors used the frayed end of an old anchor line. Basically they turned to whatever was handy.

What about the early settlers of the American West? Corncobs were used by some—but more fashion-conscious pioneers preferred the Sears catalogue. This even inspired some such humorous spinoffs as the "Rears and Sorebutt" catalogue. *The Farmer's Almanac* had a hole in it so it could be hung on a hook, but this was considered "cheap and tacky" by elite New Englanders.

When was toilet paper officially called "Toilet Paper?" "Official" toilet paper—that is, paper which was produced specifically for the purpose—dates back at least to the late 14th Century. Chinese emperors ordered it in two-foot by three-foot sheets. Yowser!!!

Who was the first person to package and sell toilet paper? Joseph C. Gayetty of New York started producing the first packaged toilet paper in the U.S. in 1857. It consisted of pre-moistened flat sheets medicated with aloe—five hundred sheets of "therapeutic paper" went for about fifty cents. As disturbing as this might sound, Gayetty's name was printed on every sheet. Ooh!

When did rolled and perforated toilet paper come on the market? Depending on who you're listening to, it could be the Albany Perforated Wrapping (A.P.W.) Paper Company in 1877 or the Scott Paper Company in 1890. Scott Paper—too embarrassed to be associated with this "unmentionable" product—sold its paper through intermediaries, cutting and labeling to each buyer's specifications.

Who were the great innovators of the toilet paper industry? In 1935, Northern Tissue advertised "splinter-free" toilet paper. Yep, you read that right; early paper production techniques sometimes left splinters embedded in the paper. And in 1942, St. Andrew's Paper Mill in Great Britain introduced two-ply toilet paper. In the late 1990s, a Seattle-based company came out with toilet paper made entirely of cotton and water—no wood! Kimberly Clark introduced—in 2001—the first dispensable pre-moistened wipe on a roll. Wow! We've come a long way, Baby!

What do today's quality-conscious consumers look for in toilet paper? A terrific paper has "SASV"—Softness, Absorbency, Strength, and Value.

Is there a fortune to be made in toilet paper? Oh yes! Global sales now exceed $20 billion and going strong—despite the introduction of the "paperless toilet" by Japan in 1999. Those little beauties come complete with a washing/rinsing mechanism, a blow-drying component, and a heating element.

JOKES, RIDDLES, TRIVIA, AND HUMOROUS STORIES

Try this!
Think of a number—
Double it.
Add 10.
Divide by 2.
Subtract the number you first thought of.

Your answer is 5.

Question: What metal will burn in water?
Answer: When sodium, a metal, is placed in water, a violent reaction occurs, causing the metal to be consumed. Hydrogen gas is liberated, and sodium hydroxide is formed.

Did you know?
Oranges, watermelons, and lemons are neither fruit nor vegetables. They are berries!

A "black eye" is called a "blue eye" in Germany and a "poached eye" in France.

While enjoying an early-morning breakfast in a northern Arizona café, four elderly ranchers were discussing everything from cattle, horses, and weather to how things used to be in the "good old days."

Eventually the conversation moved on to their spouses. One gentleman turned to the fellow on his right and asked, "Roy, aren't you and your bride celebrating your 50th wedding anniversary soon?"

"Yup, we sure are," Roy replied.

"Well, are you going to do anything special to celebrate?" another man asked.

The old man pondered this for a moment, then replied, "For our 25th anniversary, I took Bea to Tucson. I was thinking for our 50th I'd go back down there and get her!"

Did you know?

The windows in an empty house will never frost no matter how low the temperature.

What is it?

The more it dries, the wetter it gets. What is it?
A towel.

The more you have of it, the less you see. What is it?
Darkness.

The more you take away, the bigger it gets. What is it?
A hole.

The one who makes it, sells it. The one who buys it, never uses it. The one who uses it never knows that he's using it. What is it?
A coffin.

Match these Bible characters with their statement from the scriptural text:

1. "Ah, Lord God! Behold, I cannot speak, for I am a youth."

2. "The foolishness of God is wiser than men, and the weakness of God is stronger than men."

3. "My little children, let us not love in word or in tongue, but in deed and in truth."

4. "Entreat me not to leave you, or to turn back from following after you; for wherever you go, I will go; and wherever you lodge, I will lodge; your people shall be my people, and your God, my God."

5. "I have surely built You an exalted house, and a place for You to dwell in forever."

    A. Ruth (Ruth 1:16 NKJV)
    B. Apostle Paul (1 Corinthians 1:25 NKJV)
    C. Solomon (1 Kings 8:13 NKJV)
    D. Jeremiah (Jeremiah 1:6 NKJV)
    E. Apostle John (1 John 3:18 NKJV)

Answers: 1 (D), 2 (B) 3 (E) 4 (A) 5 (C)

During a family reunion, a small boy looked at his great-grandfather and asked his mother, "What's his name?"

"That's Grandpa Miller," his mother replied,

"No," the little boy said. "What's his REAL name?"

"His first name is Harry," his mother answered.

Loudly he shouted, "Well, no wonder they call him Grandpa Miller!"

Vague Newspaper Headlines

The following are real newspaper headlines from newspapers around the globe. Can you see what the journalist meant to say? Can you also see a more humorous interpretation?

"Eye Drops Off Shelf"
"Kids Make Nutritious Snacks"
"Queen Mary Having Bottom Scraped"
"Dealers Will Hear Car Talk at Noon"
"Miners Refuse to Work after Death"
"Milk Drinkers Are Turning to Powder"
"Drunk Gets Nine Months in Violin Case"
"Juvenile Court to Try Shooting Defendant"
"Complaints about NBA Referees Growing Ugly"
"Panda Mating Fails; Veterinarian Takes Over"
"Killer Sentenced to Die for Second Time in 10 Years"
"Safety Experts Say School Bus Passengers Should Be Belted"
"Sisters Reunited after 18 Years at Checkout Counter"
"Man-Eating Piranha Mistakenly Sold as Pet Fish"
"Astronaut Takes Blame for Gas in Spacecraft"
"Hospitals Are Sued by Seven Foot Doctors"
"Two Soviet Ships Collide, One Dies"
"Lack of Brains Hinders Research"
"Hershey Bars Protest"

The sun bakes them, the hand breaks them, the foot treads on them, and the mouth tastes them. What are they?
Grapes

In what year did Christmas Day and New Year's Day fall on the same year?
It happens every year.

What book was once owned by only the wealthy, but now everyone can have it? You can't buy it in a bookstore or take it from a library.

A telephone book.

Reading is FUNdamental

A pair of chickens walk up to the circulation desk at a public library and say, "Buk Buk BUK." The librarian decides that the chickens desire three books, and gives them the books . . . and the chickens leave shortly thereafter.

Around midday, the two chickens return to the circulation desk quite vexed and say, "Buk Buk BuKKOOK!" The librarian decides that the chickens desire another three books and gives the books to them. The chickens leave as before.

The two chickens return to the library in the early afternoon, approach the librarian, looking very annoyed and say, "Buk Buk Buk Buk Bukkooook!" The librarian is now a little suspicious of these chickens. She gives them what they request and decides to follow them.

She followed them out of the library, out of the town, and to a park. At this point, she hid behind a tree, not wanting to be seen. She saw the two chickens throwing the books at a frog in a pond, to which the frog was saying, "Rrredit, rrredit, rrredit!"

Short Quips

Never, under any circumstances, take a sleeping pill and a laxative on the same night.

Never lick a steak knife.

Generous Gifts

A tour bus driver is driving down a highway with a bus full of seniors, when a little old lady taps him on his shoulder. She offers him a handful of almonds, which he gratefully munches.

Fifteen minutes later, she taps him on his shoulder again and hands him another handful of almonds. She repeats this gesture about eight times.

At the ninth tap on his shoulder, the bus driver asks the little old lady why they don't eat the almonds themselves, whereupon she replies that it is not possible because of their old teeth. They are not able to chew them. "Why do you buy them, then?" he asks, puzzled. The old lady answers, "We just love the chocolate around them."

A-Z Dictionary for Moms

AIRPLANE: What Mom impersonates to get a one-year-old child to eat strained beets.

APPLE: Nutritious lunchtime dessert, which children will trade for cupcakes.

BATHROOM: A room used by the whole family, believed by all except Mom to be self-cleaning.

BECAUSE: Mom's reason to make kids do things that can't be explained logically.

CARPET: Expensive floor covering used to catch spills and clean mud off shoes.

CHINA: Legendary nation reportedly populated by children who love leftover vegetables.

DATE: Infrequent outings with Dad where Mom can enjoy worrying about the kids in a different setting.

DRINKING GLASS: Any carton or bottle left open in the fridge.

EAR: A place where kids store dirt.

EAT: What kids do between meals but not during them.

FABLE: A story told by a teenager arriving home after curfew.

FOOD: The response Mom usually gives when asked, "What's for dinner tonight?"

GARBAGE: Refuse items that Mom winds up taking out herself.

GUM: Adhesive for the hair.

HAMPER: A container, usually with a lid, surrounded by but not containing dirty clothing.

HANDI-WIPES: Pants, shirtsleeves, drapes, etc.

INSIDE: That place that immediately looks attractive once Mom has cleaned every room in the house.

JACKPOT: When all the kids stay at friends' homes for the night.

JOY RIDE: Going somewhere without the kids.

KETCHUP: Goop kids use to drown a dinner that Mom spent years perfecting to get the seasoning just right.

KISS: Medicine by Mom.

LEMONADE STAND: Business venture in which Mom buys powdered mix, sugar, lemons, and paper cups, and sets up a table, chairs, pitchers, and ice for kids who sit there for three to six minutes and net a profit of fifteen cents.

LOVE: Overwhelming feeling on the occasion when kids do something nice for Mom.

MAYBE: No.

"MOMMMMMMMMY!": The cry of a child on another floor of the house who wants something.

OCEAN: What the bathroom floor looks like after the kids' bath time.

PANIC: What a mother does when the wind-up swing stops.

PETS: Small, furry creatures that follow kids home so Mom will have something else to care for.

PURSE: A bag Mom carries that doubles as a diaper bag when children are small.

QUIET: A state of household peace that occurs only before the birth of the first child and again after the last child leaves for college.

RAINCOAT: Article of clothing Mom bought to keep a child dry and warm, rendered ineffective because it's in the bottom of a locker.

REFRIGERATOR: Combination art gallery and air-conditioner in the kitchen.

SPIT: All-purpose cleaning fluid especially good to use on kids' faces.

TERRIBLE TWO'S: Having both kids at home all summer.

TOWELS: Floor coverings.

UMPTEENTH: Highly conservative estimate of the number of times Mom must instruct her offspring to do something before it actually is done.

VACATION: Where you take the family to get away from it all, only to find it there, too.

"WHEN YOUR FATHER GETS HOME": Standard measurement of time between crime and punishment.

XOXOXOXO: Mom's salutation guaranteed to make the already embarrassing note in a kid's lunch box even more mortifying.

"YIPPEE!": What Mom would jump up and shout if the school year were changed to twelve months.

ZILLION: Amount of times Mom has gone to the grocery store this week.

If You Were
If you were locked in a concrete room with no windows and no doors, and all you had inside the room was a bed and a calendar, how would you eat and drink?

Get "dates" from the calendar and water from the (bed) "springs."

If you were locked in a concrete room with no windows and no doors, and all you had inside the room was a table and a mirror, how would you get out?

Look in the mirror, see what you saw, take the saw, cut the table in half; two halves make a "whole," then climb out the "hole."

If you were standing directly on Antarctica's South Pole facing north, which direction would you travel if you took one step backward?

North; from the South Pole, all directions are north.

If you were to take two apples from three apples, how many would you have?

Two. What you take is what you have.

What Am I?

I'm as small as an ant, as big as a whale. I'll approach like a breeze, but can come like a gale. By some I get hit, but all have shown fear. I'll dance to the music, though I can't hear. Of names I have many, of names I have one. I'm as slow as a snail, but from me you can't run. What am I?

A shadow

The more you take, the more you leave behind. What are they?

Footsteps.

Driver's Ed

While riding with three students in a driver's education vehicle, the instructor did his best to remain calm and patient during each student's turn at the wheel. The first driver of the semester was a young man, and he did quite well. As they entered the downtown area of the city, he had the students switch seats, and a young lady took the wheel.

As they approached the first stoplight, the young lady gave no sign that she saw the pedestrian making his way through the crosswalk. Finally, the instructor used the instructor's brake pedal on his side of the car and came to a complete stop.

Exasperated with her instructor, the young lady said, "The light was still green!" The instructor silently pointed to the man still standing, but apparently shaken, at the driver's front bumper.

Letters to the Pastor

Dear Pastor, I think a lot more people would come to your church if you moved it to Disneyland.

Loreen, age 9, Tacoma

Dear Pastor, I liked your sermon on Sunday. Especially when it was finished.

Ralph, age 11, Akron

Dr. Billy Graham

The Reverend Billy Graham tells of a time early in his ministry when he arrived in a small town to preach. Wanting to mail a letter, he asked a young boy where the post office was. When the boy had told him, Dr. Graham thanked him and said, "If you'll come to the church this evening, you can hear me telling everyone how to get to Heaven."

"I don't think so," the boy said. "You don't even know your way to the post office."

Right Impressions

A young businessman had just started his own firm. He'd rented a beautiful office and had it furnished with antiques. Sitting there, he saw a man come into the outer office. Wishing to appear busy, the businessman picked up the phone and started to pretend he had a big deal working. He threw huge figures around and made giant commitments. Finally, he hung up and asked the visitor, "Can I help you?" The man said, "Sure. I've come to install the phone!"

A Simple Message

The little church in the suburbs suddenly stopped buying from its regular office supply dealer. So the dealer telephoned Deacon Brown to ask why.

"I'll tell you why," shouted Deacon Brown. "Our church ordered some pencils from you to be used in the pews for visitors to register."

"Well," interrupted the dealer, "didn't you receive them yet?"

"Oh, we received them all right," replied Deacon Brown.

"However, you sent us some golf pencils *. . . each stamped with the words, 'Play Golf Next Sunday.'"*

Bible Q & A

Question: Where is the first baseball game in the Bible?

Answer: *In the big inning, Eve stole first, Adam stole second. Cain struck out Abel, and the Prodigal Son came home. The Giants and the Angels were rained out.*

Question: Who is the greatest babysitter mentioned in the Bible?

Answer: *David. He rocked Goliath to sleep.*

Question: Why didn't Noah go fishing?

Answer: *He only had two worms!*

Question: When was the longest day in the Bible?

Answer: *The day Adam was created, because there was no Eve.*

Great Faith

An elderly lady was well-known for her faith and for her boldness in talking about it. She would stand on her front porch and shout, "PRAISE THE LORD!"

Next door to her lived an atheist who would get so angry at her proclamations he would shout, "There ain't no Lord!"

Hard times set in on the elderly lady, and she prayed for God to send her some assistance. She stood on her porch and shouted, "PRAISE THE LORD! GOD, I NEED FOOD! I AM HAVING A HARD TIME. PLEASE, LORD, SEND ME SOME GROCERIES!"

The next morning the lady went out on her porch, noted a large bag of groceries, and shouted, "PRAISE THE LORD."

The neighbor jumped from behind a bush and said, "Aha! I told you there was no Lord. God didn't buy those groceries—I did!"

The lady started jumping up and down and clapping her hands and said, "PRAISE THE LORD! He not only sent me groceries, but He made the devil pay for them. Praise the Lord!"

Why Ask Why?

If a 7-11 is open 24 hours a day, 365 days a year, why are there locks on the doors?

If a cow laughed, would milk come out her nose?

Why is it that when you're driving and looking for an address, you turn down the volume on the radio?

How did a fool and his money get together in the first place?

How do they get the deer to cross at that yellow road sign?

What was the best thing before sliced bread?

"Experience is what you get when you didn't get what you wanted."

Why do they lock gas station bathrooms? Are they afraid someone will clean them?

Why do people who know the least know it the loudest?

If a turtle doesn't have a shell, is he homeless or naked?

Like Mother, Like Daughter

One day a little girl was sitting and watching her mother do the dishes at the kitchen sink. She suddenly noticed that her mother had several strands of white hair sticking out in contrast on her brunette head. She looked at her mother and inquisitively asked, "Why are some of your hairs white, Mom?"

Her mother replied, "Well, every time you do something wrong and make me cry or unhappy, one of my hairs turns white."

The little girl thought about that for a few moments and then said, "Momma, how come ALL of grandma's hairs are white?"

There is a word in the English language in which the first two letters signify a man, the first three signify a woman, the first four signify a great man, and the whole word represents a great woman. The word is *heroine.*

Is an old hundred-dollar bill better than a new one?
It's ninety-nine dollars better!

No sooner spoken than broken. What is it?
Silence.

Past mountain, meadow, field, and hill, it follows a river while standing still.
A riverbank.

What always speaks the truth but doesn't say a word?
A mirror.

Romance Trivia

Coffee Break Romance
It's reported that more than ten thousand marriages a year now are directly traceable to romances that begin during coffee breaks.

Diamond Engagement Rings
The first diamond engagement ring was presented in 1477 by Archduke Maximillian of Austria to Mary of Burgundy.

Engagement Lengths
The average engagement lasts six months.

First Love
Two out of five people marry their first love.

Forgotten Romance
Recent research indicates that about nine thousand romantic couples each year take out marriage licenses, then fail to use them.

Honeymoons
The word honeymoon first appeared in the sixteenth century. Honey is a reference to the sweetness of a new marriage and moon is a bitter acknowledgment that this sweetness, like a full moon, would quickly fade.

Longest Marriage
Canadian hunter and trapper Joseph Henry Jarvis (b. 6/15/1899) and wife, Annie (b. 10/10/1904), were married for seventy-nine years.

Mating Birds
It was believed that birds chose their mates on February 14, and because doves mate for life, they have become a symbol of fidelity.

Median Age for Marriage
In 1970, brides were on average 20.8 years old when they married, while grooms were 23.2. Americans are now marrying later in life. In the year 2000, brides were on average 25.1, with their grooms averaging 26.8.

Morning Kissing
Studies indicate that a man who kisses his wife good-bye when he leaves for work every morning averages a higher income than those who don't. Husbands who exercise the rituals of affection tend to be more painstaking, more stable, more methodical, thus, higher earners. Studies also show that men who kiss their wives before leaving in the morning live five years longer than those who don't.

Oldest Bride
Minnie Munro became the world's oldest bride when she married Dudley Reid at the age of 102 on May 31, 1991. Reid, the groom, was 83 years old.

Oldest Groom
Harry Stevens was 103 when he married 84-year-old Thelma Lucas at the Caravilla Retirement Home in Wisconsin on December 3, 1984.

On Bended Knee
One in five men proposes on one knee.

Phone Proposals
Six percent of men propose to their girlfriends over the phone.

Red Roses
Red roses are the most popular flower to give on
Valentine's Day, and although they may all look the same to
the untrained eye, there are actually more than nine
hundred different varieties of dark-red and medium-red
roses.

The Longest Engagement
Sixty-seven years, according to the Guinness Book of World
Records. The happy couple finally wed at age eighty-two!

Tying the Knot
The expression "tying the knot" dates back to Roman
times, when the bride wore a girdle that was tied in knots—
which the groom then had the fun of untying.

U.S. Marriage Rates
The Wall Street Journal, citing U.S. Census Bureau research,
reports that the U.S. marriage rate is significantly higher in
the Mountain States (thanks primarily to
Nevada's wedding industry), along with the
East South-Central States of Mississippi,
Tennessee, Kentucky, and Alabama. The
Northeast region of the country has the lowest marriage
rate.

Your Hand in Marriage
Only 4 percent of men ask for the parents' approval for
their bride's hand in marriage.

How to Make Friends in an Elevator
Whistle the first seven notes of "It's a Small World" inces-
santly.

Crack open your briefcase or purse and, while peering
inside, ask, "Got enough air in there?"

Offer name tags to everyone getting on the elevator. Wear yours upside down.

Wear a puppet on your hand and use it to talk to the other passengers.

When the elevator is silent, look around and ask, "Is that your beeper?"

Say "DING!" at each floor.

Say "I wonder what all these do . . ." and push any and all red buttons.

Stand silent and motionless in the corner, facing the wall, without getting off.

Greet everyone getting on the elevator with a warm handshake and ask them to call you Admiral.

Stare, grinning at another passenger for a while, and then announce: "I've got new socks on!"

Bet the other passengers you can fit a quarter in your nose.

When arriving at your floor, grunt and strain to yank the doors open, then act embarrassed when they open by themselves.

Walk on with a cooler that says "Human Head" on the side.

Stare at another passenger for a while, and then announce: "You're one of THEM!" and move to the far corner of the elevator.

Listen to the elevator walls with a stethoscope.

Draw a little square on the floor with chalk and announce to the other passengers that this is your "personal space."

Make explosion noises when anyone presses a button.

CLASSIC FAIRY TALES

The Bell

HANS CHRISTIAN ANDERSEN

In the evening at sunset, when glimpses of golden clouds could just be seen among the chimney pots, a curious sound would be heard, first by one person, then by another. It was like a church bell, but it only lasted a moment because of the rumble of vehicles and street cries.

"There is the evening bell," people would say. "The sun is setting."

Those who went outside the town where the houses were more scattered, each with its garden or little meadow, saw the evening star and heard the tones of the bell much better. It seemed as if the sound came from a church buried in the silent, fragrant woods, and people looked in that direction, feeling quite solemn.

Time passed and still people said one to the other, "Can there be a church in the woods? That bell has such a wonderfully sweet sound! Shall we go and look at it closer?" The rich people drove and the poor ones walked, but it was a very long way. When they reached a group of willows which grew on the outskirts of the wood, they sat down and looked up among the long branches, thinking that they were really in the heart of the forest. A confectioner from the town came out and pitched a tent there, and then another confectioner, and he hung a bell up over his tent. This bell was tarred so as to stand the rain, and the clapper was wanting. When people went home again, they said it had been so romantic, and that meant something beyond mere tea. Three persons protested that they had penetrated right through the forest to the other side. They said that they heard the same curious bell all the time, but that then it sounded as if it came from the town.

One of them wrote a poem about it and said that it sounded

like a mother's voice to a beloved child. No melody could be sweeter than the chimes of this bell.

The Emperor's attention was also drawn to it and he promised that anyone who really discovered where the sound came from should receive the title of "World's Bell Ringer," even if there were no bell at all.

A great many people went into the woods for the sake of earning an honest penny, but only one of them brought home any kind of explanation. No one had been far enough, not even he himself, but he said that the sound of the bell came from a very big owl in a hollow tree. It was a wise owl that perpetually beat its head against a tree, but whether the sound came from its head or from the hollow tree he could not say with any certainty. All the same he was appointed the "World's Bell Ringer," and every year he wrote a little treatise on the owl, but nobody was much the wiser for it.

Now on a certain confirmation day the priest had preached a very moving sermon, and all the young people about to be confirmed had been much touched by it. It was a very important day for them. They were leaving childhood behind and becoming grown-up persons. The child's soul was, as it were, to be transformed into that of a responsible being. It was a beautiful, sunny day and after the confirmation, the young people walked out of the town, and they heard the sound of the unknown bell more than usually loud coming from the wood. On hearing it, they all felt anxious to go and see it—all except three.

The first of these had to go home to try on her ball dress. It was this very dress and this very ball that were the reason of her having been confirmed this time; otherwise it would have been put off. The second was a poor boy who had borrowed his tailcoat and boots of the landlord's son and had to return them at the appointed time. The third said that he had never been anywhere without his parents, that he had always been a good child and he meant to continue so, although he was confirmed. Nobody ought to have made fun of this resolve, but he did not escape being laughed at.

So these three did not go. The others trudged off. The sun shone and the birds sang, and the newly confirmed young people took each other by the hand and sang with them. They had not yet received any position in life. They were all equal in the eyes of the Lord on the day of their confirmation. Soon two of the smallest ones got tired and returned to town. Two little girls sat down and made wreaths, so they did not go either. When the others reached the willows where the confectioners had their tents, they said, "Now then, here we are. The bell doesn't exist. It is only something people imagine."

Just then the bell with its deep rich notes was heard in the woods and four or five of them decided after all to penetrate further into the wood. The underwood was so thick and close that it was quite difficult to advance. The woodruff grew almost too high. Convolvulus and brambles hung in long garlands from tree to tree, where the nightingales sang and the sunbeams played. It was deliciously peaceful but there was no path for the girls; their clothes would have been torn to shreds. There were great boulders overgrown with many-colored mosses, and fresh springs trickled among them with a curious little gurgling sound.

"Surely that cannot be the bell," said one of the young people as he lay down to listen. "This must be thoroughly looked into." So he stayed behind and let the others go on.

They came to a little hut made of bark and branches overhung by a crab apple, as if it wanted to shake all its blooms over the roof, which was covered with roses. The long sprays clustered round the gable, and on it hung a little bell. Could this be the one they sought? Yes, they were all agreed that it must be, except one. He said it was far too small and delicate to be heard so far away as they had heard it, and that the tones that moved all hearts were quite different from these. He who spoke was the King's son and so the others said, "That kind of fellow must always be wiser than anyone else."

So they let him go on alone, and as he went he was more and more overcome by the solitude of the wood, but he still heard the little bell with which the others were so pleased. And now and then when the wind came from the direction of the confectioners, he could hear demands for tea. But the deep-toned bell sounded above them all, and it seemed as if there were an organ playing with it; and the sounds came from the left where the heart is placed.

There was a rustling among the bushes, and a little boy stood before the King's son. He had on wooden shoes and such a small jacket that the sleeves did not cover his wrists. They knew each other, for he was the boy who had had to go back to return the coat and boots to the landlord's son. He had done this, changed back into the shabby clothes and wooden shoes, and then, drawn by the deep notes of the bell, had returned to the wood again.

"Then we can go together," said the King's son.

But the poor boy in the wooden shoes was too bashful. He pulled down his short sleeves and said he was afraid he could not walk quickly enough and besides he thought the bell ought to be looked for on the right, because that side looked the most beautiful.

"Then we shan't meet at all," said the King's son, nodding to the poor boy, who went into the thickest and darkest part of the wood, where the thorns tore his shabby clothes and scratched his face, hands, and feet till they bled. The King's son got some good scratches too, but he at least had the sun shining upon his path. We are going to follow him, for he is a bright fellow.

"I must and will find the bell," said he, "if I have to go to the end of the world."

Some horrid monkeys sat up in the trees grinning and showing their teeth. "Shall we pelt him?" they said. "Shall we thrash him? He is a King's son."

But he went confidently on, further and further into the wood, where the most extraordinary flowers grew. There were white star-like lilies with blood-red stamens, pale blue tulips that glistened in the sun, and apple trees on which the apples looked like great shining soap bubbles. You may fancy how these trees glittered in the sun. Round about were beautiful green meadows where stags and hinds gamboled under the spreading oaks and beeches. Mosses and creepers grew in the fissures where the bark of the trees was broken away. There were also great glades with quiet lakes, where white swans swam about flapping their wings. The King's son often stopped and listened, for he sometimes fancied that the bell sounded from one of these lakes. Then again he felt sure that it was not there, but further in the wood.

Now the sun began to go down, and the clouds were fiery red.

A great stillness came over the wood and he sank upon his knees, sang his evening psalm, and said, "Never shall I find what I seek, now the sun is going down. The night is coming on—the dark night. Perhaps I could catch one more glimpse of the round, red sun before it sinks beneath the earth. I will climb up onto those rocks. They are as high as the trees."

He sized up the root and creepers and climbed up the slippery stones where the water snakes wriggled and the toads seemed to croak at him, but he reached the top before the sun disappeared. Seen from this height, ho, what splendor lay before him! The ocean, the wide beautiful ocean, with its long waves rolling toward the shore! The sun still stood like a great shining altar, out there where sea and sky met. Everything melted away into glowing colors. The wood sang, the ocean sang, and his heart sang with them. All nature was like a vast holy temple, where trees and floating clouds were as pillars, flowers and grass a woven tapestry, and the heaven itself a great dome. The red colors vanished as the sun went down, but millions of stars peeped out. They were like countless diamond lamps, and he spread out his arms toward heaven, sea, and forest.

At that moment, from the right hand path came the poor boy with the short sleeves and wooden shoes. He had reached the same goal just as soon by his own road. They ran toward each other and clasped each other's hands in that great temple of nature and poetry, and above them sounded the invisible holy bell. Happy spirits floated round it to the strains of a joyous hallelujah.

The Old Man and His Grandson

Jacob Grimm

There was once a very old man, whose eyes had become dim, his ears dull of hearing, his knees trembled. When he sat at the table. he could hardly hold the spoon, and spilt the broth on the tablecloth or let it run out of his mouth.

His son and his son's wife were disgusted at this, so the old grandfather had to sit in the corner behind the stove. They gave him his food in an earthenware bowl, and not even enough of it. On occasion, the old man would look toward the table with his eyes full of tears.

One day, the old man's trembling hands could not hold the bowl, and it fell to the ground and broke. The young wife scolded him, but he said nothing and only sighed. Then the couple bought him a wooden bowl for a few half-pence, out of which he had to eat.

They were once sitting this way when the little grandson of four years old began to gather together some bits of wood upon the ground. "What are you doing there?" asked the father. "I am making a little trough," answered the child, "for father and mother to eat out of when I am big."

The man and his wife looked at each other for a while, and presently began to cry. Then they helped the old grandfather up and seated him at the table. Thereafter, he was always allowed to eat with the family—and if he spilled a little of anything, they said nothing at all.

The Ants and the Grasshopper

AESOP'S TALE

The ants were spending a fine winter's day drying grain collected in the summertime when a grasshopper, perishing with hunger, passed by and earnestly begged for a little food.

The ants inquired of him, "Why did you not treasure up food during the summer?"

"I had not leisure enough," the grasshopper answered. "I passed the days in singing."

The ants then answered in derision, "If you were foolish enough to sing all the summer, you must dance supperless to bed in the winter."

The Cobbler Who Would Be a Doctor

AESOP'S TALE

A cobbler unable to make a living by his trade and made desperate by poverty, began to practice medicine in a town in which he was not known. He sold a drug, pretending that it was an antidote for all types of poisons. Before long, he had made a name for himself through advertising and long-winded self promotion.

When the cobbler happened to fall sick himself of a serious illness, the governor of the town determined to test his skill. For this purpose, he called for a cup, and while filling it with water, pretended to mix poison with the cobbler's antidote. He then offered the cobbler a reward if he would drink it.

The cobbler, under the fear of death, confessed that he had no knowledge of medicine and was only made famous by the clamor of the crowd. The governor then called a public assembly and addressed the citizens.

"Of what folly have you been guilty? You have not hesitated to entrust your heads to a man to whom no one could employ to make even the shoes for their feet."

Damon and Pythias

BY VALERIUS MAXIMUM

O nce upon a time, a powerful king named Dionysius ruled the Greek island of Sicily with an iron fist. He was a cruel tyrant, a man of little mercy. And because he had many enemies, the king was in constant fear that he would be assassinated.

The king had reason to worry. Many honorable men sought to end his life and with it the harsh rule constraining the people of the beautiful Grecian island. One day, a likely assassin was captured—a man named Pythias. In point of fact, this young man and his dear friend Damon had conspired together, but only Pythias was found out.

When Pythias asked the king to allow him to return home and arrange his affairs before his execution was carried out, the ruler sneered. Dionysius was not inclined to allow the kindness, but he was intrigued by the man's bold request.

"How could I be sure you would return," the king asked with a haughty laugh.

"You have my word," Pythias answered.

Quite understandably, the king was not inclined to trust the word of an assassin. "Perhaps there is someone, however, you would feel comfortable placing their life in your hands. Is there someone present who would be willing to face the executioner on your behalf if you should not return at the appointed time?"

To the king's surprise, a young man stepped up from the crowd. "I am willing," he told the king. "Pythias is my dear friend. I trust him with my life. I will remain here as your prisoner until he returns, and if he doesn't return, I will even face the execution in his place."

"Are you crazy?" the king responded. "Don't think I won't execute you if he returns even one minute late!"

They were fearsome words, but Damon would not be dissuaded. The king ordered Pythias released and Damon thrown into his cell.

Pythias wasted no time leaving to take care of his obligations. The king had given him only five days to complete his task and return.

The first two days of his long journey were quite difficult. Torrential rains dogged his every step. He had to navigate washed out roads and ruined bridges. At last, he came to a rushing river and was forced to turn back.

Back at the palace, the king chided Damon again and again as the days passed. "Your pledge was a foolish one, and it will surely be the end of you. In a few more hours you will die—and for what? Your friend is like all other men, who speak of friendship and trust, but in the end, give higher priority to their own interests."

Despite the king's ridicule, Damon's faith in Pythias did not waver—even as he was led out of his cell and placed on the block.

"Fool," said the king. "I told you he would not come. You have only yourself to blame!"

The executioner was preparing to swing the axe when a voice rang out. "Do not harm him. I am here."

Every head turned as Pythias ran and threw himself at the feet of the king. The cruel and merciless king was amazed and seemed strangely moved by the drama that had played out before his throne.

The crowd stood amazed as Dionysius waved the executioner away. "I have never seen such friendship—a friendship that trusts beyond the grave. You shall both live," the king exclaimed.

The Valiant Little Tailor

THE BROTHERS GRIMM

One summer's morning a little tailor was sitting at his table by the window; he was in good spirits, and sewed with all his might. Then came a peasant woman down the street crying, "Good jams, cheap. Good jams, cheap."

This rang pleasantly in the tailor's ears; he stretched his delicate head out of the window, and called, "Come up here, dear woman. Here you will get rid of your goods."

The woman came up the three steps to the tailor with her heavy basket, and he made her unpack all the pots for him. He inspected each one, lifted it up, put his nose to it, and at length said, "The jam seems to me to be good. Weigh me out four ounces, dear woman, and if it is a quarter of a pound that is of no consequence."

The woman who had hoped to find a good sale, gave him what he desired, but went away quite angry and grumbling.

"Now, this jam shall be blessed by God," cried the little tailor. "It will give me health and strength." So he brought the bread out of the cupboard, cut himself a piece right across the loaf and spread the jam over it. "This won't taste bitter," said he, "but I will just finish the jacket before I take a bite."

139

He laid the bread near him, sewed on, and in his joy, made bigger and bigger stitches. In the meantime, the smell of the sweet jam rose to where the flies were sitting in great numbers, and they were attracted and descended on it in hosts.

"Ah! Who invited you," said the little tailor, driving the unbidden guests away. The flies, however, would not be turned away, but instead returned in ever-increasing companies. The little tailor at last lost all patience, and drew a piece of cloth from the hole under his work-table. "Wait, and I will give it to you," he shouted and struck it mercilessly on them. When he drew it away and counted, there lay before him no fewer than seven, dead and with legs stretched out. "You must be quite a fellow," he said, and could not help admiring his own bravery. "The whole town shall know of this."

With gusto, the little tailor hastened to cut himself a girdle, stitched it, and embroidered on it in large letters, "Seven at One Blow. This town," he continued, "indeed, the whole world shall hear of it." And his heart wagged with joy like a lamb's tail.

The tailor put on the girdle, and resolved to go forth into the world, because he thought his workshop was too small for his valor. Before he went away, he sought about in the house to see if there was anything he could take with him. He found nothing, however, but an old cheese, and that he put in his pocket. In front of the door, he observed a bird that had caught itself in the thicket. It had to go into his pocket with the cheese. Now he took to the road boldly, and as he was light and nimble, he felt no fatigue. The road led him up a mountain, and when he had reached the highest point of it, there sat a powerful giant looking peacefully about him.

The little tailor went bravely up, spoke to him, and said, "Good day, Comrade. I see you are sitting here looking out at the great wide world. I am just on my way to see it. Have you any inclination to go with me?

The giant looked contemptuously at the tailor, and answered, "You ragamuffin. You miserable creature."

"Oh, indeed," answered the little tailor. Unbuttoning his coat, he showed the giant the girdle. "You may read right here what kind of man I am."

The giant read, "Seven in One Blow," and thinking they were men the tailor had killed, began to feel some respect for the tiny fellow. Nevertheless, he wished to try him first, and took a stone in his hand and squeezed it together so that water dropped out of it.

"Let's see you do that," said the giant, "if you're so strong."

"Is that all?" said the tailor. "Why that's little more than child's play for a man like me." He then reached into his pocket, took out the soft cheese and pressed it until the liquid ran out of it. "What do you think of that?"

The giant did not know what to say, and could not believe it of the little man. Then the giant picked up a stone and threw it so high that the eye could scarcely follow it. "Now, little mite of a man, can you do that as well?"

"Well thrown," said the tailor. "But after all the stone came down to earth again, I will throw one so high that it shall never come back at all." Placing his hand in his pocket, the tailor took out the bird and threw it into the air. The bird, delighted with its new-found liberty, rose, flew away and did not come back.

"How does that shot please you, Comrade?" asked the tailor.

"You can certainly throw," said the giant. "But now we will see if you are able to carry anything properly."

The giant took the little tailor to a mighty oak tree that lay on the ground, and said, "If you are strong enough, help me carry this tree out of the forest."

"Certainly," answered the little man. "Take the trunk on your shoulders, and I will raise up the branches and twigs. After all, they are the heaviest."

The giant took the trunk on his shoulder, while the tailor seated himself on a branch. Because he could not see what was happening, the giant carried away the whole tree and the little tailor into the bargain. Meanwhile, the tailor was quite merry and happy. He whistled the song, "Three Tailors Rode Forth from the Gate," as if carrying the tree were child's play.

The giant, after he had dragged the heavy burden part of the way, could go no further. "Hey you," he shouted. "I shall have to let the tree fall."

At that moment, the tailor sprang nimbly down, seized the

tree with both arms as if he had been carrying it all along, and said to the giant, "You are such a great fellow, and yet you can't seem to manage this little tree!"

The two went on together, and as they passed a cherry-tree, the giant grabbed the top of the tree where the ripest fruit was hanging, bent it down, put it into the tailor's hand, and told him to eat. But the little tailor was much too weak to hold the tree. When the giant let go, it sprang back, and the tailor was tossed into the air with it.

When the tailor picked himself up, the giant said, "What is this? Aren't you strong enough to hold onto a twig?"

"Nothing to it," answered the tailor. "Do you honestly think that would be a problem for a man who killed seven with one blow? I leapt over the tree because the huntsmen are shooting down there in the thicket. Jump as I did, if you can do it." The giant made the attempt, but could not get over the tree, and remained hanging in the branches. Once again the tailor had the upper hand.

Once the giant had pulled himself from the tree, he said, "If you're such a valiant fellow, why don't you come with me into our cavern and spend the night with us?" He seemed surprised when the little tailor was willing and followed him into the cave.

Inside the cave, the other giants were sitting by the fire. Each had a roasted sheep in his hand and was eating it. The little tailor looked around and thought, *It is much more spacious here than in my workshop.*

The giant showed him a bed, and said he was to lie down in it and sleep. The bed, however, was too big for the little tailor. Instead of lying down, he crept into a corner.

At midnight, thinking the little tailor would be in a sound sleep, the giant got up, took a great iron bar, and cut through the bed with one blow. He was certain he had finished off the annoying, little man for good.

With the earliest dawn the giants went into the forest, and had quite forgotten the little tailor, when all at once he walked up to them quite merrily and boldly. The giants were terrified. Thinking he might strike them all dead, they ran away in a great hurry.

The little tailor went onward, always following his own

pointed nose. After he had walked for a long time, he came to the courtyard of a royal palace. Feeling weary, he lay down on the grass and fell asleep.

While he lay sleeping, people from the palace discovered him and inspected him on all sides. They quickly read the words on his girdle, "Seven with One Blow."

"Oh my," they said. "What is a great warrior doing here in the midst of peace? He must be a mighty lord!" Wasting no time, they announced him to the king, and gave it as their opinion that if war should break out, this would be a weighty and useful man who ought on no account to be allowed to depart. Their counsel pleased the king, and he sent one of his courtiers to the little tailor to offer him military service. The ambassador stood by the sleeper, waiting for him to stretch his limbs and open his eyes. Then he conveyed the king's proposal.

"I've come here for that very purpose," the little tailor responded. "I am ready to enter the king's service." He was therefore honorably received and a special dwelling was assigned him.

The soldiers, however, were set against the little tailor, and wished him to be a thousand miles away. "What are we to do?" they said among themselves. "If we quarrel with him, and he strikes about him, seven of us will fall at every blow. Not one of us can stand against him." Finally, they came to a conclusion. They would present themselves as a body to the king and beg to be dismissed. "We are not prepared," said they, "to stay with a man who kills seven at one stroke."

The king was sorry that for the sake of one he should lose all his faithful servants. He now wished he had never set eyes on the tailor, and would have been glad to be rid of him again. But he did not venture to dismiss him. The king reasoned that the little tailor might strike him dead, along with all his people. He might even place himself on the royal throne.

The king pondered his dilemma for some time. Finally, he came up with a plan. He would send for the little man and ask for his help.

"Since you are such a great warrior," he told the tailor, "I would like to make a request. In the forest, live two giants who have caused great mischief with their robbing, murdering, ravaging, and burning. None of my warriors are able to approach them without being in danger of death. If you will conquer and kill these two giants," the king promised, "I will give my only daughter to be your wife and half my kingdom as her dowry. And one more thing, I will send one hundred horsemen to assist you."

That would be a fine thing for a man like me, thought the little tailor. *One is not offered a beautiful princess and half a kingdom every day of one's life.* "Oh, yes," he replied, "I will soon subdue the giants, and I will not need the help of the hundred horsemen to do it. He who can hit seven with one blow has no need to be afraid of two."

The little tailor went forth, and the hundred horsemen followed him. When he came to the outskirts of the forest, he said to his followers, "Wait here. I alone will soon finish off the giants." Then he bounded into the forest and looked about right and left. After a while he saw both giants sleeping under a tree. Their snores caused the branches to wave up and down.

The little tailor, not idle, gathered two pocketsful of stones, and with these climbed up the tree. When he was half-way up, he slipped down by a branch, until he sat just above the sleepers' heads. He then let one stone after another fall on the breast of one of the giants. For a long time the giant felt nothing, but at last he awoke, pushed his comrade, and said, "Why are you hitting me?"

"You must be dreaming," said the other. "I am not hitting you."

The two had no sooner laid themselves down to sleep than the little tailor began to throw rocks down on the second giant. "What is the meaning of this," the second giant cried out. "Why are you pelting me."

"I'm not pelting you," growled the first giant. They argued for a time, but being weary, they finally let the matter rest and closed their eyes once more.

The little tailor quickly took up his game again, picking out the biggest stone, and throwing it with all his might onto the breast of the first giant.

"This is so wrong," the giant cried out, springing up like a madman and pushing his companion against the tree until it shook. The other paid him back and then some. Soon they were both so enraged that they tore up trees, fighting so ferociously that they both fell down dead on the ground at the same time. Then the little tailor leapt down. "It is a lucky thing," said he, "that they did not tear up the tree on which I was sitting. I would have had to spring on to another like a squirrel, but we tailors are nimble."

The little tailor drew out his sword and gave each of the giants a couple of thrusts in the breast, and then went out to tell the horsemen that the job was done. "I have finished both of them off, but it was hard work," he told them. "They tore up trees in their sore need, and defended themselves with them, but all that is to no purpose when a man like myself comes along. Who can kill seven at one blow?"

"But you have not a single wound," exclaimed the horsemen.

"You need not concern yourself with that," answered the tailor. "They have not bent one hair of mine." The horsemen, unbelieving, rode into the forest, found the giants swimming in their blood, and the forest torn up all around.

The little tailor demanded of the king the promised reward. But the king tried instead to think of a way to get rid of the little tailor turned national hero. "Before you receive my daughter and the half of my kingdom," he said to the tailor, "you must perform one more heroic deed.

"A unicorn has been roaming through the forest, causing a great deal of damage. You must catch it."

"Only one unicorn," the tailor exclaimed. "That's much less than two giants. After all, seven in one blow is my kind of affair."

Taking rope and an axe with him, the little tailor went into the forest, and again bade those who were sent with him to wait outside. He had not long to wait. The unicorn soon came forward and rushed directly at him as if it intended gore him with its horn without more ado.

"Softly, softly, it can't be done as quickly as that," the little tailor said. Then he stood still and waited for the animal to get quite close before springing nimbly behind a tree. The unicorn rammed against the tree with all its strength, and struck its horn so fast in the trunk that it had not strength enough to draw it out again. I've got it now, the tailor said to himself. Coming out from behind the tree, he put the rope round the animal's neck, and then with his axe he hewed the horn out of the tree. When all was ready, he led the beast away to the king.

Still the stubborn king would not give him the promised reward, and made a third demand. Before the wedding the tailor was to catch him a wild boar that was making great havoc in the forest. Once again, the king's men would give him their help.

"That's child's play," the tailor answered. Once again, he chose not to take the king's men into the forest, and they were well pleased that he did not. The wild boar had several times received them in such a manner that they had no inclination to lie in wait for him.

When the boar saw the tailor, it ran on him with foaming mouth and whetted tusks. It was about to throw him to the ground, but the hero fled and sprang into a nearby chapel. As quickly as he ran in, the tailor climbed up to a window and in one bound was back outside again. When the boar ran in after him, the tailor ran up and shut the door behind it. The raging beast, much too heavy and awkward to leap out of the window, was caught. The little tailor called the king's men so that they could see the prisoner with their own eyes.

The hero then returned to the king, who was now, whether he liked it or not, obliged to keep his promise—and keep it he did. The king gave the little tailor his daughter's hand in marriage and half of his kingdom. What would he have thought had he known that the man before him was no war-like hero but rather a little tailor? The wedding was held with great magnificence and small joy, and out of a tailor a king was made.

After some time, the young queen heard her husband say in his dreams at night, "Boy, make me the doublet, and patch the pantaloons, or else I will rap the yard-measure over your ears." Only then did she discover in what state of life the young lord had been born. The next morning, she complained of her wrongs to her father and begged him to help her to get rid of her husband, who was nothing else but a tailor.

The king comforted her and said, "Leave your bedroom door

open this night, and my servants shall stand outside. When he has fallen asleep, they shall go in, bind him, and take him on board a ship that shall carry him into the wide world."

The woman was satisfied with this, but the king's armor-bearer, who had heard all, was friendly with the young lord, and informed him of the whole plot. "I'll put a screw into that business," said the little tailor. At night he went to bed with his wife at the usual time. When she thought that he had fallen asleep, she got up, opened the door, and then lay down again. The little tailor, who was only pretending to be asleep, began to cry out in a clear voice, "Boy, make me the doublet and patch me the pantaloons, or I will rap the yard-measure over your ears. I smote seven at one blow. I killed two giants, I brought away one unicorn and caught a wild boar. Am I to fear those who are standing outside the room?"

When the men heard the tailor speaking thus, they were overcome by a great dread, and ran as if the wild huntsman were behind them, and none of them would venture anything further against him. So the little tailor was and remained a king to the end of his life.

The Greedy Wife

Author Unknown

There was once a married couple. He was thin—thin. She was fat—fat.

Now every afternoon when the husband came home for dinner, the wife would say, "I am not hungry, husband."

"How so?" he would ask.

"That so," she would answer him.

Yet, with every day that passed, she would gain another pound or so. At last the husband grew suspicious, and vowed that he would keep a close watch and see what happened while he was away.

So one day, instead of going to work, he hid under the house, bored a hole through the floor, and fixed his eye to it. He had not been long watching when his wife came to the kitchen, took a large bowl, and filled it with bread crumbs. Then she poured a jug of milk over them and added sugar and ate it all.

"What shall I eat now?" she asked. "I'm still hungry."

It began to rain, and since she could not go out to the store, she took a dozen eggs, some peppers and tomatoes, and made herself an omelet. Then she sat and ate it. She washed and dried the dishes, and then sat in her rocking chair and fell asleep. When she awoke, the rain was coming down in torrents.

"I cannot go out," she said, "and I am still hungry." So she went to the chicken coop, killed a chicken, fricasseed it with potatoes and onions, and ate it, bones, sauce, and all. Then she prepared a salad for her husband.

In the afternoon the husband went into the house.

"Why, husband," said the wife, "how is it that your clothes are so dry when you work out in the fields and it has been raining all morning?"

And the husband answered, "You see, wife, the drizzle in the field was as fine as the bread crumbs you had for breakfast, and yet I spent the time under a tree whose branches were as broad and wide as the size of the omelet you ate. Had it not been for that, I would have gotten as wet as the chicken in the rich sauce that you have just eaten."

The wife hung her head, for she knew her husband had found her out.

Since that day she never ate by herself again. But always waited for her husband to come home, and the two of them grew fat—fat!

The Pen and the Inkstand

Hans Christian Andersen

In a poet's room, where his inkstand stood on the table, the remark was once made, "It is wonderful what can be brought out of an inkstand. What will come next? It is indeed wonderful."

"Yes, certainly," said the inkstand to the pen, and to the other articles that stood on the table; "that's what I always say. It is wonderful and extraordinary what a number of things come out of me. It's quite incredible, and I really don't know what is coming next when that man dips his pen into me. One drop out of me is enough for half a page of paper, and what cannot half a page contain? From me, all the works of a poet are produced; all those imaginary characters whom people fancy they have known or met. All the deep feeling, the humor, and the vivid pictures of nature. I myself don't understand how it is, for I am not acquainted with nature, but it is certainly in me. From me have gone forth to the world those wonderful descriptions of troops of charming maidens, and of brave knights on prancing steeds; of the halt and the blind, and I know not what more, for I assure you I never think of these things."

"There you are right," said the pen, "for you don't think at all; if you did, you would see that you can only provide the means. You give the fluid that I may place upon the paper what dwells in me, and what I wish to bring to light. It is the pen that writes: no man doubts that; and, indeed, most people understand as much about poetry as an old inkstand."

"You have had very little experience," replied the inkstand. "You have hardly been in service a week, and are already half worn out. Do you imagine you are a poet? You are only a servant, and before you came I had many like you, some of the goose family, and others of English manufacture. I know a quill pen as well as I know a steel one. I have had both sorts in my service, and I shall have many more when he comes—the man who performs the mechanical part and writes down what he obtains from me. I should like to know what will be the next thing he gets out of me."

"Inkpot!" exclaimed the pen contemptuously.

Late in the evening the poet came home. He had been to a concert, and had been quite enchanted with the admirable performance of a famous violin player whom he had heard there. The performer had produced from his instrument a richness of tone that sometimes sounded like tinkling waterdrops or rolling pearls; sometimes like the birds twittering in chorus, and then rising and swelling in sound like the wind through the fir-trees. The poet felt as if his own heart were weeping, but in tones of melody like the sound of a woman's voice. It seemed not only the strings, but every part of the instrument from which these sounds were produced. It was a wonderful performance and a difficult piece, and yet the bow seemed to glide across the strings so easily that it was as if any one could do it who tried. Even the violin and the bow appeared to perform independently of their master who guided them; it was as if soul and spirit had been breathed into the instrument, so the audience forgot the performer in the beautiful sounds he produced. Not so the poet; he remembered him, and named him, and wrote down his thoughts on the subject. "How foolish it would be for the violin and the bow to boast of their performance, and yet we men often commit that folly. The poet, the artist, the man of science in his laboratory, the general—we all do it; and yet we are only the instruments which the Almighty uses; to Him alone the honor is due. We have nothing of ourselves of which we should be proud." Yes, this is what the poet wrote down. He wrote it in the form of a parable, and called it "The Master and the Instruments."

"That is what you have got, madam," said the pen to the inkstand, when the two were alone again. "Did you hear him read aloud what I had written down?"

"Yes, what I gave you to write," retorted the inkstand. "That was a cut at you because of your conceit. To think that you could not understand that you were being quizzed. I gave you a cut from within me. Surely I must know my own satire."

"Ink-pitcher!" cried the pen.

"Writing-stick!" retorted the inkstand. And each of them felt satisfied that he had given a good answer. It is pleasing to be convinced that you have settled a matter by your reply; it is something to make you sleep well, and they both slept well upon it. But the poet did not sleep. Thoughts rose up within him like the tones of the violin, falling like pearls, or rushing like the strong wind through the forest. He understood his own heart in these thoughts; they were as a ray from the mind of the Great Master of all minds.

"To Him be all the honor."

WORD POWER

Elegant Words

Imbroglio—n., a confused heap, a confusing and involved situation, a state of confusion or complication, a confused misunderstanding or disagreement.
Example: "I wished I had never come to the reunion, much less stated my political opinion, as the resulting imbroglio was not resolvable."

Appassionata—adj., an Italian word meaning impassioned music, impassioned, deeply emotional as directed in musical scores.
Example: "The most heart-wrenching part of the opera is the appassionata in the final scene when the child dies."

Meander—adj., to wander at random; wind about gracefully.
History: This word comes from the name of a river in the western part of Turkey called Menderes, known in ancient times as Maeander. The river was not remarkable for length or width; it was notable for the great number of twists and turns it pursued through low flat country toward the ocean.
Example: "The ladies spent the entire afternoon meandering through the booths of the craft fair."

Comestible—adj., edible, food suitable to be eaten.
Example: "Despite our fears, we found the food aboard ship to be not only comestible, but delightful."

Easel—n., stand with three legs used by an artist to hold his canvas while painting.
History: Surprisingly, this word comes from the Dutch word for ass, as many people name tools or implements for a resemblance they found to some animal. The Dutch name was adopted and

modified into English spelling, easel.
Example: "The artist placed her easel in the center of the plaza."

Pastiche—n., a jumbled mixture, hodgepodge; potpourri, a literary, artistic or musical composition made up of bits and pieces from various sources, sometimes done to ridicule another artist's style.
Example: "The artist was offended to learn a pastiche of his work was used to decorate the museum brochure's cover."

Parable—n., allegory, comparison, similitude; specifically: a usually short fictitious story that illustrates a moral attitude or a religious principle.
History: From Middle French *parable, parabole,* from Late Latin *parabola,* from Greek *parabol* comparison, parable, superposition. Parables have been used through the ages to teach a doctrine or truth by storytelling. They were stories that presented a moral through fictional persons or situations.
Example: "Jesus told the parable of the prodigal son to teach God's love for the rebellious."

Verisimilitude—n., appearance of being true or real; like or resembling reality.
History: The root of this word is the Latin *versimilis,* from *verus* (very), meaning true, plus *similar,* meaning alike.
Example: "A mirage was to the thirsty traveler, the verisimilitude of a tree-encircled oasis."

Stochastic—adj., of, pertaining to, or arising from chance; involving probability, random. In the math realm this word refers to a procession of jointly distributed random variables.
History: This word comes from a Greek word *stochastikos* that means proceeding by guesswork, literally skillful in aiming.
Example: "Earning money on the stock market, for a person who is unlearned in money matters, is purely stochastic."

Religious Words

Sanctification—n. treat as holy, free from sin.
History: The dominant idea of sanctification is separation from the secular and sinful, and setting apart for a sacred purpose. As the holiness of God means His separation from all evil, so sanctification—in the various Scripture applications of the term—has a kindred lofty significance.

In the Old Testament economy, things, places, times, as well as people, were sanctified and consecrated to holy purposes. These rites, however, when applied to people were only ceremonial and did not extend to the purifying of the moral and spiritual nature. They were symbolical, and thus were intended not only to remind of the necessity of spiritual cleansing, but also of the gracious purpose of God to actually accomplish the work.
Example: "May God himself, the God of peace, sanctify you through and through. May your whole spirit, soul, and body be kept blameless at the coming of our Lord Jesus Christ. The one who calls you is faithful and He will do it" (1 Thessalonians 5:23-24).

Trespass—n. to go off a path, fall, or slip aside.
History: In secular usage, the word *trespass* means "to encroach on someone else's property," but it has an entirely different meaning in the religious context. The Greek *paraptoma*, from which it is taken, literally means "to go off a path, fall or slip aside." When it is applied to moral and ethical issues, it means to deviate from the right way, to wander.

When we understand the terms God inspired to describe sin, we can easily see why sin is so universal. Because the robber, murderer, drunkard, rapist, and child-abuser are so obviously evil, we readily agree that they are sinners. In our hearts we consider ourselves to be respectable citizens since we do none of these things. These terms, though, bring us face-to-face with the reality of sin—that it is not always obvious.
Example: "If by the trespass of one man, death reigned through that one man, how much more will those who receive God's

abundant provision of grace and of the gift of righteousness reign in life through the one man, Jesus Christ" (Romans 5:17).

Adonai—n., name for God used in its place because the real names of God were considered too holy for mortals to pronounce.
History: From the Hebrew word *adon*, it means "my Lord" and was used in place of the word Jehovah when reading aloud. Jehovah was considered to be "ineffable" or wrong to say out loud because of its holiness.

Laud—v., to sing songs or praise God with words and voice.
Example: "Laud and honor God for He is full of mercy."
History: From the Middle French or Medieval *laudes*, from Latin *laud* meaning "praise."

Precisian—n., person who is strict and precise in keeping rules and customs, especially of religious nature, as a 17th century English Puritan.
Example: "The rain fell and the wheat lay ruining in the field because the Sabbath must be kept. Papa was a precisian, even to the point of losing the entire crop."

Obdurate—adj., hard-hearted, not easily moved to pity; a hardening of feelings against moral influences; resistant to persuasion or softening influences; unyielding, inflexible; harsh or rough; unrepenting, impenitent.
Example: "The defendant seemed completely obdurate when questioned about the murder."

Zucchetto—n., a skullcap worn by Roman Catholic Ecclesiastes.
History: It is a light, close-fitting brimless cap usually worn indoors, the color denoting the standing of the cleric. A priest wears a black zucchetto. A bishop wears a purple cap. A cardinal's is red and the pope's is white. This word comes from the Italian *zucca* for gourd.
Example: "The cardinal's zucchetto made his religious attire complete."

Archaic Words

Ruly—adj., obedient, the opposite of unruly; a word still in use.
Example: "It is refreshing to see such ruly, well-mannered children."

Snirtle—v., to attempt to suppress one's laughter; from snirt, a short suppressed laugh.
Example: "The teenagers began to snirtle during the funeral service."

Nazzle—n., female child who has earned a reputation for being deceitful; never applied to males.
Example: "You cannot trust the 'little nazzle' out of your sight, nor in it!"

Magsman—n., well-dressed and accomplished man who watched for opportunities to swindle gullible people and rob them; con artist.
Example: "There was not one clue that we were being approached by a magsman, until he had disappeared with our bags."

Papelard—n., flatterer or hypocrite; from the word from the Italian *pappalardo* for a glutton.
Example: "I would not trust a word of praise from that papelard."

Snogly gear'd—adj., handsomely dressed.
Example: "The president rose to give his speech, snogly gear'd."

Maffle—v., to stutter or stammer.
Example: "In his stage fright, the young man maffled his well-planned speech."

Cowclash—n., state of confusion.
Example: "A small fire in the building turned the meeting quickly into a cowclash."

Cockerate—v., to brag and boast.
Example: "The young man strutted about the room, cockerating about his newly won contest."

Quckerwodger—n., wooden toy doll that is manipulated with strings that jerk its limb up and down.
History: The term was used for a politician who was manipulated by someone else.
Example: "I fear the new governor will prove to be nothing more than a quckerwodger."

Snow-blossom—n., snowflake.
Example: "Maggie raced outside and caught a downy snow-blossom on the tip of her tongue."

Snoutfair—n., person of handsome countenance.
Example: "The wealthy man's daughters are snoutfairs and good-hearted girls."

Sparrow's ticket—n., the act of climbing a fence or sneaking in a back way to gain admission to a ball game or circus or show.
Example: "I got in on a sparrow's ticket as I was too broke to pay a cent."

Ruricolist—n., person who lives in a rural area; a resident of the country.
Example: "Farmers and ranchers make up the greater proportion of ruricolists in this state."

Rumbustical—adj., boisterous, overbearing, loud and raucous, from the French word *robaster.*
Example: "That child is so rumbustical, he could not sit quietly for the concert."

Clapperclaw—v., to scold, abuse verbally, maul or scratch, fighting in unskilled manner; generally used for women.
Example: "The women got into an argument and began to clapperclaw one another."

Linctus—n., soft substance of a thick and viscous consistency like syrup or molasses that must be eaten by licking off a spoon.

Example: "Mom, may I have a spoon of linctus?"

Miscreant—n., person who believed wrongly, a heretic, an unbeliever. Later the word came to mean a criminal, robber, thief, murderer, or evil-doer.
Example: "The preacher showed the miscreant the error of his ways."

Quisling—n., traitor to one's country.
History: The word comes from the name Vidkum Abraham Quisling, a Norwegian who betrayed his country and helped the Germans invade Norway in 1940. He was later tried and executed, and his name became synonymous with a traitor.
Example: "We couldn't believe the man who fought beside us was a quisling."

Liversick—n., person who is lovesick or heartsick, or has a diseased liver, from the belief that the liver was the seat of affections.
Example: "My darling agreed to marry me for I was liversick for her."

Swazz—v., to swagger.
Example: "After accepting the award, the arrogant man swazzed to his seat."

Cowboy Phrases and Western Words

Scissorbill—someone who does not do his job well.

Seam-squirrels—the term for body-lice, also called pants rats.

Plumb cultus—The word *cultus* came from the Chinook word which meant "worthless," thus this expression means as bad as they come, cussed, worthless, lowdown, good for nothing.

His cinch is gettin' frayed—said of a person who has outstayed his welcome.

Hive off—an expression meaning to leave, go away, back off.

Pig's vest with buttons—salt pork.

Hobble your lip—advice to quit talking so much.

Alkalied—grissel-heel, old-timer, entitled to a warm corner, no spring colt.

Peddler of loads—a teller of tall tales, a fireside storyteller.

Slipped his hobbles—said of a horse who has escaped his hobbles or of a person who has fallen from grace.

Swamp seed—a slang name for rice.

Texas butter—a cowboy's term for gravy made by mixing flour in the hot grease he has fried meat in and stirring in water.

Throat-tickling grub—the term for fancy foods he would never be fed on the range.

Waddy—a man who is hired on to fill out a ranch crew during a busy season.

Visiting harness—a cowboy's good clothes reserved for going to town.

Gritty as fish eggs laid in sand—reference to one possessing courage.

Hair in the butter—a delicate situation.

No breakfast forever—said of a person caught in a prairie fire.

One foot in the stirrup—done half-heartedly or, in another context, ready to face any emergency.

Slang Words

Gung-ho—going about an endeavor with enthusiasm.

Bogart—to hog it all.

Church key—the pull-up tab on a soda can.

Props—respect, appreciation.

Copasetic—everything is all right.

Negs—a short form of negative, NO.

Nerbie—a person who is book-smart but street-dumb.

Ditz—a dumb-acting person.

Dude—in the '60s this term meant a sissy. Later it meant cool or macho.

Earthy-crunchy—person with hippie or tree-hugging tendencies, stuck in the '60's lifestyle.

Warez—piece of pirated software copied from a friend or downloaded from the Internet.

Dibs—to claim first chance at possessing some item.

Scarf—to eat very fast (narf, snarf).

Bag—to steal something.

Fab—wonderful short word for fabulous.

Newbie—newcomer or beginner, novice at some skill.

Namedrop—to mention a high-status person in a conversation in order to gain the attention or respect of the listeners.

Hobby Words

Spelunker—person who spends time exploring caves.

Naturalist—person who studies nature by direct observation of animals and plants.

Semaphorist—person who employs a method of using flags as signals—two flags, one held in each hand, represent the alphabet when held in various positions by the arms.

Rockhound—collector of rocks and fossils.

Topiarist—person who is skilled in the art of topiary gardening; that is, the training, cutting, and trimming of trees and shrubs into odd and ornamental shapes.

Apiarist—person who keeps a collection of hives or colonies of bees for their honey.

Blogger—computer diarist who shares their thoughts and opinions over the Internet on a blog spot or opinion Web site.

Bibliomaniac—collector of books.

Avian Nomenclaturist—person who studies and is intrigued by place names that come from bird names.

Vexillologist—person who studies flags.

Birder—person who birdwatches, studies, feeds, houses, and loves birds.

Storm chaser—person who follows storms or speeds toward a tornado, attempting to photograph it.

Railbird—enthusiast who sits on or near the rail to watch a race.

Scrapbooker—person involved in the making of photo albums with decorated pages.

Philatelist—collector of postage stamps, from two Greek

words, *philos*, meaning "loving," and *atelos*, meaning "free of tax" or "paid." Stamps are a sign that the tax has been paid.

Professional Words

Playwright—person who writes plays or who adapts materials for stage, radio, television, or motion-picture production.

Enigmatologist—professional who makes and studies the art and science of constructing puzzles.

Dialectologist—person who studies the science of regional dialects.

Pathologist—doctor or scientist who deals with the nature of a disease and the results and conditions resulting from the disease.

Folk Etymologist—person who studies the changes that develop in words over a prolonged period of usage so as to give it an apparent association with another word. Example: "'Cole slaw' became 'cold slaw' in some regions because it is served cold."

Paleoclimatologist—scientist who studies climate conditions in geological eras of ancient times.

Pyrographer—artist who uses the process of burning designs into wood or leather by use of heated tools.

Necrologist—person who produces listings of people who have died within a certain time period, as that in a newspaper, death notices, obituaries.

Organographer—person who studies the organs of animals and plants, especially the outer parts of plants.

Semasiologist—person who studies the significance of words.

Cartologist—mapmaker.

Taxonomist—person who studies the laws and principles of classification of living things, namely, in the field of biology, someone who arranges animals and plants into naturally related groups based on factors common to each, such as structure, embryology, chemical makeup, color, and shape.

Herpitologist—person who studies snakes.

College-World Slang

The language on college campuses can leave the average person dumbfounded. Students use shortened terms— clipped words or slang—for everything. Use this as an informal cheat sheet.

The names of courses are lopped off:
- psychology becomes psych
- anthropology becomes anthro
- American history becomes Am hist
- human personality becomes hum per
- geometry becomes geo
- trigonometry becomes trig
- calculus becomes calc
- physical education becomes phys ed

Students *snarf za*—eat pizza. Their food is *munchies* and *feeds* served at the *trough*. *Yamming* is collective *pigging-out*. If the meal is *hurtin'*, you will *yack, gag, barf, toss your biscuits*, or *puke*.

Positive slang words: *awesome, gnarly, rad, intense, jock, copin'*, or *chill*.

Negative reviews: *rasty, rude, heinous, just not dealin', gomer, rast show, lame*, or *hurtin'*.

A dorm room has *inverviz* time when students are allowed to visit freely in rooms in coed dormitories. You sleep on a *rack* (bed) and your room has a *tesh* corner for *hangin' out, chillin'*. This would be a place to get *cofy, snarf* some chips, and *tube out.*

Socially inept students are *gomers, bwebs, nerds, geeks.* They might be called *moon-men, space-cadets,* or *in a real fog.* New, green students who haven't yet learned the ropes are called *newbies* or *newbs.*

If you pass an exam you *aced it.* If you fail the exam, you got *smoked, torched, burned, roasted* or *toasted, blown away,* or *shot down.* Teachers who give hard exams *dissed you* or *wiped you out.* You got *harshed* or *latered.* It was probably the fault of the government—*White House.*

Girls want to date the *jocks,* guys who play sports. Some like *puck* (ice hockey). Others go for *Pit* or they shoot *hoops.* Never date a *scuzz.*

Business Jargon

bell cow—sales item that makes a good profit.

bangtail—coupon or order form that comes attached to the billing envelope.

headhunter—recruiter for executive positions.

paper-pusher—desk-job employee.

buckle down—make an effort to get work done.

hang it up—give up on a job, quit trying, throw in the towel, be done with.

kowtow—bow to or cater to someone's every desire, usually out of fear or a desire to gain advancement.

powwow—hold a meeting.

scuttlebutt—gossip, current scandalous rumors exchanged during breaks at the water fountain.

pounding the pavement—out of work and looking for another job.

gopher—worker who runs errands for the higher-ups.

lead time—the allotted time for a project to be accomplished or before an event will take place.

put on hold—postpone a job or project.

slack off—shirk responsibilities on the job.

schmooze—take advantage of a party for socializing with influential persons who may be able to advance your position.

talks a good game—shows self-confidence in his or her abilities.

CLASSIC CHRISTIAN WRITING

God Loved First

CHARLES SPURGEON

(1832-1892)

God thought of you before you had a being, when the sun, moon and stars slept in the mind of God, like unborn forests in an acorn cup, and the old sea was not yet born. God thought of you long before this infant world lay in its swaddling bands of mist. It was then that God inscribed your name upon the heart and upon the hands of Christ indelibly, to remain forever (Ephesians 1:4). Does this not make you love God?

Soar back through all your own experiences. Think of how the Lord has led you in the wilderness and has fed and clothed you every day. How God has borne with your ill manners, and put up with all your murmurings and all your longings after the "sensual pleasures of Egypt!" Think of how the Lord's grace has been sufficient for you in all your troubles. Think of how Christ's blood has been a pardon to you in all your sins. How the Lord's rod and staff have comforted you!

When the time comes for you to die, you need not be afraid, because death cannot separate you from God's love. When you shall come into the mysteries of eternity, you do not need to tremble. Is not your love for God refreshed? Does not this make you love God?

You never hear Jesus say in Pilate's judgment hall one word that would let you imagine that he was sorry that he had undertaken so costly a sacrifice for us. When his hands are pierced, when he is parched with fever, his tongue dried up like a shard of pottery, when his whole body is dissolved into the dust of death, you never hear a groan or a shriek that looks like Jesus is going to go back on his commitment. It was love that could not be stayed by death, but overcame all the horrors of the grave.

Go forth today, by the help of God's Spirit, vowing and declaring that in life—come poverty, come wealth, in death—come pain or come what may, you are and ever must be the Lord's. For this is written on your heart, "We love Him because He first loved us."

A Peaceable Spirit

THOMAS WATSON

(c. 1600- c.1689)

To be a peaceable spirit is highly prudent. "The wisdom . . . from above is . . . peaceable" (James 3:17 NKJV). A wise man will not meddle with strife. It is like putting one's finger into a hornets' nest—or to use Solomon's example, "the beginning of strife is like releasing water" (Proverbs 17:14 NKJV). To seek out the folly of strife is like releasing water in two respects. First, when water begins to be let out there is no end of it. So there is no end of strife when once begun. Second, the letting out of water is dangerous.

If a person should break down a bank and let in an arm of the sea, the water might overflow their fields and drown them in the flood. It is the same with those that meddle with strife. They may cause mischief to themselves and open such a current that may engulf and swallow them up. True wisdom promotes peace. The prudent will keep away from conflict as much as they can.

To be of a peaceable spirit brings peace along with it. The contentious annoy themselves and destroy their own comfort. They are like the bird that beats itself against the cage. The wicked one "troubles his own flesh" (Proverbs 11:17 NKJV). They are just like one that cuts off the sweet of the apple and eats nothing but the core. So a quarrelsome person cuts off all the comfort of their life and feeds only upon the bitter core of unrest.

They are self-tormentors. The wicked are compared to "a troubled sea" (Isaiah 57:20 NKJV). And it follows "there is no peace . . . for the wicked" (verse 21). The Septuagint renders it "There is no joy to the wicked."

Pushy people do not enjoy what they possess, but the peace-loving spirit brings the sweet music of peace along with them. It makes a calm and harmony in the soul. Therefore the psalmist says, it is not only good, but pleasant, to live together in unity. (See Psalm 133:1.)

Life Instead of Law

CATHERINE BOOTH

(1829-1890)

Where does the Law fail us? It does all this for me: It brings me right up opening my eyes, creating an intense desire after holiness and the effort behind it, and then it just fails me. Where? At the essential point. It cannot give me power. That is where the Law fails. It cannot give me power to fulfill itself.

Oh! But there is a Gospel nowadays, a Law-Gospel. A great deal of the Gospel these days never gets any further than the Law, and some people tell me that it is never intended to do so. Then I ask, "How then does Christ Jesus help me? How am I better for such a Gospel, if my Gospel cannot deliver me from the power of sin? If through the Gospel I cannot get deliverance from this "I-would-if-I-could religion," this "Oh!-wretched-man-that-I-am religion," how am I benefited by it? (See Romans 7:24.)

How does your Gospel do more for me than the Law? The Law convinced me of sin, and set me desiring and longing after righteousness; but where is the superiority of Jesus Christ, if He cannot lead me further than that?" And I say, "Very well; your faith is vain, and Christ died in vain, and you are yet in your sins, if that is all it can do." If that is all Jesus Christ can do, His coming is vain, and I am yet in my sins, and am doomed to hug this dead corpse to the last, and go down to hell; for death will never do for me what the blood and sacrifice of Jesus Christ cannot do for me. If Christ cannot supersede the Law, then I am lost, and lost for ever.

Oh! but the real Gospel does. The Gospel that represents Jesus Christ, not as a system of truth to be received, into the mind, as I should receive a system of philosophy, or astronomy, but it represents Him as a real, living, mighty Savior, able to save me now.

Triumphant

BOOKER T. WASHINGTON

(1856-1915)

It has been my fortune to be associated all my life with a problem—a hard, perplexing, but important problem. There was a time when I looked upon this fact as a great misfortune. It seemed to me a great hardship that I was born poor, and it seemed to me a greater hardship that I should have been born a Negro *[sic]*. I did not like to admit, even to myself, that I felt this way about the matter, because, it seemed to me an indication of weakness and cowardice for any man to complain about the condition he was born to.

Later, I came to the conclusion that it was not only weak and cowardly, but that it was a mistake to think of the matter in the way in which I had done. I came to see that, along with his disadvantages, the Negro in America had some advantages, and I made up my mind that opportunities that had been denied him from without could be more than made up by greater concentration and power within.

Perhaps I can illustrate what I mean by a fact I learned while I was in school. I recall my teacher's explaining to the class one day how it was that steam or any other form of energy, if allowed to escape and dissipate itself, loses its value as a motive power. Energy must be confined; steam must be locked in a boiler in order to generate power.

The same thing seems to have been true in the case of the Negro. Where the Negro has met with discrimination and with difficulties because of his race, he has invariably tended to get up more steam. When this steam has been rightly directed and controlled, it has become a great force in the up building of the race. If, on the contrary, it merely spent itself on fruitless agitation and hot air, no good has come of it.

Power When We Pray

R. A. TORREY

(1856-1928)

If we are to obtain from God all that we ask from Him, Christ's words must abide or continue in us. We must study His words, fairly devour His words, let them sink into our thought and into our heart, keep them in our memory, obey them constantly in our life, let them shape and mold our daily life and our every act.

This is really the method of abiding in Christ. It is through His words that Jesus imparts Himself to us. The words He speaks unto us, they are spirit and they are life. (See John 6:33.) It is vain to expect power in prayer unless we meditate much upon the words of Christ, and let them sink deep and find a permanent home in our hearts.

It is not by times of mystical meditation and rapturous experiences that we learn to abide in Christ; it is by feeding upon His Word, His written word as found in the Bible, and looking to the Holy Spirit to plant these words in our hearts and to make them a living thing in our hearts.

If we then let the words of Christ abide in us, they will stir us up in prayer. They will be the mold in which our prayers are shaped, and our prayers will be necessarily along the line of God's will, and will triumph with Him. Triumphant prayer is almost impossible where there is neglect of the study of the word of God.

George Müller, one of the mightiest men of prayer of the present generation, would begin by reading and meditating upon God's Word until out of the study of the Word a prayer began to form itself in his heart. Thus God Himself was a real author of the prayer, and God answered the prayers which He Himself had inspired.

The Dwelling Place of God

A. W. TOZER

(1897-1963)

Deep inside every man there is a private sanctum where dwells the mysterious essence of his being. This far-in reality is that in the man which is what it is of itself without reference to any other part of the man's complex nature. It is the man's "I Am," a gift from the I AM who created him.

The I AM which is God is underived and self-existent; the "I Am" which is man is derived from God and dependent every moment upon His creative fiat for its continued existence. One is the Creator, high over all, ancient of days, dwelling in light unapproachable. The other is a creature and, though privileged beyond all others, is still but a creature. ...

The deep-in human entity of which we speak is called in the Scriptures the spirit of man. "For what man knoweth the things of man, save the spirit of man which is in him? even so the things of God knows no man, but the Spirit of God" (2 Cor. 2:11) . As God's self-knowledge lies in the eternal Spirit, so man's self-knowledge is by his own spirit, and his knowledge of God is by the direct impression of the Spirit of God upon the spirit of man.

The importance of all this cannot be overestimated. ... It reveals the essential spirituality of mankind. It denies that man is a creature having a spirit and declares that he is a spirit having a body. That which makes him a human being is not his body but his spirit, in which the image of God originally lay.

One of the most liberating declarations is this: "The true worshippers shall worship the Father in spirit and in truth: for the Father seeks such to worship him. God is a Spirit: and they that worship him must worship him in spirit and in truth" (John 4:23, 24). True religion is removed from diet and days, from garments and ceremonies, and placed where it belongs—in the union of the spirit of man with the Spirit of God.[1]

God Alone

CHARLES SPURGEON

(1834-1892)

My Rock." How noble a title for God. It is so suggestive. With awe we look upon giant aged rocks, for they are among nature's first-born. Even so, our God is pre-eminently ancient. Long before creation was begotten, God is "from everlasting to everlasting" (Psalm 90:2).

Other things change, but a giant aged rock stands as steadfast as if it were the very foundation of the whole world. So with God. How faithful God is to keep Divine promises! God is the same, and God's kingdom shall have no end.

"He is my fortress." We see a fortress standing on a high rock, up where the clouds themselves can scarcely climb and up whose precipices the assault cannot be carried out. So is our God a sure defense.

Many a giant rock is a source of admiration from its elevation, because on the summit we can see the world spread out below, like some small map. The mighty God is such a rock. God is our refuge and our high observatory from which we see the unseen and have the evidence of things not yet enjoyed.

If we are delivered and made alive in Christ, still our preservation is the Lord alone. If we are prayerful, God makes us prayerful. If we have graces, God gives us graces. If we have spiritual fruit, God gives us spiritual fruit. If we have repulsed an enemy, God's strength nerved our arm. Do we live to God a holy life? It is not us, but Christ who lives in us. Are we sanctified? God's Holy Spirit sanctifies us. Do we grow in knowledge? The great Instructor teaches us. "He alone is my rock and my salvation."

If God only be your rock, and you know it, are you not bound to put all your trust in God, to give all your love to God? If God be all you have, surely, all you have shall be God's. If God alone is your hope, surely, you will put all your hope upon God. God has put all salvation in God, to bring all yourself unto God.

Intercession

OSWALD CHAMBERS

(1874-1917)

When the exiles of Israel returned from their captivity in Persia (now Iran and Iraq), they had high hopes about the future. However, efforts back home to move forward in rehabilitating their lives were often met with the scornful laughter of enemies. The psalmist confesses that contempt, with its scornful bitterness, began monopolizing his inner thought life. God's breakthrough was desperately needed to restore a healthier disposition of the mind. Have you been there? Are you there now?

The thing of which we have to be beware is not so much damage to our belief in God as damage to our Christian disposition. There are certain dispositions of the mind in which we never dare indulge. If we do, we find they have distracted us from faith in God. Until we get back to the quiet mood before God, our faith in Him is nil and our confidence in the flesh and in human ingenuity is the thing that rules.

Beware of "the cares of this world," because they are the things that produce a wrong disposition of the soul. It is extraordinary what an enormous power there is in simple things to distract our attention from God! Refuse to be swamped with the cares of this life.

Another thing that distracts us is the lust for vindication. That disposition of mind destroys the soul's faith in God. "I must explain myself! I must get people to understand!" Our Lord never explained anything. He left mistakes to correct themselves.

When we discern that persons are not spiritually progressing, and we allow the discernment to turn to criticism, we block our way to God. God never gives us discernment in order that we may criticize, but that we may intercede.[2]

Spiritual Hunger

GEORGE MÜLLER

(1805-1898)

As our bodies are not fit for work for any length of time except with regular food, and as this is one of the first things we do in the morning, so it should be with our souls.

Now what is food for our souls? Not prayer, but the word of God. And here again, it is not the simple reading of the Bible, so that it only passes through our minds, just as water runs through a pipe, but instead considering what we read, pondering over it and applying it to our hearts.

I began to meditate on the New Testament from the beginning, early in the morning. The first thing I did, after having asked in a few words the Lord's blessing on His precious word, was, to begin to meditate on the word of God. By meditate, I mean, searching every verse, to get blessing out of it . . . not for the sake of preaching on what I had read, but for the sake of obtaining food for my own soul. The result I have found to be almost always this, that after a very few minutes my soul has been led to confession, or to thanksgiving, or to intercession, or to supplication; so that, though I did not give myself to prayer, but to meditation, yet it turned almost immediately more or less into prayer.

When I have been praying for a while, I go on to the next words or verse, turning all, as I go on, into prayer for myself or others, as the Bible may lead to it. But I still continually keep before me that my purpose for meditation is food for my own soul. The result of this is that there is always a good deal of confession, thanksgiving, supplication, or intercession mingled with my meditation, and that my soul is almost always nourished and strengthened. By breakfast time, with rare exceptions, I am in a peaceful if not happy state of heart.

Full Redemption

SMITH WIGGLESWORTH

(1859-1947)

The Bible is full of entreaty for you to come and partake and receive the grace, and the full redemption of Jesus Christ. He never fails to hear when we believe.

A lame man was brought to me who had been in bed for two years, with no hope of recovery. His boy was also afflicted in the knees and they had four crutches between the two of them. The man's face was filled with torture. There is healing virtue in the Lord and He never fails to heal when we believe. In the name of Jesus—that name so full of virtue—I put my hand down that leg that was so diseased. The man threw down his crutches and all were astonished as they saw him walking up and down without aid. The little boy called out to his father, "Papa, me; papa, me, me, me!" The little boy who was withered in both knees wanted a like touch. And the same Jesus was there to bring a real deliverance for the little captive. He was completely healed.

If God will stretch out His mighty power to loose afflicted legs, what mercy will He extend to that soul of yours that must exist forever? Hear the Lord say, "The Spirit of the Lord is upon me, because be hath anointed me to preach the gospel to the poor; he hath sent me to heal the broken hearted, to preach deliverance to the captive, and recovering of sight to the blind, to set at liberty them that are bruised."

He invites you, "Come unto me, all ye that labor and are heavy laden, and I will give you rest." God is willing in His great mercy to touch you with His mighty vital power, and if He is willing to do this, how much more anxious is He to deliver thee from the power of Satan and to make thee a child of the King. God is willing to give the double cure.

Restitution

D. L. MOODY

(1837-1899)

I was once preaching, and a man came up to me. He said, "I want you to notice that my hair is gray, and I am only thirty-two years old. For twelve years I have carried a great burden."

"Well," I said, "what is it?" He looked around as if afraid someone would hear him.

"Well," he answered, "my father died and left my mother with the county newspaper, and left her only that. That was all she had. After he died the paper began to waste away; and I saw my mother was fast sinking into a state of need. The building and the paper were insured for a thousand dollars, and when I was twenty years old I set fire to the building, and obtained the thousand dollars, and gave it to my mother. For twelve years that sin has been haunting me. I have tried to drown it by indulgence in pleasure and sin; I have cursed God; I have gone into infidelity; I have tried to make out that the Bible is not true; I have done everything I could—but all these years I have been tormented."

I said, "There is a way out of that."

He inquired, "How?"

I said, "Make restitution. Let us sit down and calculate the interest, and then you pay the company the money."

It would have done you good to see that man's face light up when he found there was mercy for him. He said he would be glad to pay back the money and interest if he could only be forgiven. There are men today who are in darkness and bondage because they are not willing to turn from their sins and confess them; and I do not know how a man can hope to be forgiven if he is not willing to confess his sin.

Inspiration of Hope

FREDERICK DOUGLASS

(1817-1895)

The good old man had told me, that the "Lord had a great work for me to do;" and I must prepare to do it; and that he had been shown that I must preach the Gospel. His words made a deep impression on my mind, and I verily felt that some such work was before me, though I could not see how I should ever engage in its performance. "The good Lord," he said, "would bring it to pass in his own good time," and that I must go on reading and studying the scriptures.

The advice and the suggestions of Uncle Lawson were not without their influence upon my character and destiny. He threw my thoughts into a channel from which they have never entirely diverged. He fanned my already intense love of knowledge into a flame, by assuring me that I was to be a useful man in the world. When I would say to him, "How can these things be—and what can I do?" his simple reply was, "Trust in the Lord." When I told him that "I was a slave, and a slave FOR LIFE," he said, "the Lord can make you free, my dear. All things are possible with him, only have faith in God."

"Ask, and it shall be given."

"If you want liberty," said the good old man, "ask the Lord for it, in faith, AND HE WILL GIVE IT TO YOU."

Thus assured, and cheered on, under the inspiration of hope, I worked and prayed with a light heart, believing that my life was under the guidance of a wisdom higher than my own. With all other blessings sought at the mercy seat, I always prayed that God would, of His great mercy, and in His own good time, deliver me from my bondage.

Extinguish the Fire

John Chrysostom

(347-407)

T he other person did wrong and is the cause of the hostility." For this reason, then, you first must go and be reconciled. Since you were not the cause of the hostility, neither be the cause of extending it further.

"But the other person is haughty." If the other person's ailment is both haughtiness and anger, then, because of these very things you ought to be the first to go to the other person. That person is in darkness, for darkness is anger and false pride. But you, the physician who is free from these and healthy, go to that sick person.

Does any physician say, "Because this person is sick, I don't go to him"? No, this is especially the reason why a physician does go when a sick person is unable to come to him. For when sick persons are able to come, the physician assumes they are not extremely ill. But not so for those who lie at home sick. Are not pride and anger, don't you think, worse than any illness? Is not the one like a severe fever and the other like a body swollen with inflammation? Go, extinguish the fire, because by the grace of God you can. Go, assuage the heat, as it were, with water.

"What if the other person becomes more upset by my doing this?" You have done your part. Let the other person take account for himself. Only, don't let your conscience condemn you....

Go, not that you may heap coals of fire, but that the other person, knowing that future consequence for keeping up the enmity, may be appeased by your kindness. For you do not hurt the "hater" so much by showing your resentment as an enemy, as by doing good and showing kindness.

If the other person persists in keeping up the enmity when you are doing that person good and honoring that person and offering to be reconciled, that person has kindled the fire for himself or herself. You are guiltless.

The Simple Light of the Soul

MEISTER ECKHART

(c.1260–c.1328)

What God makes in the simple light of the soul is more beautiful and more delightful than all the other things He creates. Through that light comes grace.

Grace never comes in the intelligence or in the will. If it could come in the intelligence or in the will, the intelligence and the will would have to rise above themselves. The true union between God and the soul takes place in the little spark, which is called the spirit of the soul. Grace doesn't take any work to unite. It is an indwelling and a living together of the soul in God.

Every gift of God makes the soul ready to receive a new gift, greater than itself.

God has never given any gift, so people might rest in the possession of the gift, but gives every gift that He has given in heaven and on earth, in order that He might be able to give one main gift, which is Himself. So with this gift of grace, and with all His gifts, He will make us ready for the one gift, which is Himself.

No one is so coarse or stupid or awkward, that they cannot, by God's grace, unite their will wholly and entirely with God's will. And nothing more is necessary than that they should say with earnest longing: O Lord, show me Your dearest will, and strengthen me to do it.

And God does it, as sure as He lives, and gives them grace in ever richer fullness, until they come to perfection.

O almighty and merciful Creator and good Lord, be merciful to me for my poor sins, and help me that I may overcome all temptations and shameful desires, and may be able to avoid utterly, in thought and deed, what You forbid. And give me grace to do and to hold all that You have commanded. Help me to believe, to hope, and to love, and in every way to live as You will, as much as You will, and what You will. Amen.

What Is Revival?

BILLY SUNDAY

(1862-1935)

Revival is a purely philosophical, common-sense result of the wise use of divinely appointed means, just the same as water will put out a fire; the same as food will appease your hunger; just the same as water will slake your thirst; it is a philosophical common-sense use of divinely appointed means to accomplish that end.

A revival does two things. First, it returns the Church from her backsliding and second, it causes the conversion of men and women; and it always includes the conviction of sin on the part of the Church. A revival helps to bring the unsaved to Jesus Christ. God Almighty never intended that the devil should triumph over the Church.

When is a revival needed? When carelessness and unconcern keep the people asleep. It is as much the duty of the Church to awaken and work and labor for the men and women of this city as it is the duty of the fire department to rush out when the call sounds. What would you think of the fire department if it slept while the town burned? You would condemn them, and I will condemn you if you sleep and let men and women go to hell. It is just as much your business to be awake. The Church of God is asleep today; it is turned into a dormitory; and has taken the devil's sleeping pills.

When may a revival be expected? When the wickedness of the wicked grieves and distresses the Christian. Sometimes people don't seem to mind the sins of other people. Don't seem to mind while boys and girls walk the streets of their city and know more of evil than gray-haired men. We are asleep.

When is a revival needed? When Christians have lost the spirit of prayer.

Burnt Offering

FRANCOIS FENELON

(1651-1715)

There is scarce any one who desires to serve God, but does so for selfish reasons; we expect gain and not loss, consolation and not suffering, riches and not poverty, increase and not diminution. But the whole interior work is of an opposite character; to be lost, sacrificed, made less than nothing, and despoiled of an excessive delight, even in the gifts of God, that we may be forced to cling to Him alone.

We are like a patient eagerly desiring returning health, who feels his own pulse forty times a day, and requires his physician to prescribe frequent doses of various remedies, and to give him a daily assurance that he is getting better. Such is almost the only use we make of our spiritual conductors. We travel in a little round of everyday virtues, never gathering sufficient courage to pass generously beyond it, and our guides, like the doctor, flatter, console, encourage and strengthen our selfish sensitiveness, and administer pleasant remedies, to the effects of which we soon become insensible.

The moment we find ourselves deprived of the delights of grace, that milk for babes, we are at once in despair; a manifest proof that we were looking to the means, instead of to the end, and solely for selfish gratification.

Privations are meat for men; by them the soul is rendered hardy, is separated from self, and offered in a pure sacrifice to God; but we give up all, the moment they commence. We cannot but think that everything is going to ruin, when, in fact, the foundations are just beginning to be solidly laid. Nothing would give us more delight than that God should do all his pleasure with us, provided it should always be to magnify and perfect us in our own eyes. But if we are not willing to be destroyed and annihilated, we shall never become that whole burnt offering, which is entirely consumed in the blaze of God's love.

We desire to enter into a state of pure faith, and retain our own wisdom! To be a babe, and great in our own eyes! Ah! what a sad delusion!

God Is Everywhere

Frances de Sales

(1567-1622)

God's Presence is universal. There is no place in the world—not one—that is devoid of God's Most Holy Presence. Even as birds in flight continually meet the air, so also wherever we might go, we will meet with that Presence always and everywhere. This is a truth that all followers of Jesus readily admit, but all are not equally alive to its importance.

A blind person, when in the presence of a king, will preserve a reverential demeanor if told that the king is there, although he or she is unable to see him. But, practically speaking, what persons do not see, they easily forget, and, therefore, readily lapse into carelessness and irreverence. In this same way, we do not see our God, although faith warns us that God is present. Because we are not seeing God with our physical eyes, we are too apt to forget God and act as though God is way far away.

While knowing perfectly well that God is everywhere, if we do not think about it, it is the same as if we did not know it. Therefore, before beginning to pray, it is always necessary to rouse your entire being to a constant, unswerving remembering and thinking about the Presence of God. In Old Testament days, when Jacob beheld the ladder that went up to Heaven, he cried out, "Surely the Lord is in this place, and I wasn't even aware of it" (Genesis 28:16). By saying this, he meant that he had not thought about it, because, surely, he could not fail to know that God was everywhere and in all things. Therefore, when you are preparing to pray, you must say with your whole heart, "God is indeed here."

Set Apart

ANDREW MURRAY

(1828-1917)

Our great Commander organizes every campaign, and His generals and officers do not always know the great plans. They often receive sealed orders, and they have to wait on Him for what He gives them as orders.

Some years ago, at Wellington, South Africa, where I live, we opened a Mission Institute. At our opening services the principal said something that I have never forgotten. He remarked:

"Last year we gathered here to lay the foundation stone, and what was there then to be seen? Nothing but rubbish, and stones, and bricks, and ruins of an old building that had been pulled down. There we laid the foundation stone, and very few knew what the building was that was to rise. No one knew it perfectly in every detail except one man, the architect. In his mind it was all clear, and as the contractor and the mason and the carpenter came to their work, they took their orders from him. The humblest laborer had to be obedient to orders. Therefore the structure rose, and this beautiful building has been completed. And just so," he added, "this building that we open today is but laying the foundation of a work of which only God knows what is to become."

But God has His workers and His plans clearly mapped out, and our position is to wait, that God should communicate to us as much of His will as each time is needful.

We have simply to be faithful in obedience, carrying out His orders. God has a plan for His Church upon earth. But alas, we too often make our plan, and we think that we know what ought to be done. We ask God first to bless our feeble efforts, instead of absolutely refusing to go unless God go before us.

God has planned for the work and the extension of His kingdom. The Holy Ghost has had that work given in charge to Him: "the work to which I have called them" (Acts 13:2 NKJV).

Immersed in Grace

JOHANNES TAULER

(1300-1361)

All the works which people and animals could ever accomplish without the grace of God—all of them together, however great they may be, are an absolute nothing, as compared with the smallest thing which God has worked in people by His grace. As much as God is superior to all His creatures, so much more superior are His works than all the works, or wisdom, or designs, which all people could devise. Even the smallest drop of grace is better than all earthly riches that are beneath the sun.

A drop of grace is nobler than all angels and all souls, and all the natural things that God has made. And yet grace is given more richly by God to the soul than any earthly gift. It is given more richly than brooks of water, than the breath of the air, than the brightness of the sun; for spiritual things are far finer and nobler than earthly things. The whole Trinity, Father, Son, and Holy Ghost, give grace to the soul, and flow immediately into it. Even the highest angel, in spite of its great nobility, cannot do this.

Grace looses us from the snares of many temptations. It relieves us from the heavy burden of worldly anxieties, and carries our spirit up to heaven, the land of spirits. It kills the worm of conscience, which makes sins alive. Grace is a very powerful thing. The person who receives even a tiny drop of grace is ruined for all else.

Grace makes, contrary to nature, all sorrows sweet, and brings it about that a person no longer feels any enjoyment for things that formerly gave great pleasure and delight. On the other hand, what formerly was found to be disgusting, now delights and is the desire of the heart—for instance, weakness, sorrow, inwardness, humility, self-abandonment, and detachment from others. All of this is very dear to a person, when this visitation of the Holy Ghost—grace—has in truth come to them.

Creation

JAMES WELDON JOHNSON

(1871-1938)

Then God walked around,
And God looked around
On all that He had made.
He looked on His world
With all its living things
And God said: I'm lonely still.

Then God sat down—
On the side of a hill where He could think;
By a deep, wide river He sat down;
With His head in His hands,
God thought and thought,
Till He thought: I'll make me a man!

Up from the bed of the river
God scooped the clay;
And by the bank of the river
He kneeled Him down;
And there the great God Almighty
Who lit the sun and fixed it in the sky,
Who flung the stars to the most far corner of the night,
Who rounded the earth in the middle of His hand,
This Great God,
Like a mammy bending over her baby,
Kneeled down in the dust
Toiling over a lump of clay
Till He shaped it in His own image;

Then into it He blew the breath of life,
And man became a living soul.
Amen. Amen.

Love

GEORGE MACDONALD

(1824-1905)

How can we love a man or a woman who is cruel and unjust to us—who sears with contempt, who is mean, unlovely, fault-finding, self-righteous, self-seeking and self-admiring? These things cannot be loved. But are these the person? Lies there not within the man and the woman something lovely and lovable? It may be slowly dying away under the fierce heat of vile passions, or the yet more fearful cold of selfishness, but isn't something still there?

It is the very presence of this fading humanity that makes it possible for us to hate. We hate the person just because we cannot embrace. For to embrace is the necessity of our deepest being. That foiled, we hate. Instead of admonishing ourselves that there is our enchained brother, that there lies our enchanted, disfigured, scarce recognizable sister, captive of the devil, we recoil into the hate which would fix them there. And the dearly lovable reality of them we sacrifice to the outer falsehood of Satan's incantations, thus leaving them to perish.

If anyone says, "Can you deny that that person is unlovely? Then, how can you love that person?" I answer, "That person, with the evil thing cast out of him, will be yet more the person, for he will be his real self. The thing that now makes you dislike him is separable from him. That thing is, therefore, not him. It makes him so much less himself, for it is working death in him.

"When he is clothed and in his right mind, he will be a person indeed. Then, you could not go on hating him. Begin to love him now, and help him into the loveliness which is his. Do not hate him, although you can. The personality, I say, though clouded, besmeared, defiled with the wrong, lies deeper than the wrong."

Eternal Embrace

RICHARD BAXTER

(1615-1691)

D o not worry, dear soul. Be at peace. God's love is constant. It cannot be torn from you and it will never change except to grow stronger and stronger as you return it with love of your own.

You shall be eternally embraced in the arms of the love which was from everlasting, and, will extend to everlasting. This is the same love that brought the Son of God's love from heaven to earth, from earth to the cross, from the cross to the grave, from the grave to glory. It is the love through Christ which was weary, hungry, tempted, scorned, scourged, buffeted, spit upon, crucified, pierced; which did fast, pray, teach, heal, weep, sweat, bleed, and die. This love of God will eternally embrace you.

Let this be your everlasting comfort and peace, if God's arms have once embraced you, neither sin nor hell can grip you. You do not have to deal with an inconstant human, but with Him with whom there is no variableness nor shadow of turning. His love to you will not be as yours is on earth to Him, seldom, and cold, up, and down. He will not cease nor reduce His love, for all your hostility, neglect, and opposition. How can He cease to love you, when He has made you truly lovely? He even keeps you so stable in your love to Him, that you can challenge all that will try to separate your love from Christ—tribulation, distress, persecution, famine, nakedness, peril, and sword. How much more will He himself be constant!

Indeed you should be "convinced that nothing—nothing living or dead, angelic or demonic, today or tomorrow, high or low, thinkable or unthinkable—absolutely nothing can get between us and God's love because of the way that Jesus our Master has embraced us" (Romans 8:38-39 MSG).

Method of Prayer

Madame Jeanne Guyon

(1648-1717)

There are two ways of introducing a soul into prayer, which should for some time be pursued; the one is Meditation, the other is Reading accompanied with Meditation.

Meditative Reading is the choosing of some important practical or speculative truth, always preferring the practical, and proceeding thus: whatever truth you have chosen, read only a small portion of it, endeavoring to taste and digest it, to extract the essence and substance thereof, and proceed no farther while any savor or relish remains in the passage: when this subsides, take up your book again and proceed as before, seldom reading more than half a page at a time, for it is not the quantity that is read, but the manner of reading, that yields us profit.

Those who read fast reap no more advantage than a bee would by only skimming over the surface of the flower, instead of waiting to penetrate into it, and extract its sweets. If that method were pursued, we should become gradually habituated to, and more fully disposed for, prayer.

Meditation, which is the other method, is to be practiced at an appropriated season, and not in the time of reading. I believe the best manner of meditating is as follows: When by an act of lively faith, you are placed in the Presence of God, recollect some truth wherein there is substance and food; pause gently and sweetly thereon, not to employ the reason, but merely to calm and fix the mind: for you must observe, that your principal exercise should ever be the Presence of God; your subject, therefore, should rather serve to stay the mind, than exercise the understanding.

From this procedure, it will necessarily follow, that the lively faith in a God immediately present in our inmost soul, will produce an eager and vehement pressing inwardly into ourselves, and a restraining of all our senses from wandering abroad: this serves to extricate us speedily from numberless distractions, to remove us far from external objects, and to bring us nigh unto our God, who is only to be found in our inmost centre, which is the Holy of Holies wherein He dwelleth.

Divine Fact

WATCHMAN NEE

(1903-1972)

It is important for us to recall again facts stated in God's Word for faith to lay hold of. Sin, the old master, is still about, but the slave who served him has been put to death and is out of reach (Romans 6:6). His members are unemployed, now to be used as "instruments of righteousness"(Romans 6:13).

The life of Christ has been planted in us by the new birth, and its nature is not to commit sin (1 John 3:9). But there is a great difference between the nature of the life within us and our history. Sins in our history are historic facts, but so is the new nature that we have received in Christ.

The matter still rests upon our making real in history what is true in Divine fact. The facts of the Cross remain as real as ever. It does not need faith to make these things real in themselves.

When I am sleeping, when I am awake, when I remember it, when I forget it, I am Mr. Nee. If I were to try and pose as Miss K., I should have to keep saying to myself all the time, "You are Miss K. Now, be sure to remember that you are Miss K." Despite much reckoning, the likelihood would be that when I was off my guard and someone called, "Mr. Nee!" I would answer to my own name. Fact would triumph over fiction, and all my reckoning would break down at that crucial moment. But I am Mr. Nee. It is a fact, which nothing I experience or fail to experience can alter.

Whether I feel it or not, I am dead with Christ. Faith is always meeting a mountain of apparent contradiction in the realms of failures, feeling, and suggestion. If we refuse to accept as binding anything that contradicts God's Word, and maintain an attitude of faith in Him alone, we shall find that our experience is coming progressively to tally with the Word.[3]

Filled with Purpose

MATTHEW HENRY

(1662-1714)

The first appearance of God to Moses, found him tending sheep. This seems a poor employment for a man of his talents and background, yet he rests satisfied with it; and learned meekness and contentment—for which he is more noted in the Scriptures, than for all his learning.

Formerly Moses thought himself able to deliver Israel, and set himself to the work too hastily. Now, when he is the fittest person on earth for it, he knows his own weakness. This was the effect of more knowledge of God and of himself. Formerly, self-confidence mingled with strong faith and great zeal, now sinful distrust of God crept in under the garb of humility. But all his objections are answered by God with, "Certainly I will be with you. That is enough."

Moses continued going backward to the work God designed for him because there was much cowardice, laziness, and unbelief in him. We must not judge people by the readiness of their talk. A great deal of wisdom and true worth may be with a slow tongue. God sometimes makes choice of these people as his messengers, who have the least advantages of art or nature, so that His grace in them may appear the more glorious.

Christ's disciples were no orators, until the Holy Spirit made them such. God condescends to answer the excuse of Moses. Even self-diffidence, when it stops us from or slows down our duty, is very displeasing to the Lord. But while we blame Moses for shrinking from this dangerous service, let us ask our own hearts if we are not neglecting duties easier and less perilous. The tongue of Aaron, with the head and heart of Moses, would make one completely fit for this errand.

God promises, I will be with your mouth and with his mouth. Even Aaron, who could speak well, yet could not speak to purpose, unless God gave constant teaching and help. For without the constant aid of Divine grace, the best gifts will fail.

Standing Versus Experience

F. B. MEYER

(1847-1929)

Our experiences are fickle as April weather; now sunshine, now cloud; lights and shadows chasing each other over miles of heathery moor or foam flecked sea. But our standing in Jesus changes not. It is like Himself-the same yesterday, to day, and forever. It did not originate in us, but in His everlasting love, which, foreseeing all that we should be, loved us notwithstanding all. It has not been purchased by us, but by His precious blood, which pleads for us as mightily and successfully when we can hardly claim it, as when our faith is most buoyant. It is not maintained by us, but by the Holy Spirit. If we have fled to Jesus for salvation, sheltering under Him, relying on Him, and trusting Him, though with many misgivings, as well as we may, then we are one with Him for ever. We were one with Him in the grave; one with Him on the Easter morn; one with Him when He sat down at God's right hand. We are one with Him now as He stands in the light of His Father's smile, as the limbs of the swimmer are one with the head, though it alone is encircled with the warm glory of the sun, while they are hidden beneath the waves. And no doubt or depression can for a single moment affect or alter our acceptance with God through the blood of Jesus, which is an eternal fact.

You have not realized this, perhaps, but have thought that your standing in Jesus was affected by your changeful moods. As well might the fortune of a ward in chancery be diminished or increased by the amount of her spending money. Our standing in Jesus is our invested capital. Our emotions at the best are but our spending money, which is ever passing through our pocket or purse, never exactly the same. Cease to consider how you feel, and build on the immovable rock of what Jesus is, and has done, and is doing, and will do for you, world without end.

Means of Grace

JOHN WESLEY

(1703-1791)

By "means of grace" I understand outward signs, words, or actions, ordained of God, and appointed for this end, to be the ordinary channels whereby he might convey to men, preventing, justifying, or sanctifying grace.

The chief of these means are prayer, whether in secret or with the great congregation; searching the Scriptures (which implies reading, hearing, and meditating thereon); and receiving the Lord's Supper, eating bread and drinking wine in remembrance of Him: And these we believe to be ordained of God, as the ordinary channels of conveying his grace to the souls of men.

But we allow, that the whole value of the means depends on their actual subservience to the end of religion; that, consequently, all these means, when separate from the end, are less than nothing and vanity; that if they do not actually conduce to the knowledge and love of God, they are not acceptable in his sight; yea, rather, they are an abomination before him, a stink in his nostrils; he is weary to bear them. Above all, if they are used as a kind of commutation for the religion they were designed to subserve, it is not easy to find words for the enormous folly and wickedness of thus turning God's arms against himself; of keeping Christianity out of the heart by those very means which were ordained for the bringing it in.

We allow, likewise, that all outward means whatever, if separate from the Spirit of God, cannot profit at all, cannot conduce, in any degree, either to the knowledge or love of God. Without controversy, the help that is done upon earth, He doeth it himself. It is He alone who, by His own almighty power, worketh in us what is pleasing in His sight; and all outward things, unless He work in them and by them, are mere weak and beggarly elements.

More than Enough

HANNAH WHITALL SMITH

(1832-1911)

E verything is yours," declares the apostle. It would be impossible for any statement to be more all-embracing. "All is yours" . . . not because you are so good and so worthy, but simply and only because you belong to Christ. All things we need are part of our inheritance in Him, and they only await our claiming. Let our needs and difficulties be as great as they may. There is in these "all things" a supply exceedingly abundant, above all we can ask or think.

Because God is, all must go right for us. Because the mother is, all must go right, up to the measure of her ability, for her children. Infinitely more must this be true of the Lord. To the child there is, behind all that changes and can change, the one unchangeable fact of the mother's existence. While the mother lives, the child must be cared for. While God lives, God's children must be cared for as well. What else could God do, being what God is? Neglect, indifference, forgetfulness, ignorance are all impossible to God. God knows everything, cares about everything, can manage everything, and God loves us. What more could we ask?

Therefore, O doubting and sorrowful Christian hearts . . . nothing else is needed to quiet all your fears, but just this. God is. . . . Since God loves us, God cannot exist and fail to help us. Do we not know, by our own experience, what an urgent necessity it is for love to pour itself out in blessing on the ones it loves? Can we not understand that God, who is love, who is, if I may say so, made out of love, simply cannot help blessing us? We do not need to beg God to bless us. God simply cannot help it.

Therefore, God is enough! God is enough for time. God is enough for eternity.

Purposed to Know God

Joanna P. Moore

(1832-1916)
The following story by Joanna P. Moore from the life of
the Reverend Osborn Dickerson, a former slave, demonstrates his fixed
purpose to know God.

Once, near dark, I was sitting away back in my cabin, so interested in reading about the blessed Savior that I did not hear the master till he stood right over me. "Osborn," he said, "do you know how to read?" "Yes," I answered all in a tremble. "Did you know it's against my rules?" "Yes, I did." He then snatched the book, tore and threw it in the fire.

About a year after the loss of my Bible, a servant very close to the master got sick and died. The master was mighty sorry. As he sat by the bedside when he was dying, Stephen said, "Master, I have one request to make; will you grant it?"

"Yes, Stephen, anything you want I would do."

"Well, after I am dead, please master, let Osborn bury me. Let him sing and pray at my grave."

This the master promised. The cart came and carried the coffin to the servants' graveyard. The master was there on horseback, the other friends standing around the grave. I prayed and repeated some verses about the resurrection and sang, lining out the hymn.

When I came to the words in the song, "The tall, the wise, the reverent head must be as low as ours," the master uttered a cry and fell from his horse. The servants carried him away. The next morning he sent for me. "Osborn," he said, "you may teach your religion here on my place as much as you like and as you have time to preach, but do not go onto any other plantation, for it is against the law."

That is the way the Lord opened the Red Sea for me. I never got another Bible until the Yankees came. The first thing I said to them was, "Give me a Bible"; and I got one. That was as great a joy to me as my freedom.

Born of the Spirit

ALEXANDER WHYTE

(1836-c. 1921)

You may wonder, "What is it like to be born of the Spirit? What does it look like?"

The best way to see what it is like to be born of the Spirit is to look at Jesus Christ himself. Look at him at all times and in all places, and as you look at him, you will become like him. Things like these take place with you every day as they took place with Jesus, don't they? Someone injures you or speaks against you. Someone insults you or overlooks you. Someone treats you with contempt or shows you the worst ingratitude. But now, you have been born again, and a strange and unaccountable change has come over you, and you cannot deny it.

When once you are born of the Spirit, it will be almost as sweet to you to hear your competitor praised and promoted, as it once was to sniff up that sweet incense to yourself. Humility and patience will also begin to take the place of high looks and a proud heart. Your sudden outbursts of anger will cease, and old resentments will decay and die out. You will shed courtesy and gentleness onto persons round about you. Perhaps most miraculous of all, there will be times when your first thought will be God's glory and your neighbor's good, and you forget yourself altogether!

"But can persons be born to all that blessedness when they are as old and as old in sin as I am?" Yes! Look at Nicodemus. He was born again that very night! Do not let the number of your years weigh too heavily on your mind. Do not let the mountains of your lifetime of sin, and your whole chains of such mountains, keep you back. Let all these things compel you all the more to come to Christ on this very spot!"

Honesty Matters

CHARLES G. FINNEY

(1792-1875)

I believe it is a general impression that a person may be honest in greater matters, and deserve the character of honesty, notwithstanding he is guilty of dishonesty in small matters.

If he was actuated by a supreme regard to the authority of God, and if this was the habitual state of his mind, such a state of mind would be quite as apt to manifest itself in smaller matters as in large. Nay, where the temptation is small, he would be more certain to act conscientiously than in greater matters, because there is less to induce him to act otherwise.

What is honesty? If a man has no other motives for acting honestly than mere selfishness, the devil is as honest as he is; for I dare say he is honest with his fellow devils, as far as it is for his interest or policy to be so. Is that honesty? Certainly not. And, therefore, if a man does not act honestly from higher motives than this, he is not honest at all, and if he appears to be honest in certain important matters, he has other motives than a regard to the honor of God.

It is certain that, if an individual is dishonest in small matters, he is not actuated by love to God. If he was actuated by love to God, he would feel that dishonesty in small matters is just as inconsistent as in great. It is as real a violation of the law of God, and one who truly loves God would no more act dishonestly in one than in the other.

It is certain that he is not actuated by real love to his neighbor, such as the law of God requires. If he loved his neighbor as himself, he would not defraud him in small things any more than in great. Nay, he might do it in great things, where the temptation to swerve from his integrity was powerful. But where the temptation is small, it cannot be that one who truly loves his neighbor would act dishonestly.

The Minimum

MARTIN LUTHER

(1483-1546)

The apostles themselves did not know everything, even after they had received the Holy Spirit. Yes, and sometimes they were weak in faith. When all Asia turned from the apostle Paul, when some of his own disciples had departed from him, and when many highly esteemed false persons set themselves against him, then with sorrow of heart he said, "I was with you in weakness and in fear and in much trembling" (1 Corinthians 2:3). Also, "We were afflicted on every side: conflicts without, fears within" (2 Corinthians 7:5). By these verses it is evident that Paul was not always strong in faith. Moreover, the Lord was obliged to comfort him, saying, "My grace is sufficient for you, for power is perfected in weakness" (2 Corinthians 12:9).

This is to me, and to all true followers of Jesus, a comforting teaching. I persuade myself also that I have faith, though it is but so-so, and might well be better. Yet, I teach faith to others, and know that my teaching is right. Sometimes I say to myself, "Indeed, you preach God's word. This ministry is committed to you and you are called unto it without your seeking. Your ministry is not fruitless, for many are changed by it." But when I consider and behold my own weakness, that, I eat, drink, am sometimes merry, yes, also now and then overtaken, (being off my guard), then I begin to doubt and say, 'Ah! If I could but only believe!'

Confident professors of faith are troublesome and dangerous people. When they have but only looked on the outside of the Bible or heard a few sermons, they immediately think they have the Holy Spirit and understand and know all. But good and godly hearts are of another mind, and they pray daily, "Lord, increase our faith."

True Love

HENRY SCOUGAL

(1650-1678)

We see how easily couples or friends slide into the imitation of the one they adore; and how, even before they are aware, they begin to resemble them, not only in their actions, but also in their voice and gesture, and their expression or manner. Certainly we should also copy the virtues and inward beauties of the soul, if they were the true object and motive of our love. But because all people we encounter have their mixture of good and bad, we are always in danger to be corrupted by placing our affections on them.

The true way to improve and ennoble our souls is by fixing our love on the divine perfection of God, that we may have them always before us, and derive an impression of them on ourselves; and "beholding as in a mirror the glory of the Lord, are being transformed into the same image from glory to glory, just as by the Spirit of the Lord" (2 Corinthians 3:18 NKJV). Those who, with a generous and holy ambition, have raised their eyes towards that uncreated beauty and goodness, and fixed their affection there, are of quite another spirit and of a more excellent and heroic temper, than the rest of the world. They cannot help but infinitely dislike all unworthy things and will not entertain any low or base thoughts that might disparage their high and noble purpose.

Love is the greatest and most excellent thing we are masters of and therefore it is folly and baseness to give it unworthily. It is indeed the only thing we can call our own: other things may be taken from us by violence, but none can ravish our love. If any thing else be counted ours by giving our love, we give all, so far as we make over our hearts and wills, by which we possess our other enjoyments. It is not possible to refuse Him anything, to whom by love we have given ourselves. . . . Certainly love is the worthiest present we can offer unto God.

The Word of God

E. W. BULLINGER

(1837-1913)

Arevelation in writing must necessarily be given in "words." The separate words, therefore, in which it is given must have the same importance and authority as the revelation as a whole. If we accept the Bible as a revelation from God, and receive it as inspired by God, we cannot separate the words of which that inspired revelation is made up, or admit the assertion "that the Bible contains the Word of God, but is not the Word of God." The position conveyed by such an expression is both illogical and impossible.

As we design this work for those who accept the Scriptures as the Word of God, we do not propose to offer any arguments in proof of its inspiration.

The Bible is its own best proof of its inspiration. It claims to be "the Word of God"; and if it be not what it claims to be, then it is not only not a "good book," but is unworthy of our further attention.

We cannot understand the position of those who assert and believe that many of its parts are myths and forgeries, while at the same time they continue to write commentaries upon it, and accept their emoluments and dignities for preaching or lecturing about it.

If we were told and believed that a bank-note in our possession is a forgery, we certainly should take no further interest in it, beyond mourning the loss which we had sustained. Our action would thus be consistent with our belief.

We write, therefore, for those who, receiving the claims of the Scriptures as being the Word of God, desire to study it so as to understand it and enjoy it.

When this claim is admitted, and a course of study is undertaken in this spirit, we shall be at once over-whelmed with proofs as to its truth; and on almost every page find abundant confirmation of our faith.

The Bible simply claims to be the Word of God. It does not attempt to establish its claim, or seek to prove it. It merely assumes it and asserts it. It is for us to believe it or to leave it.

The Highest Degree of Quiet

Teresa of Avila

(1515-1582)

It is well to seek greater solitude so as to make room for the Lord and allow His Majesty to do His own work in us. The most we should do is occasionally, and quite gently, to utter a single word, like a person giving a little puff to a candle, when he sees it has almost gone out, so as to make it burn again; though, if it were fully alight, I suppose the only result of blowing it would be to put it out. I think the puff should be a gentle one because, if we begin to tax our brains by making up long speeches, the will may become active again.

It may come about that the soul is enjoying the highest degree of quiet, and that the understanding has soared so far aloft that what is happening to it seems not to be going on in its own house at all. . . . Perhaps this is only my own experience and other people do not find it so. But, speaking for myself, I sometimes long to die because I cannot cure this wandering of the mind. At other times the mind seems to be settled in its own abode and to be remaining there with the will as its companion. When all three faculties work together it is wonderful.

This state of prayer is different from that in which the soul is wholly united with God, for in the latter state it does not even swallow its nourishment: the Lord places this within it, and it has no idea how. But in this state it even seems to be His will that the soul should work a little, though so quietly that it is hardly conscious of doing so. What disturbs it is the understanding and this is not the case when there is union of all the three faculties, since He Who created them suspends them: He keeps them occupied with the enjoyment that He has given them, without their knowing, or being able to understand, the reason.

Continual Prayer

ALEXANDER MACLAREN

(1826-1910)

The apostle Paul literally writes in Colossians 4:2, "Be continually, busily engaged in prayer and continually stay awake in the same with thanksgiving."

How can such a precept be obeyed? We must seek obedience to this precept in a more inward and spiritual notion of prayer.

What is prayer? Not the utterance of words. They are but the vehicle of prayer. Prayer is the attitude of a person's spirit, and the elements of prayer may be diffused throughout our daily lives.

Prayer can be a constant consciousness of God's presence and our contact with Him. In such communion, when God's Spirit and our spirit draw closer together, there is frequently no need for speech. Silently our hearts may be kept fragrant with God's felt presence and sunny with the light of His face.

There can be a continual presence of a desire after God. All our daily experiences of God's grace, combined with all our communion with Him that unveils His beauty to us, can stir longings within us for more of Him.

Our continual submission to God's will is also essential for all prayer. Many persons have the notions that praying is urging our wishes on God, and answered prayer is God giving us what we desire. The deepest expression of true prayer is not, "Do this, because I desire it, O Lord." Rather, it is, "I do this because You desire it, O Lord."

So there should run all through our daily lives the music of continual prayer beneath our various occupations, like some prolonged, deep, bass note that bears up and dignifies the lighter melody rising, falling, and changing above it. Then our lives can be woven into a harmonious unity based upon a continual communion, a continual desire after God, and a continual submission to Him.

Pure Heart

WILLIAM BOOTH

(1829-1912)

First, a Pure Heart is not a heart that is never tempted. Possibly there is no such thing in this world, nor ever has been, as a non-tempted heart, that is, a man or a woman who has never been exposed to temptation to commit sin. Not only was our Blessed Lord tempted by the Devil in the wilderness, but He was beset with evil attractions all the way through His life. St. Paul expressly tells us that our Savior was in all points tempted like as we are, but He effectually resisted the world, the flesh, and the devil, and came through the trying ordeal without a stain.

Second, a Pure Heart is not a heart that cannot suffer. Beyond question, Jesus Christ had a Pure Heart. He was Holy and undefiled, and yet He was "The Man of Sorrows."

Third, a Pure Heart is not a heart that cannot sin. Adam was pure when he came from the hands of his Maker. God pronounced him to be good. But, led away by Satan, He lost His purity, and was cast out of Eden into a world of sin and sorrow and death.

Finally, a Pure Heart does not mean any experience of Purity, however blessed it may be, cannot increase in enjoyment, usefulness, and power. Pull the weeds out of your garden, and the flowers . . . will grow faster, flourish more abundantly, and become more fruitful.

Just so, this very moment, let Jesus Christ purge the garden of your souls of envy and pride, and remove the poisonous plants of malice and selfishness and every other evil thing. Then faith and peace, and hope and love, and humility and courage, and all the other beautiful flowers of Paradise will flourish in more charming beauty and more abundant fruitfulness.

What, then, is a Pure Heart? A Pure Heart is a heart that has been cleansed by the Holy Spirit from all sin, and enabled to please God in all it does; to love Him with all its powers, and its neighbor as itself.

Christian Behavior

JOHN BUNYAN

(1628-1688)

God's people are fruitful in good works according to the proportion of their faith; if they be slender in good works, it is because they are weak in faith. Little faith is like small candles, or weak fire, which though they shine and have heat; yet but dim shining and small heat, when compared with bigger candles and greater fire. The reason why Sardis had some in it whose works were not perfect before God, it was, because they did not hold fast by faith the word that they had formerly heard and received (Rev 3:1-3).

There may be a great mistake in our judging of our own fruitfulness. The soul that indeed is candid and right at heart, is taught by grace to judge itself, though fruitful, yet barren upon two accounts.

(1) When it compares its life to the mercy bestowed upon it: for when a soul does indeed consider the greatness and riches of the mercy bestowed upon it, then it must cry out, 'O wretched man that I am,' (Rom 7:24) for it sees itself wonderfully to fall short of a conversation becoming one who has received so great a benefit.

(2) It may also judge itself barren, because it falls so far short of that it would attain unto, 'it cannot do the thing that it would' (Gal 5:17).

The heart of a Christian is naturally very barren; upon which, though the seed of grace, that is the fruit fullest of all seeds, be sown, yet the heart is naturally subject to bring forth weeds (Mat 15:19). To have a good crop from such ground does argue the fruitfulness of the seed. Wherefore I conclude upon these three things,

(1) That the seed of faith is a very fruitful seed, in that it will be fruitful in so barren a soil.

(2) That faith is not beholden to the heart, but the heart to it, for all its fruitfulness.

(3) That therefore the way to be a more fruitful Christian, it is to be stronger in believing.

The Highest Model

E. M. BOUNDS

(1835-1913)

Prayer is to carry out the will of God. Our prayers must be the creation and exponent of God's will. We are to grasp humanity in our praying as God grasps humanity in his love, his interest, and his plans to redeem humanity Our sympathies, prayers, wrestling and ardent desires must run parallel with the will of God, broad, generous, worldwide, and Godlike. The Christian must in all things, first of all, be conformed to the will of God, but nowhere shall this royal devotion be more evident than in the salvation of the race of men. This high partnership with God, as his deputies on earth, is to have its fullest, richest, and most efficient exercise in prayer for all men.

We are to pray for all people, but to pray especially for rulers in Church and state, that we "may lead a quiet and peaceable life in all godliness and honesty" (1 Timothy 2:2 NKJV). Peace on the outside and peace on the inside. Praying calms disturbing forces, allays tormenting fears, brings conflict to an end. Prayer tends to do away with turmoil.

But even if there be external conflicts, it is well to have deep peace within the citadel of the soul. "That we may lead a quiet and peaceable life." Prayer brings inner calm and furnishes outward tranquility. If praying rulers and praying subjects were worldwide, they would allay turbulent forces, make wars to cease, and peace to reign. We must pray for all people that we may lead lives "in all godliness and honesty"—that is, with godliness and gravity.

Godliness is to be like God. It is to be godly, to have God-likeness, having the image of God stamped upon the inner nature, and showing the same likeness in conduct and in temper. Almighty God is the very highest model, and to be like Him is to possess the highest character. Prayer molds us into the image of God; and at the same time tends to mold others into the same image just in proportion as we pray for them.

Affections

JONATHAN EDWARDS

(1703-1758)

The reason given why the house of Israel would not obey God, was, that they were hardhearted: Ezekiel 3:7, "But the house of Israel will not hearken unto thee; for they will not hearken unto me: for all the house of Israel are impudent and hard-hearted."

A hard heart is plainly meant an unaffected heart, or a heart not easy to be moved with virtuous affections, like a stone, insensible, stupid, unmoved, and hard to be impressed. Hence the hard heart is called a stony heart, and is opposed to a heart of flesh, that has feeling, and is sensibly touched and moved.

We read in Scripture of a hard heart, and a tender heart; and doubtless we are to understand these, as contrary the one to the other. But what is a tender heart, but a heart which is easily impressed with what ought to affect it?

God commends Josiah, because his heart was tender; and it is evident by those things which are mentioned as expressions and evidences of this tenderness of heart, that by his heart being tender is meant, his heart being easily moved with religious and pious affection: 2 Kings 22:19, "Because thine heart was tender, and thou hast humbled thyself before the Lord, when thou heardest what I spake against this place, and against the inhabitants thereof, that they should become a desolation and a curse, and hast rent thy clothes, and wept before me, I also have heard thee, saith the Lord."

And this is one thing, wherein it is necessary we should "become as little children, in order to our entering into the kingdom of God," even that we should have our hearts tender, and easily affected and moved in spiritual and divine things, as little children have in other things.

Upon the whole, I think it clearly and abundantly evident, that true religion lies very much in the affections. Yet it is evident, that religion consists so much in affection, as that without holy affection there is no true religion; and . . . no external fruit is good, which does not proceed from such exercises.

Urgency of the Soul

JOHN B. MEACHUM

(1789-1854)

O do not let the judgment find the soul unprepared! Feet, where are you carrying the soul to? Are you not walking in forbidden paths? Death may be in some of these paths. Hands, how often have you warred against the soul, doing the very thing that God hath forbidden? Mouth, have you not helped to damn the soul, by cursing and swearing and lying?

All these things lead down to the pit of damnation. Eyes, what are you about, that you cannot watch for the soul, and not suffer these feet and hands and mouth to do so much mischief to the soul? because, if you do not watch these many members, they will damn the soul to all eternity. It seems that the tongue is an unruly member; James says, "it cannot be tamed; it is unruly, and full of deadly poison; set on fire of hell." Cannot the eye watch the other members, and keep them from damning the soul, by running headlong into forbidden paths? I condemn all the members, eye, hand and foot; they are all agreed together, to go on and war against the soul. Then the mind must be changed. God keep thy tongue from evil and thy lips from speaking guile.

It is out of the abundance of the heart that the mouth speaketh, and with the heart men believe unto righteousness, and with the mouth confession is made unto salvation. These things do not war against the soul; you have fruit unto holiness, and the end is everlasting life. How much better, then, it is to endeavor to save the soul!

Let all seek to have the mind changed, that we may be led by the Spirit of Christ. In order to be led by the Spirit of Christ, we must be born again; born of that Spirit that can lead us from earth to that blessed world of rest, that remains for the people of God. We must live godly and soberly in Christ Jesus the Lord, which is your salvation.

Peace's Presence

THOMAS À KEMPIS

(c. 1379-1471)

God's peace is with the humble and meek of heart: your peace will be found in much patience. If you hear Christ and follow His voice, you will be able to enjoy much peace.

First, watch yourself in all things, in what you do and what you say. Direct your every intention toward pleasing God alone, and desire nothing outside of God. Do not be quick to judge the deeds and words of others, and do not entangle yourself in affairs that are not your own. Thus, it will come about that you will be disturbed little and seldom.

Then realize that the lack of conflict is not the presence of peace. Do not think that you have found true peace if you feel no depression, or that all is well because you suffer no opposition. Do not think that all is perfect if everything happens just as you wish. And do not imagine yourself great or consider yourself especially beloved if you are filled with great love and sweetness. For the progress and perfection of a Christian does not consist in a life of ease.

Instead, spiritual growth consists in offering yourself with all your heart to God's will, not seeking what is yours either in small matters or great ones, either in temporary or eternal things.

In brief, seek to do the will of others rather than your own. Always choose to have less rather than more. Look always for the last place and seek to be beneath all others. Always wish and pray that the will of God be fully carried out in you. Then you will enter into the realm of peace and rest.

LOTS AND LOTS OF LISTS

Top 20 Highest-Grossing Movies of All Time

Titanic
Star Wars: Episode IV—A New Hope
Shrek 2
E. T.: The Extra-Terrestrial
Star Wars: Episode I—The Phantom Menace
Spider-Man
The Lord of the Rings: The Return of the King
Spider-Man 2
The Passion of the Christ
Jurassic Park
The Lord of the Rings: The Two Towers
Finding Nemo
Forrest Gump
The Lion King
Harry Potter and the Sorcerer's Stone
The Lord of the Rings: The Fellowship of the Ring
Star Wars: Episode II—Attack of the Clones
Star Wars: Episode VI—Return of the Jedi
Independence Day
Pirates of the Caribbean

10 Most Populous States in the U.S.

California	(35,484,453)
Texas	(22,118,509)
New York	(19,190,115)
Florida	(17,019,068)
Illinois	(12,653,544)
Pennsylvania	(12,365,455)
Ohio	(11,435,798)
Michigan	(10,079,985)
Georgia	(8,684,715)
New Jersey	(8,638,396)

5 Fabulous Fad Hobbies

Knitting
Yoga
Dance Revolution
Scrapbooking
Kickboxing

Top 10 Love Songs

"At Last" by Etta James
"You Are the Sunshine of My Life" by Stevie Wonder
"Everything I Do" by Bryan Adams
"Unchained Melody" by The Righteous Brothers
"Unforgettable" by Nat King Cole
"With or Without You" by U2
"Thank You" by Dido
"Every Breath You Take" by The Police
"Your Song" by Elton John
"Can't Help Falling in Love" by Elvis

20 Foundation Stones for Success

The wisdom of preparation
The value of confidence
The worth of honesty
The privilege of working
The discipline of struggle
The magnetism of character
The radiance of health
The forcefulness of simplicity
The winsomeness of courtesy
The attractiveness of modesty
The inspiration of cleanliness
The satisfaction of serving
The power of suggestion
The buoyancy of enthusiasm
The advantage of initiative
The virtue of patience
The rewards of cooperation
The fruitfulness of perseverance
The sportsmanship of losing
The joy of winning

5 Longest Books in the Bible

Psalms (150 chapters, 2,461 verses, 43,743 words)
Jeremiah (52 chapters, 1,364 verses, 42,659 words)
Ezekiel (48 chapters, 1,273 verses, 39,407 words
Genesis (50 chapters, 1,533 verses, 38,267 words)
Isaiah (66 chapters, 1,292 verses, 38,044 words)

Top 10 Musical Movies

The Sound of Music
Singing in the Rain
Evita
Chicago
Fiddler on the Roof
Phantom of the Opera
Moulin Rouge
Grease
Some Like It Hot
Stormy Weather

14 Must-Read Novels for Teens

The Emily Series by Lucy Maud Montgomery
The Ordinary Princess by M. M. Kaye
The 13 Clocks by James Thurber
The Trouble with Lemons by Daniel Hayes
Freak the Mighty by Rodman Philbrick
When My Name Was Keoko by Linda Sue Park
Archer's Goon by Diana Wynne Jones

Seven Famous Must-Read Novels for Teens

A Wrinkle in Time by Madeleine L'Engle
The Devil's Arithmetic by Jane Yolen
The Chronicles of Narnia by C. S. Lewis
The Neverending Story by Michael Ende
The Princess Bride by William Goldman
To Kill a Mockingbird by Harper Lee
The Secret Garden by Frances Hodgson Burnett

American Wars

Spanish-Indian War (1754-1763)—Final conflict in the ongoing struggle between the British and French for control of eastern North America.

American Revolution (1775-1782)—Led by General George Washington, Americans faced off against the British Empire led by General George Washington. We won this one!

War of 1812 (1812-1814)—U.S. declares war on Britain over British interference with American maritime shipping and westward expansion. The British attack and burn the White House in Washington, D.C., forcing the Madisons to flee, but are then defeated when they try to take over Baltimore.

The Mexican-American War (1846-1848)—U.S. declares war on Mexico in an effort to gain California and other territory in the Southwest.

Civil War (1861-1865)—America's bloodiest war. The North fought against the South to settle the dispute over national authority versus states' rights. In the process, the legal practice of slavery was abolished.

Spanish-American War (1898)—*USS Maine* is blown up in Havana harbor, prompting U.S. to declare war on Spain. U.S. annexes Hawaii to better fight Spain in Cuba. U.S. wins. Spain allows Cuba to be free. The U.S. gains Guam, Puerto Rico, and the Philippines.

World War I (1914-1918)—also known as the First World War, the Great War, the War of the Nations, and the War to End All Wars—Alliances between nations in Europe (intended to discourage one European nation from waging war on another) backfired when Austria, Hungary, and Serbia became embroiled in a conflict drawing in other nations. The U.S. entered at the urging of President Woodrow Wilson by declaring war on Germany.

World War II (1939-1945)—also known as the Second World War and the War to Make the World Safe for Democracy. The U.S. entered the war when it was attacked by the Japanese at Pearl Harbor. This brought down Nazi Germany and Adolf Hitler. It also brought the defeat of the Japanese when the first atomic bombs ever used in warfare were dropped on the cities of Hiroshima and Nagasaki.

Korean War (1950-1953)—Cold War conflict between Communist and non-Communist forces on Korean Peninsula. North Korean communists invade South Korea. President Truman, without the approval of Congress, committed American troops to battle.

Vietnam War/Conflict (1961-1975)—The U.S. never officially declared war so the dates are ambiguous. The first "official" casualty was listed in 1961, though two Americans were killed and one wounded in an attack north of Saigon in 1959. The last "official" casualty was listed in 1975. Official end of the war was 1975, when U.S. troops were withdrawn and U.S. prisoners released. (Many believe that a number of U.S. prisoners were never returned.)

Desert Storm (1991)—U.S. intervention in attempted takeover of Kuwait by Iraqi forces.

Operation Enduring Freedom (2001-Ongoing)—The U.S. confronts the perpetrators of terrorism: The Taliban and Osama bin Ladin's Al-Qaida.

Operation Iraqi Freedom (2003-Ongoing)—Largest special-forces operation since the Vietnam War waged against Saddam Hussein's Iraq in second phase of The War against Terror.

Top 10 Most-Frightening Pets

Emperor scorpion

Alligator snapping turtle

Tarantula

Hissing cockroach

Boa constrictor

Pit bull

Iguana

Rat/mouse

Parrot

Hairless cat

Top 5 Urban Myths about Spiders

The daddy longlegs has the world's most powerful venom, but fortunately its jaws (fangs) are so small that it can't bite you. All the spiders known as daddy longlegs are either not poisonous or have very weak poison.

You can identify "brown recluse" spiders by a violin-shaped mark on its body. Many harmless brown spiders also have a violin-shaped mark on them. Recluses are part of only 1 percent of all spider types that have six eyes in three pairs.

Some spiders are venomous, and others aren't. Almost all spiders have venom, but of around 50,000 spider species known, only about twenty-five (1/20 of 1 percent) have venom capable of causing illness in humans.

A deadly exotic spider has been found lurking under toilet seats in airports and airplanes. In August 1999, this began as an Internet hoax, and the spider species, airport, hospital, and doctor were all false names and didn't exist. In October 2002, another story came out, and this time the spider species mentioned was a harmless variety that likes the sunlight, but not dark, cold toilets.

"I'm very kind to spiders; when I find one in the house, I put it back outside instead of killing it." Most house spiders were always house spiders. Putting them "back" outside usually kills them because they aren't suited for the outside climate.

10 Most-Popular Pet Names

Max
Maggie
Buddy
Bailey
Jake
Sam
Molly
Nicky
Coco
Sadie

10 Most-Popular Romantic Scents

Vanilla
Roses
Scent of spouse
Scent of spouse after shower
Strawberries
Musk
Fresh flowers
Lavender
"Obsession" cologne for men
Peaches

Top 5 Children's TV Shows

Sesame Street
Dora the Explorer
SpongeBob SquarePants
Blue's Clues
The Backyardigans

Top 10 Fears or Phobias

Glossophobia (fear of public speaking)
Acrophobia (fear of heights)
Brontophobia (fear of storms)
Claustrophobia (fear of enclosed spaces)
Ophidiophobia (fear of snakes)
Enetophobia (fear of needles or pins)
Cnidophobia (fear of insect stings)
Agoraphobia (fear of open spaces)
Arachnophobia (fear of spiders)
Coulrophobia (fear of clowns)

7 Deadly Sins

Pride
Greed
Envy
Anger
Lust
Gluttony
Sloth

20 Great Cheap-Date Ideas

Make pizza together.

Go window-shopping. Discuss what you would buy if you had lots of money.

Just sit in a busy bus or train station, airport, or park, and watch people.

Go to the children's section of a library or bookstore and read children's books aloud.

Paint a room or do gardening together.

Go ice-skating or roller-skating (or rollerblading) at a local rink.

Locate a large piece of cardboard. Curve the end up like a toboggan. Find a sloping hill of dry grass and slide down. Wear older clothes because of potential grass stains.

Attend the local high school's musical.

Have a weekly game night. Break out the cards, board games, and other fun activities (Uno works well for all ages), and have chips, dip, etc.

Make a couple of pans of brownies. Then drive to friends' houses and deliver a brownie or two and visit for a while. Then go to another house. When it gets late, go home and finish off the brownies yourselves.

On a sunny Saturday morning, travel around the countryside and photograph special sites and serene scenery.

Attend church functions together. Dances, discussion groups, and potlucks really help couples grow closer to each other.

Go to a free concert in a mall or local school.

Go for a walk—even if it's cold outside. It gives you an excuse to have a cup of hot cocoa or hot spiced cider when you get back.

Go to a museum, aquarium, or zoo.

Listen to live music or a lecture at a bookstore.

Fly a kite.

Have a car picnic. Pack a nice picnic (no alcohol for the driver, please) and park the car at a scenic overlook or where you can watch planes take off or wildlife amble by. Play some music or a book on tape. Or sit and simply talk to each other.

Go to a thrift shop and buy board games (less than two dollars a game, usually) or a puzzle and spend an evening playing.

Have a BBQ in the snow.

9 Christian Virtues
Love

Joy

Peace

Patience

Kindness

Goodness

Faithfulness

Gentleness

Self-control

9 Most-Popular Bible Characters
God/Jesus

Abraham

Moses

Mary

David

Esther

Joseph

Paul

Elijah

5 Great Ways to Increase Hope

Sing loudly. Praise music is best, but oldies are also good.

Take a walk. The exercise, air, and hopefully sunshine will give energy and joy.

Drink hot cocoa or eat a banana. Chocolate cures most problems, and it's been said that bananas cure existential dread.

Read children's books alone, or read them to children.

Pray. And if you're having trouble praying, read some psalms out loud.

8 Interesting Foods Listed in the Bible

Bread

Fish

Manna

Honey and locusts

Figs

Olive oil

Pomegranates

Leeks

10 Largest Church Congregations in the World

Full Gospel Church, Seoul, Korea (253,000 members)

Yotabeche Methodist P. Church, Santiago, Chile (150,000 members)

Deeper Life Bible Church, Lagos, Nigeria (120,000 members)

Elim Church, San Salvador, El Salvador (117,000 members)

Mision Carismatica Internacional, Bogota, Columbia (90,000 members)

Vision de Futuro, Santa Fe, Argentinia (70,000 members)

Nak Presbyterian Church, South Korea (60,000 members)

Winners Chapel, Ota, Nigeria (50,000 members)

Allahabad Agricultural Institute, India (40,000 members)

Chattisgarh/MPradesh Housechurchnet, India (30,000 members)

10 Amazing Scenic Drives in the U.S.

Blue Ridge Parkway from Virginia to Tennessee offers more than 450 miles of gorgeous trees, lush valleys, and wildlife.

Route 7 and Vermont's many back roads and byways are extraordinarily beautiful, especially in the fall.

Route 169/Norwich-Woodstock Turnpike in Connecticut passes through many small historic towns with buildings, homes, and churches from the mid-1800s.

US 30 through Lancaster County, Pennsylvania, provides visitors with a glimpse of the intriguing Amish, Mennonite, and Brethren cultures.

Florida Keys Scenic Highway US 1 is great if you want to experience warm temperatures and see spectacular sunrises and sunsets.

Historic National Road in Illinois along US 40 is known as the "Main Street of America" because of its many historic towns and buildings.

Bear Lake-Caribou Scenic Byway, which stretches across the borders of Utah and Idaho, offers visitors the chance to enjoy camping, fishing, boating, and amazing scenery.

Highway 101 from northern California north along the coast of Oregon to Washington's Olympic Peninsula.

Highway 1 along the California coastline from San Diego to San Francisco is a treat for those who enjoy warm temperatures and breathtaking ocean views.

Historic Columbia River Highway in Oregon, referred to by some as the "King of the Roads," provides many trails for bikers and hikers and is a favorite among outdoor enthusiasts.

5 Good Reasons to Learn Spanish

It equips you for travel.

More than 400 million other people speak it—why not you?

It's impressive when ordering dinner in a Mexican restaurant.

It helps you understand that little Taco Bell dog.

It expands your cultural horizons.

5 Clever (Though Weird) Uses for Duct Tape

Fabulous fashions. (Even the big designers are discovering what can be done with a drab, boring outfit when strategically placed pieces of delightfully hued duct tape are applied.)

Keeping track of small parts like nuts and bolts, screws and washers. (Lay a small strip on the floor sticky side up. As you take the parts out, lay them on the tape. They won't roll around, and they won't roll off!)

Marking luggage. (When it comes flying off the luggage conveyor belt looking just like all the other baggage, yours will be the one with the brightly colored duct tape on the side—mystery solved!)

Reinforcing disposable diapers. (When your quintuplets discover the fun of taking off their diapers as quickly as you put them on, there simply is no better remedy.)

Removing cactus stickers. (You already have a workable plan in place? Get serious!)

14 Most-Loved Hymns

"How Great Thou Art"

"The Old Rugged Cross"

"What a Friend We Have in Jesus"

"Be Thou My Vision"

"And Can It Be"

"Amazing Grace"

"Great Is Thy Faithfulness"

"To God Be the Glory"

"Just As I Am"

"Blessed Assurance"

"Rock of Ages"

"Holy, Holy, Holy"

"There Is a Redeemer"

"I Come to the Garden Alone"

15 Things God Sees and Knows

God sees all things (Proverbs 15:3).

God knows the size and scope of the universe (Psalm 147:4).

God knows about animals (Matthew 10:29).

God knows people (Matthew 10:30).

God knows our thoughts (Psalm 139:2; 44:21).

God knows our words (Psalm 130:2).

God knows our deeds (Psalm 139:2).

God knows our sorrows (Exodus 3:7).

God knows our needs (Matthew 6:32).

God knows our devotions (Genesis 18:17-19; 2 Chronicles 16:9).

God knows our frailties (Psalm 103:14).

God knows our foolishness (Psalm 60:5)

God knows His own (John 10:14; 2 Timothy 2:19).

God knows the past, present, and future (Acts 15:18).

God knows what might or could have been (Matthew 11:23).

5 Regrettable Fashion Fads

Bell-bottoms

Miniskirts

Tie-dyeing

Hammer pants

Leggings

10 Great Things to Buy Used

Books

DVDs, CDs, and videos

Kids' toys

Jewelry

Clothing

Time-shares

Cars

Personal computers (not laptops)
Office furniture
Hand tools

14 Great Ways to Pray

Recite the Lord's Prayer or other verses.

Sing praises to your God and King.

Ask for help throughout your day.

Go through the ACTS prayer: Adoration, Confession, Thanksgiving, and Supplication.

Focus on God's love.

Thank God for the things He does.

Contemplate a passage of scripture, slowly reading and responding to it.

Marvel at God's creation.

Help the poor, the widows, and the orphans.

Write letters to God in a journal.

Try different prayer positions: kneeling, standing, sitting comfortably, walking, raising your hands, or lying down.

Silently listen to God.

Pray for others: missionaries, leaders, celebrities, friends, family, and politicians.

Speak out loud and talk to God.

Top 10 Chocolate-Makers

See's Candy
Ghirardelli
Hershey's
Godiva Chocolatier
Kinder Surprise
Lindt Master Chocolatier
Cadbury
Rocky Mountain Chocolate Factory
Nestlé
Toblerone

Top 10 Fictional Detectives

Sherlock Holmes
Nancy Drew and the Hardy Boys
Perry Mason
Dick Tracy
Lord Peter Wimsey
Hercules Poirot
Jessica Fletcher of *Murder She Wrote*
Lieutenant Columbo
Sergeant Joe Friday of *Dragnet*
Philip Marlowe

5 Most-Hated Chores

Changing diapers
Cleaning toilets
Hanging wallpaper
Changing the litter box
Cleaning grout

Top 10 Extreme Hairdos

Beehive
Mullet
Mohawk
Shag
Pixie
Afro
The big hair of rock
Crimped '80s hair
Farah Fawcett waves
Flower bangs

10 Must-Read Christian Autobiographies

The Journal of John Wesley
C. S. Lewis's *Surprised by Joy*
Elizabeth Sherrill's *All the Way to Heaven*
Brother Andrew's *God's Smuggler*
Corrie ten Boom's *The Hiding Place*
George Müller's Journal
Hudson Taylor's *Spiritual Secret*
Catherine Marshall's *Beyond Ourselves*
Confessions of Saint Augustine
Just As I Am: The Autobiography of Billy Graham

Top 5 Rules for Making a Mix CD

Don't include an artist more than once.
Include an equal number of classic and current songs.
Start out and end well.
Keep the listener in mind when choosing songs.
Listen to it first before giving it away.

5 Great Ways to Exercise and Have Fun

Play Frisbee with a friend, an animal, or an animal that's
    a friend.
Play tag with children.
Take a kickboxing, Pilates, or aerobics class.
Go to a video arcade and try playing Dance Dance
    Revolution.
Walk or run in a beautiful park.

10 Must-Have Power Tools

Cordless drill
Band saw
Table saw
Drill press
Air compressor
Bench grinder

Combination disk and belt sander
Circular saw
4-inch portable sander/grinder
Soldering iron

10 Great Ways to Change Your World

Pray.
Help the poor, the widows, and orphans.
Forgive those who hurt you.
Give generously.
Work responsibly.
Rest well.
Dream.
Mentor and be mentored.
Invest wisely.
Plant a tree.

10 Amusing Things That Show God Has a Sense of Humor

The platypus
The digestive system
Bumblebees
Baby animals
The appendix
Solar eclipses
The story of Baalam and his talking donkey (Numbers 22)
Hammerhead sharks
Snowflakes
Oklahoma weather

10 Cool Things about Science

Volcanoes
Black holes
Robots

Rockets

Awesome vocabulary words like *mitochondria* and *endoplasmic reticulum*

Lasers

String Theory

Deep-sea exploration

The Aurora Borealis

Supernovas

10 Great Ways to Improve Your Life

Pray.

Read your Bible.

Brush and floss your teeth.

Exercise.

Get enough sleep.

Bathe.

Smile.

Spend time with wise and encouraging people.

Help others.

Pray again.

5 Best Flowers for Non-Stop Summer Blooming

Dahlia

Stella d'oro daylily

Geranium

Roses

Red salvia

5 Dreaded College Courses

English Composition 1

Organic chemistry

Statistics

Speech

Differential equations

WHAT'S IN A NAME?

Place Names—Cities

Chicago—one of the largest cities in the world was named for the Chicago River. In the 1600s, the first white men arrived on the banks of a river the Potawatomi Indians called "Checagou"—their word meaning wild onion. Later a fur-trading settlement and military base built on the river was given a variation of the river's Indian name.

Philadelphia—meaning "brotherly love" in Greek, was founded in 1682 by William Penn, an English Quaker, whose intention was to make it a center of religious freedom.

Boston—named by the Puritans after the town of Boston, England. Puritan housewives prepared baked beans every Saturday to be served for dinner on Sunday (work of any kind on Sunday was forbidden by the Puritans). This practice earned Boston the nickname "Beantown."

Seattle—named for Chief Sealth, a Duwamish Indian who had befriended the settlers.

San Diego—named for San Diego de Alcala, a Spanish saint. The city was founded by soldiers who built California's first military fort on the site. In 1769, a Franciscan priest, Junipero Serra, established California's first mission in the fort.

Denver—founded in 1858 by gold prospectors and named for James W. Denver, governor of the Kansas Territory at the time. Its nickname, "Mile High City," refers to the fact that the state capitol stands on land one mile above sea level.

Des Moines, Iowa—named for the Des Moines River, which was originally called Moingona—meaning river of the mounds (Indian mounds). French explorers changed the river's name to Moin and called it la Riviere des Moines. In 1843, the army built Fort Des Moines to protect Indians in the area.

Dallas—founded by John Neely Bryan, a lawyer and trader, in 1841 as a trading post on the Trinity River. Historians believe the city was named for George M. Dallas, vice-president of the United States from 1845 to 1849 under President James Polk.

Phoenix—named for the Greek mythological bird that burned himself every five hundred years and rose to life again—after Darrell Duppa, one of the white pioneers who first settled there in the 1860s, realized that an ancient civilization had flourished on the site.

Gary, Indiana—named after Judge Elbert H. Gary, chairman of the board of the United States Steel Corporation in 1906. The settlement was established at the base of Lake Michigan for the benefit of steelworkers.

Mobile, Alabama—founded as Fort Louis de la Mobile, a trading and military outpost, in 1702 by Jean Baptiste LeMoyne, Sieur de Bienville, a French-Canadian explorer. In 1711 flooding caused the post to be moved twenty-seven miles downriver to its present site.

Duluth, Minnesota—named in honor of David Greysolon, a French explorer who went by the title Sieur Duluth. It became a city in 1870 after making peace with the Chippewa and Sioux Indians and exploring the headwaters of the Mississippi River. It is one of the largest natural ports in the U.S.

Place Names—States

Kentucky—Wyandot Indian word for "great meadow." First region west of the Allegheny Mountains to be settled by American pioneers.

Florida—named by Ponce de Leon and the Spaniards who discovered it close to Easter Day and believed it to be an island. "Pasqua de Flores" is their name for this holiday.

Dakota—Sioux Indian's word for "friend" or "ally." Both the North and South territories of Dakota vied for statehood and wanted to use the name. When statehood was granted, the controversy was resolved by the North and South Compromise.

Hawaii—Means "homeland" in Polynesian: (*hawa*) meaning "place of residence" and (*ii*) meaning "smaller and raging" (because of the volcanoes). At one time these islands were called the Sandwich Islands, so named by Captain James

Cook. King Kamehameha I insisted that each island should have its own name, thus they are Hawaii, Maui, Oahu, Kauai, Molokai, Lanai, Niihau, and Kahoolawe. The chain is named Islands of the King of Hawaii.

Kansas—named for the Kanze tribe of Indians. Kansas is the French spelling with an English "s" ending.

Missouri—named for a small Algonkian tribe who lived at the mouth of the river of the Algonkian River, it means "canoe haver." In 1673, an explorer and missionary named Jacques Marquette drew a map on which he named the tribe and river "8emess8rit." "8"—the number was used for the French "ou" sound.

Ohio—Iroquis Indians called the river Ohiiyo, which means in Seneca "beautiful" or "magnificent."

Oklahoma—Choctaw word meaning "red people," it became the state name for the place once called Indian Territory.

Oregon—French word meaning "ouragan," which means "hurricane." Explorers thought the Columbia River, "the river of squalls," would lead to a northwest passage to the Orient.

Texas—Caddo Indians' word for friends—*Tehsha*.

Idaho—name means "salmon tribe" or "salmon eaters" for the Shoshone Indians. The territory was first named Colorado. Later the people petitioned for the Indian name Idaho.

Iowa—first named Quaouiatonon—then Quaouia—then Iowa, meaning "one who puts to sleep," referring to the Iowa Indians' use of hypnotism.

Utah—named for the Ute Indians, who as their name signifies, lived "higher up" in the mountains than the other tribes.

Vermont—first named New Connecticut, Congress renamed it 150 years later. The "green mountains" or "verd monts" were first noted by French explorer Samuel Champlain in 1609.

Arkansas—Quapaw Indians lived in this area and the Algonkian Indians called them Oo-ka-na-sa. A Jesuit missionary recorded the name as Arkansea, meaning "downstream people." The region became the Arkansaw Territory in 1819. When it became a state, it was spelled Arkansas.

Place Names—Mountains

Khmer Chuir Phnum Dâmrei—formerly the Elephant Mountains, in Cambodia. The name literally translated means "The mountains round which the clouds turn." The Dâmrei Mountains were once the principal center of Cambodia's pepper-growing industry.

Mackenzie Mountains—the northern extension of the Rocky Mountains, these Canadian mountains were named for Sir Alexander Mackenzie, who explored the Mackenzie River in 1789. These mountains became known when an oil field at Norman Wells on the Mackenzie River was developed and a four hundred-mile pipeline was built to Whitehorse, Yukon Territory, to fuel U.S. military bases in the Pacific Northwest.

Selkirk Mountains—named after Thomas Douglas, 5th Earl of Selkirk, sponsor of Canadian settlements. This major subdivision of the Columbia Mountains extends for two hundred miles, mostly in British Columbia, Canada, and just across the U.S. border into northern Idaho and Montana. Bounded by the Purcell Mountains and the Columbia River, they are sometimes considered part of the Rocky Mountain system.

Chisos Mountains—*Chisos* may be a Native American word meaning "ghost" or "spirit," or it may derive from the Castilian hechizos "enchantment." Covering forty-square miles along the Rio Grande in southwestern Texas, U.S., these mountains were a favored stronghold of bandits and robbers. Later, the area was used for cattle ranching until it was made part of the national park in 1944.

Wicklow Mountains—mountain range in County Wicklow, Ireland. Little Sugar Loaf and the Great Sugar Loaf Mountains, named because of their shapes, are part of this chain.

Jotunheim Mountains—named Jotunfjell ("Giant's Mountains") in 1822, this mountain range has been known as the Jotunheimen ("Giant's Home") since the turn of the century. Located in Oppland fylke (county), south-central Norway, this is the highest range in Scandinavia. Its tallest peak is Glitter Mountain.

Place Names—Rivers

Fraser River—Sir Alexander Mackenzie discovered this British Columbian river and named it after a German Canadian trader who followed the river to the Pacific in 1808.

De Grey River—Australian explorer Francis Gregory visited this river in northwestern Australia in 1861 and named it for the 3rd Earl de Grey. In 1888 the rich Pilbara goldfield attracted many settlers to the river's valley. Australia's Great Northern Highway crosses the river near the village of De Grey, a few miles from the ocean.

Okavango River—The river, formerly called the Okovango, takes its name from the Okavango (Kavango) people of northern Namibia. It is also called Kubango River, fourth longest river system in southern Africa, running basically southeastward for one thousand miles from central Angola, where it is known as the Kubango, to the Kalahari in northern Botswana. The river terminates in an immense inland delta known as the Okavango Swamp. David Livingstone, the Scottish missionary and explorer, and first European known to have seen the Okavango, reached its swampy delta in 1849.

Cache la Poudre River—The story of this Colorado river's name is that some trappers needing to lighten their wagons in a snowstorm hid their supplies by the river. A cache (or stash) included, along with other supplies, a considerable amount of gun powder.

Manicouagan River—Indian name meaning "where there is bark." This refers to the river's long-term use as an important lumbering artery supporting pulp and paper factories. The name is also spelled Manikuagan River, French Rivière Manicouagan River in the (North Shore) region, eastern Quebec province, Canada. The Manicouagan drains more than sixteen-thousand square miles of the heavily forested region.

Oconaluftee River—This North Carolina river gets its name from the Cherokee word for "soapy water."

Tweed River—This river in the Scottish Borders council area of southeastern Scotland, flows eastward for ninety-seven miles, and for seventeen miles it forms the border with England. For the last two miles of its course, the Tweed flows through England before entering the North Sea at Berwick-upon-Tweed. The towns of the Tweed valley are woolen-manufacturing towns and markets.

The Betwa River—Sanskrit Vetravati, "Containing Reeds," this river in northern India flows generally northeast through Madhya Pradesh and Uttar Pradesh states and empties into the Yamuna just east of Hamirpur after a 380-mile course.

Pascagoula River—Caddo Indian word for "singing river," this river is formed by the union of the Leaf and the Chickasawhay Rivers in Mississippi and flows into the Gulf of Mexico. The legend says the water sings a death song for an Indian woman who, heartbroken, committed suicide by walking into the river.

Red River—Named for the red clay soil that forms the banks, this river flows from New Mexico across Texas and Louisiana to the Mississippi.

Judith River—Discoverers, Lewis and Clark, named this Montana river for Judith Hancock, Clark's sweetheart back in Virginia.

Place Names—Streets

Wall Street—named for an earthen wall built by Dutch settlers in 1653 to repel an expected English invasion, this name refers to the southern section of the borough of Manhattan, in New York City, which has long been the location of many U.S. financial institutions. Even before the American Civil War the street was recognized as the financial capital of the nation.

Watling Street—named by a group of Anglo-Saxon settlers who called Verulamium by the name of Wætlingaceaster, this local name passed to the whole of the Roman road (Wæclinga stræt) by the 9th century. Roman Road in England ran from Dover west-northwest to London and then northwest via St. Albans to Wroxeter. Watling Street was one of Britain's greatest arterial roads of the Roman and post-Roman periods.

Via del Corso—named for the horseraces (*corse*) that were part of the Roman carnival celebrations. It has been an important thoroughfare in central Rome since classical times, when it was the Via Flaminia, the road to the Adriatic. Along the Corso are shops, churches, palaces, and the column of Marcus Aurelius.

Tin Pan Alley—named for a genre of American popular music that arose in the late 19th century from the American song-publishing industry in New York City. This type of music—ballads, dance music, and vaudeville—took its name from the byname of the street on which the industry was based. The phrase tin pan referred to the sound of pianos played by musicians attempting to sell their songs to music publishers. The phrase "Tin Pan Alley" eventually became synonymous with American popular music.

Place Names—Countries

Hong Kong—taken from the Chinese words *hong*, meaning "fragrant," and *kong*, meaning "harbor." It won its name from the incense trade which helped the port develop.

Guyana—derived from the word *Guaya-na*, which means "we, the esteemed." It was formerly called British Guiana and is the largest of the three countries in the Guiana region of South America, along with Suriname and French Guiana.

Ethiopia—taken from the Greek words *aitho* meaning "burn" and *ops* meaning "face." It is the "land of the people with sunburned faces."

Georgia—taken from the Greek word *georgos* which means "farmer." It was once a part of the Soviet Union, which supports agriculture.

Belize—derived from *Belice*, an old French word that meant "beacon." It was formerly the British Honduras. It was named for its principal town, which grew from a colony known to use a beacon to guide ships into the harbor.

Albania—comes from the Latin *albus*, meaning "white," and

means "white land." This mountainous country is often white with a blanket of ice and snow. Albanians call it *Shqiperia*, which means "land of the eagle."

Tanganyika—comes from the Bantu word *tanganya*, meaning "to gather" and *nyika*, which is a water chestnut. It was once called Tanzania.

Zimbabwe—means "dwelling place of the chief." It was named Southern Rhodesia until 1980, when it gained its independence.

Taiwan—Chinese word meaning "terraced bay." It is located on the island of Formosa. Farmers there terrace the slopes of the island to provide level ground for their crops and buildings.

Venezuela—named for a village built on wooden poles above a shallow lake. It was discovered by Spanish explorers, who named this South American country Little Venice—Venezuela in Spanish.

Uruguay—Guarani word meaning "bird's tail." The country took its name from the Uruguay River, which refers to a fan-shaped waterfall in the river.

Brazil—derived from the Portuguese word *braza*, meaning "burnt wood" or "live coal." *Braza* was a wood used to produce a valuable purple dye.

Names—Planets and Heavenly Bodies

Earth—name derived from the Middle English word *eorthe* and from the Greek word *era, earth,* which means "soil." It is the only planet able to sustain life because of its perfect distance from the sun, perfect tilt and rotation, abundant water, and atmosphere of oxygen.

Mercury—named for a winged Roman god. The surface of Mercury is incredibly hot because it is so near the sun. It is pockmarked with craters and has no air or water.

Mars—named for the Roman god of war. It is an orange-red planet with canyons and volcanoes, mountains and polar ice caps, and a surface like a cold, dry desert. The atmosphere is too thin to breathe, yet violent dust storms blow across the Martian landscape.

Venus—named for the Greek goddess of love. Most of the features of the planet are named after real or imaginary women. Two of its continents are named for the goddesses Ishtar and Aphrodite, and one crater is named after jazz singer Billie Holiday.

Jupiter—named for the king of the Roman gods. It is a planet three hundred times heavier than Earth, surrounded by hydrogen, ammonia, and methane gases, and bitter cold, swirling cloud zones. Many storms of fiery gases have raged unceasingly about the surface. The planet is encircled by a ring of rock or ice fragments and has sixteen moons. The largest are named Ganymede and Callisto.

Pluto—named for the Greek god of the dark underworld. It is a mysterious planet with a spooky name, too far away to afford much investigation.

Uranus—named for the Greek god of the sky. It is a greenish planet first observed by William Hershel in 1781. Its moon is named Miranda.

Neptune—named for the powerful god of the sea. It is two billion miles from the sun. This planet has many faint rings and eight moons. The largest moon is named Triton, after Neptune's son.

Saturn—named after the Romans' mythological god of agriculture. It has three large rings and thousands of narrow ringlets made up of ice particles.

Names—Trees

Paloverde—*Cercidium torreyanum* Sargent, the green-barked Acacia. The "Sargent," third part of the scientific name, refers to the botanist responsible for naming the species.

Southern pine—*Pinus palustris* Mill. Other names are longleaf yellow pine, pitch pine, hard pine, heart pine, turpentine pine, rosemary pine, fat pine, longstraw pine.

California redwood—*Sequoia sempervirens* Endl, refers to the coast redwood. It is also called *Sequoia giganteum* Buchholz, the giant redwood, bigtree, Sierra redwood, mammoth tree. This tree's largest specimen is thirty-six and a half feet in diameter and about three to four thousand years old. Its nickname is "General Sherman."

Blue spruce—*Picea sungens* Engelm is also called Colorado blue spruce, balsam, prickly spruce, white spruce, silver spruce, Parry's spruce, or Colorado spruce.

American holly—*Ilex opaca* Aiton may be called holly, white holly, evergreen holly, or boxwood.

Sabal palmetto palm—*Sabal palmetto* Lodd is called cabbage palmetto, palmetto, tree palmetto, or bank palmetto.

Kukui tree—*Aleurites moluccana* of Hawaii is commonly called the candlenut tree.

Cottonwood—*Populus deltoides* Bartr is known as eastern poplar, Carolina poplar, necklace poplar, big cottonwood, Vermont poplar, whitewood, cotton tree, or yellow cottonwood.

Tulip tree—*Liriodendron tulipifera* goes by several names: yellow poplar, blue poplar, hickory poplar, basswood, cucumber tree, whitewood, white poplar, or old-wife's-shirt.

Names—Flowers

Black-Eyed Susan—*Rudbeckia hirta,* an herb and member of the thistle family, is also called by the name yellow daisy.

Lady slipper—*Cypripedum reginae* is an orchid, also known as pink lady slipper or moccasin-flower.

American dogwood—*Corus florida* is a small tree with greenish yellow flowers, scarlet fruit, and red leaves in the fall. It is also known as boxwood, white cornel, Indian Arrowhead, and nature's mistake.

Red clover—*Trifolium pretense* from the pea family of plants also goes by the names cowgrass, sugar plum, and honey-suckle clover.

Bird-of-Paradise—*Strelitziaceae,* also called "crane flower," is an ornamental plant native to southern Africa. The flower has two erect, pointed petals, and five stamens. One main bract, shaped like a boat, is green with red borders. It holds many long-stemmed orange and blue flowers, shaped and colored like bright tropical birds.

Periwinkle—Vinca of the dogbane family (*Apocynaceae*) may be taken from *pervinka,* the Russian name of the flower, which in turn is derived from *pervi,* "first," as it is one of the first flowers of spring.

Rose of Sharon—*Hibiscus syriacus* is also called Althaea. From the mallow family, this flower is native to eastern Asia but widely planted as an ornamental for its showy flowers. The mallowlike flowers range in the different varieties from white and pinkish lavender to purple, generally with a crimson base.

Nasturtium—*Tropaeolum majus,* the common nasturtium, is also known as Indian cress. T. peregrinum is commonly known as the canary creeper.

Zinnias—*Zinnia elegans* presents solitary flower heads borne at the ends of branches, growing at the junction of a bract (leaf-like structure) and the receptacle. The flowers occur in a wide range of colors except blue.

Hydrangea—Native to the Western Hemisphere and eastern Asia, about twenty-three species are known. Other names are Hills-of-snow or wild hydrangea.

Fuchsia—From the evening primrose family, the lovely flowers are named for Leonhard Fuchs, a 16th-century botanist and physician. They are found in shades of red and purple to white. The popular name—ladies' eardrop—comes from the shape. The color fuchsia—a deep reddish-purple—is named for the genus, not the other way around.

Figwort—*Scrophularia* refers to plants in the snapdragon family, native to woodlands in the Northern Hemisphere. The common name refers to an early use of these plants in treating hemorrhoids, an ailment once known as "figs." It is also called carpenter's square because of its four-sided grooved stems.

Yucca—Succulent plants of the lily family and native to southern North America, most species of yucca are stemless with a rosette of stiff, sword-shaped leaves at the base and clusters of waxy white flowers. This plant is also called Joshua tree, Spanish bayonet, Spanish dagger, and Adam's needle, bear grass, or "candles of the Lord."

Indian pipe—*Monotropa uniflora,* a non-green herb, is also called corpse plant, convulsion root, or fits root. It grows throughout North American, lives on the remains of dead plants, and is commonly found in moist, shady areas. The plant is white, pinkish, or red. When it dries out, it turns black. A single, odorless, cup-shaped flower with four or five petals hangs down from the tip of the stalk.

Violet—*Voila palmate* is also called a "Johnny-jump-up" or early blue violet.

Passion flower—*Passiflora incarnate* is called a maypop or a wild apricot. The Indian name was *ocoee.* Christian missionaries gave it the name because of the symbols of the Crucifixion—the crown of thorns and three crosses. In the south, little boys call the slim-filled fruits of this beautiful purple flower "snot and buggers."

Oregon grape—*Berberis aquifolium* is commonly called holly-leaf, barberry, or Rocky Mountain grape.

Big laurel—*Rhododendron maximum* is called deer-laurel, cow-plant, rose-bay, or spoon-hutch.

Indian paintbrush—*Castilleja linariaefolia* of the figwort family is known as prairie fire, bloody warrior, or nose-bleed.

American pasqueflower—*Pulsatilla hirsutissima* is also called the Mayday flower, the wild crocus, Aprilfools, rock lily, badger flower, wind flower.

Names—Boys

Alton—English name meaning excellent and kind. It is said by some to mean "old town."

Berne—German name meaning "courageous." Berne name is a form of Bernard. St. Bernard was a Christian saint, a monk who served as a missionary in the Alps and developed a breed of dogs that rescue people lost in snow.

Bryce—Welch name meaning "spunky."

Cheramy—Americanization of the name Jeremiah, which in Hebrew means "God will uplift." In its Irish form the name is Jeremy.

Damien—Irish name of Greek origin that means "fate."

Zane or Zayn—Polish version of the name John, meaning "God's gift."

Eckhardt—German name meaning "iron-willed."

Fletcher—English name denoting "occupation of arrow maker." A fletcher was skilled at fletching or putting feathers on arrows to make them fly true. The name also means "kind-hearted."

Quentin—Latin name meaning "fifth." Quintus is Spanish for fifth child. Quintavious is African-American, meaning fifth child. Quincy means fifth in French. *Quintin* from Latin means planner. Quinn is short for Quinton, Irish for bright.

Coleman—Irish name that means "little dove."

Gimpel—Jewish name of Germanic background meaning "bright."

Gilchrist—Gaelic/Irish name that means "servant of Christ."

Gerald—German name meaning "strong," literally "ruling with a spear."

Guthrie—Celtic name that means "war hero." Guthrum was a king of East Anglia in the ninth century who made treaties with Alfred the Great and converted to Christianity.

Jacquawn—African-American name that means "rock," denoting a strong stable personality.

Karolek—Polish form of Charles meaning "grown man."

Names—Girls

Yvonne—French name meaning "archer with a yew-bow."

Kylie—Aboriginal Australian name meaning "boomerang."

Charlotte—French/Saxon name meaning "little, noble woman."

Kezia or Cassia—Hebrew name meaning "cinnamon," from Job's daughter, given to him after the trying of his faith.

Monica—Latin derived name meaning "admonition, a wise counselor."

Belinda—Italian name meaning "beautiful and snake; as wise as a serpent."

Winola—Germanic name meaning "a gracious friend."

Brenna—Celtic name meaning "raven" or "maiden with dark hair."

Taryn—Greek/Welsh name meaning "innocent one."

Giselle—Teutonic name meaning "oath or pledge."

Hortense—Latin name meaning "gardener."

Malkiya—Hebrew name meaning "God is my king."

Nadia—Slavic name meaning "one with hope."

Penny—Greek name that means "weaver, silent worker, or a flower."

Sibyl—Greek name meaning "prophetess."

Thora—Norse name meaning "thunderous."

Chiamaka—African name meaning "God is splendid."

Names—Most Widely Used Surnames by Country

Sweden—Johansson, Ericksson, Andersson, Kaerlsson, Nilsson

Ireland—Monaghen, Kelly, O'Sullivan

Sri Lanka—Ninety-eight percent of population has the surname De Silva

France—Martin, Bernard, Thomas, Petit

Singapore—Hee, Hsu, Tan, Chan

Germany—Müller, Schmidt, Scheidner

Spain—Garcia, Fernandez, Gonzalez

Serbia—Petrovic, Jovanovic

Romania—Popsecu, Popa, Radu

Canada—Tremblay, Gagnon, Roy

India—Patnaik, Bhattia, Singh

Poland—Nowak, Kowalski, Wisniewski

Hungary—Nagy, Kovacs, Toth, Szabo

Mexico—Martinez, Rodriquez, Garcia

Norway—Hansen, Olsen

The Netherlands—De Jang, DeVries, Jansen

Israel—Cohen, Levi

Finland—Virtanen, Kohomen, Neiminen

Danish—Jensen, Hansen, Neilsen, Pederson

Egypt—Abanza, Sorour, Kishk

China—Wang, Chen, Li, Zhang Lin, Yang, Huang

Czech Republic—Novak, Svoboda, Novotny, Dvorak

Bulgaria—Ivanov, Petrov, Georgiev

Brazil—da Silva, da Costa, dos Santos

Belgium—Peeters, Jansens, Maes

Argentina—Gozalez, Rodrigues, Lopez

Korea—Kim, Lee, Park, Choi, Jung

Japan—Sato, Suzuki, Takahashi

Vietnam—Nguyen

Names—Celebrity Children's Names

Princess Katharina zu Waldeck und Pyrmont (royalty) & Matthias Hoyer are parents of triplets—Zita-Florentine and her brothers: Henry-Oscar and John-Moritz.

Natalie Maines (musician) & Adrian Pasdar have a son named Beckett Finn.

Angela Schijf (actress) & Tom Van Landuyt named their daughter Bloem.

Frank Zappa has children named Moon Unit, Ahmet Emuukha, Rodan, Diva, and Dweezil.

Christy Brinkley and Peter Cook named their daughter Sailor.

Cher and Gregg Allman have a son named Elijah Blue.

Mia Farrow, whose full name is Maria de Lourdes Villiers Farrow, has fourteen children: twins Matthew Phineas and Sascha Villiers, and Fletcher (all with Previn), Satchel O'Sullivan Farrow (with Allen, now called Seamus), Soon-Yi Previn, Lark Song Previn, Summer Song (called Daisy) Previn, Moses Amadeus Farrow (called Misha Farrow, adopted with

Allen), Dylan O'Sullivan Farrow (called Eliza, adopted with Allen), Isaiah Farrow, Tam Farrow, Keili-Shea Farrow, Gabriel Wilk Farrow.

John Mellancamp has children named Michelle, Teddy Jo, Speck Wildhorse, Justice, and Hud.

India and Roman Caruso are the children of Dan Cortese.

Indy driver Kenny Black named his daughter Karma.

Jayson Williams, an ex-NBA player, has children named Whizdom and Tryumph.

Jason Lee named his son Pilot Inspektor. Pilot because it was unique and Inspektor—in homage to Peter Sellers.

Names—Stage Names, Pen Names or nom de plumes, Assumed Names, Pseudonyms

George Orwell's real name was Eric Arthur Blair.

Mark Twain was Samuel Langhorn Clemens, the author of *Tom Sawyer* and *The Adventures of Huckleberry Finn*.

Emily Brontë was able to sell her writing by assuming a male pen name, Ellis Bell.

Voltaire was the pen name of Francois Marie Arouet.

Lemony Snicket, a popular writer of the children's books called *A Series of Unfortunate Events*, chose a pseudonym because his name was a plain Daniel Handler.

Charles Lutwidge Dodgson wrote the *Alice's Adventures in Wonderland*. We knew this writer as Lewis Carroll.

Woody Allen was born Allen Stewart Konigsberg.

Bing Crosby, singer, was Harry Lillis Crosby.

Pol Pot was Saloth Sar.

Pope John Paul II was born as Karol Jozef Wojtyla.

Mother Teresa of Calcutta—was Agnes Gonzha Bojaxhiu until she became a nun.

Leon Trotsky was named Lev Davidovich Bronstein.

Joseph Estrada was named Joseph Marcelo Ejercito.

Ho Chi Minh was Nguyen Tat Thanh.

Whoopi Goldberg was plain old Caryn Johnson.

Kirk Douglas dropped his long Polish name: Issur Danielovitch Demsky.

Grandma Moses was an artist whose real name was Anna Mary Robertson.

Robert Zimmerman took on the stage name of Bob Dylan.

Joyce Penelope Frankenburg is the actress we know as Jane Seymour.

Country singer Tammy Wynette was born Virginia Wynette Pugh.

Charles Atlas, a weight lifter, was born in Italy with the name Angelo Siciliano.

Conway Twitty's real name is Harold Jenkins.

Fred Astaire was Frederick Austerlitz.

John Wayne may not have captured the cowboy hero image with a name like his birth name, which was Marion Michael Morrison.

John Denver, the singer, was born Henry John Deutschendorf, Jr.

Artist Eric Sloane first painted his Americana under the name Ericard Hinrichs.

Tom Cruise makes a better acting name than Thomas Cruise Mapother IV.

Hayley Mills found her given name too cumbersome—Hayley Catherine Rose Vivien Mills.

The jazz singer Billy Holiday was Eleanora Fagan Gough.

Harry Houdini, the great escape artist was born Ehrich Weiss.

Jerry Lewis is the stage name of Joseph Levitch.

Meg Ryan's name is Margaret Mary Emily Ann Hyra.

Baroness van Lawick-Godall is known as Jane Goodall, the ethologist.

Names—American Legends

Mike Fink—Stories have been so exaggerated that truth is hard to discover. Mike was born near the frontier post of Pittsburgh around 1770. He became a keelboatman on the flatboats of the Ohio and the Mississippi Rivers. Later he became a trapper. He was noted as a marksman, fighter, and teller of tall tales. Mike Fink was said to be half horse—half alligator.

Paul Bunyan—Mythical lumberjack and subject of tall tales throughout timber country. (For example: He dug the Grand Canyon.)

Johnny Appleseed—Real name was John Chapman. He was a Massachusetts-born nurseryman, reputed to have spread seeds and seedlings out of which grew the apple orchards of the Midwest. Supposedly he walked barefoot across the new country wearing his cooking pot on his head, passing out apple seeds to pioneers.

Daniel Boone—Frontiersman and Indian fighter about whom legends of early America have been built; figured in Byron's Don Juan.

Buffalo Bill—Real name was William F. Cody. He was a buffalo hunter and Indian scout. Many of the legends about him stem from the Wild West show he operated in the late 19th century.

Davy Crockett—Frontiersman, congressman, and defender of the Alamo. His backwoods humor and larger-than-life adventures, such as wrestling grizzly bears, etc., made him synonymous with the Wild West. His clothes were made of fringed buckskin, and he wore a coonskin cap.

Casey Jones—John Luther Jones was a heroic locomotive engineer given to feats of prowess. He died in a wreck when his Illinois Central "Cannonball" Express hit a freight train in Vaughan, Mississippi.

Pecos Bill—Mythical cowboy character of the Wild West. His first and favorite of dozens of wives was Slue-foot Sue. He had to shoot her to keep her from starving because she tried to ride Widow Maker. The horse bucked her so high she hit the moon and then her hoopskirt kept her bouncing.

Febold Feboldson—Swedish settler who hauled logs and built fires around a lake so the water would evaporate and form clouds to make rain. The settlers were unhappy because their swimming hole was dried up, but their friend Febold brought them rain.

John Henry—Freed slave who went to work driving steel, laying railroad tracks. This took great strength. John Henry was the winner of a competition against a steel-driving machine, but sadly, the contest killed him. "He died with a hammer in his hand, Lawd, Lawd. He died with a hammer in his hand."

Names—Famous Immigrants

Cary Grant—After immigrating to America in 1920, the actor left behind his former name Alexander Archibald Leach.

Al Jolson—After immigrating from Russia in 1894, the singer, actor, and songwriter abandoned the name Asa Yoelson.

Bob Hope—When he came from England in 1908 via Ellis Island, the beloved American comedian was only four. Until that time, his name had been Leslie Towne Hope. When Les Hope was turned into the nickname Hopeless, the name Bob was adopted.

Stan Laurel—Arthur Stanley Jefferson, half of the famous comedy team Laurel and Hardy, was born in Ulverson, England, in 1910.

Greta Garbo—The actress came to American in 1925 and changed her name from Greta Lovisa Gustafsson.

Billy Wilder—Previously named Samuel Wilder, the movie director, producer and writer came to America from Vienna, Austria, in 1934.

Father Edward Flanagan—Edward Flanagan added Father to his name when he became a priest. He came from Ireland to America in 1903 and later founded Boys' Town, homes for the benefit of boys who had fallen into lives of crime through poverty.

Rudolf Valentino—The dancer and actor arrived in America from Italy in 1913. He worked as a laborer and a gardener before changing his name from Rodolfo d'Antonguolla.

Irving Berlin—The songwriter who composed "White Christmas" and "God Bless America" came from Russia to the USA in 1892 with his parents. Formerly, his name was Israel Baline.

Alexander Graham Bell—The inventor, who among other things worked to develop the telephone, was named Alexander Bell after his grandfather. He adopted the name Graham for a family friend when he was a young man and was called Graham by close friends and family.

Al Capone—This infamous criminal came to the USA in the early 1900s from Italy. His name was probably Alphonse or Alphonso Caponi or Capone. He was a gangster leader of Chicago's underworld. The murderer and criminal was nicknamed "Scarface Al" after he was slashed in a knife fight.

ANECDOTES AND STORIES

A Retrieved Reformation

O. HENRY

A guard came to the prison shoe shop, where Jimmy Valentine was assiduously stitching uppers, and escorted him to the front office. There the warden handed Jimmy his pardon, which had been signed that morning by the governor. Jimmy took it in a tired kind of way. He had served nearly ten months of a four-year sentence. He had expected to stay only about three months, at the longest. When a man with as many friends on the outside as Jimmy Valentine had is received in the "stir" it is hardly worth while to cut his hair.

"Now, Valentine," said the warden, "you'll go out in the morning. Brace up, and make a man of yourself. You're not a bad fellow at heart. Stop cracking safes, and live straight."

"Me?" said Jimmy in surprise, "Why I never cracked a safe in my life."

"Oh, no," laughed the warden. "Of course not. Let's see, now. How was it you happened to get sent up on that Springfield job? Was it because you wouldn't prove an alibi for fear of compromising somebody in extremely high-toned society? Or was it simply a case of a mean old jury that had it in for you? It's always one or the other with you innocent victims."

"Me?" said Jimmy, still blankly virtuous. "Why, warden, I never was in Springfield in my life!"

"Take him back, Cronin," smiled the warden, "and fix him up with outgoing clothes. Unlock him at seven in the morning, and let him come to the bull-pen. Better think over my advice, Valentine."

At a quarter past seven on the next morning, Jimmy stood in the warden's outer office. He had on a suit of the villainously fitting, ready-made clothes and a pair of the stiff, squeaky shoes that the state furnishes to its discharged compulsory guests.

The clerk handed him a railroad ticket and a five-dollar bill with which the law expected him to rehabilitate himself into good citizenship and prosperity. The warden gave him a cigar, and shook hands. Valentine, 9762, was chronicled on the books "Pardoned by Governor," and Mr. James Valentine walked out into the sunshine.

Disregarding the song of the birds, the waving green trees, and the smell of the flowers, Jimmy headed straight for a restaurant. There he tasted the first sweet joys of liberty in the shape of a broiled chicken and a bottle of white wine—followed by a cigar a grade better than the one the warden had given him. From there he proceeded leisurely to the depot. He tossed a quarter into the hat of a blind man sitting by the door, and boarded his train. Three hours set him down in a little town near the state line. He went to the café of one Mike Dolan and shook hands with Mike, who was alone behind the bar.

"Sorry we couldn't make it sooner, Jimmy, me boy," said Mike. "But we had that protest from Springfield to buck against, and the governor nearly balked. Feeling all right?"

"Fine," said Jimmy. "Got my key?"

He got his key and went upstairs, unlocking the door of a room at the rear. Everything was just as he had left it. There on the floor was still Ben Price's collar-button that had been torn from that eminent detective's shirtband when they had overpowered Jimmy to arrest him.

Pulling out from the wall a folding bed, Jimmy slid back a panel in the wall and dragged out a dust-covered suit case. He opened this and gazed fondly at the finest set of burglar's tools in the East. It was a complete set, made of specially tempered steel, the latest designs in drills, punches, braces and bits, jimmies, clamps, and augers, with two or three novelties, invented by Jimmy himself, in which he took pride. Over nine hundred dollars they had cost him to have made at a place where they make such things for the profession.

In half an hour Jimmy went downstairs and through the café. He was now dressed in tasteful and well-fitting clothes, and carried his dusted and cleaned suit case in his hand.

"Got anything on?" asked Mike Dolan, genially.

"Me?" said Jimmy, in a puzzled tone. "I don't understand. I'm representing the New York Amalgamated Short Snap Biscuit Cracker and Frazzled Wheat Company."

This statement delighted Mike to such an extent that Jimmy had to take a seltzer-and-milk on the spot. He never touched "hard" drinks.

A week after the release of Valentine, 9762, there was a neat job of safe-burglary done in Richmond, Indiana, with no clue to the author. A scant eight hundred dollars was all that was secured. Two weeks after that a patented, improved burglar-proof safe in Logansport was opened like a cheese to the tune of fifteen hundred dollars currency; securities and silver untouched. That began to interest the rogue-catchers. Then an old-fashioned bank safe in Jefferson City became active and threw out of its crater an eruption of banknotes amounting to five thousand dollars. The losses were now high enough to bring the matter up into Ben Price's class of work. By comparing notes, a remarkable similarity in the methods of the burglaries was noticed. Ben Price investigated the scenes of the robberies, and was heard to remark:

"That's Dandy Jim Valentine's autograph. He's resumed business. Look at that combination knob—jerked out as easy as pulling up a radish in wet weather. He's got the only clamps that can do it. And look how clean those tumblers were punched out! Jimmy never has to drill but one hole. Yes, I guess I want Mr. Valentine. He'll do his bit next time without any short-time or clemency foolishness."

Ben Price knew Jimmy's habits. He had learned them while working up the Springfield case. Long jumps, quick get-aways, no confederates, and a taste for good society—these ways had helped Mr. Valentine to become noted as a successful dodger of retribution. It was given out that Ben Price had taken up the trail of the elusive tracksman, and other people with burglar-proof safes felt more at ease.

One afternoon Jimmy Valentine and his suitcase climbed out

of the mail hack in Elmore, a little town five miles off the railroad down in the blackjack country of Arkansas. Jimmy, looking like an athletic young senior just home from college, went down the board sidewalk toward the hotel.

A young lady crossed the street, passed him at the corner and entered a door over which was the sign "The Elmore Bank." Jimmy Valentine looked into her eyes, forgot what he was, and became another man. She lowered her eyes and colored slightly. Young men of Jimmy's style and looks were scarce in Elmore.

Jimmy collared a boy that was loafing on the steps of the bank as if he were one of the stockholders, and began to ask him questions about the town, feeding him dimes at intervals. By and by the young lady came out, looking royally unconscious of the young man with the suitcase, and went her way.

"Isn't that young lady Miss Polly Simpson?" asked Jimmy, with specious guile.

"Naw," said the boy. "She's Annabelle Adams. Her pa owns this bank. What'd you come to Elmore for? Is that a gold watch chain? I'm going to get a bulldog. Got any more dimes?"

Jimmy went to the Planters' Hotel, registered as Ralph D. Spencer, and engaged a room. He leaned on the desk and declared his platform to the clerk. He said he had come to Elmore to look for a location to go into business. How was the shoe business, now, in the town? He had thought of the shoe business. Was there an opening?

The clerk was impressed by the clothes and manner of Jimmy. He, himself, was something of a pattern of fashion to the thinly gilded youth of Elmore, but he now perceived his shortcomings. While trying to figure out Jimmy's manner of tying his four-in-hand he cordially gave information.

Yes, there ought to be a good opening in the shoe line. There wasn't an exclusive shoe store in the place. The dry goods and general stores handled them. Business in all lines was fairly good. Hoped Mr. Spencer would decide to locate in Elmore. He would find it a pleasant town to live in, and the people very sociable.

Mr. Spencer thought he would stop over in the town a few days and look over the situation. No, the clerk needn't call the boy. He would carry up his suitcase himself; it was rather heavy.

Mr. Ralph Spencer, the phoenix that arose from Jimmy Valentine's ashes—ashes left by the flame of a sudden and alternative attack of love—remained in Elmore, and prospered. He opened a shoe store and secured a good run of trade.

Socially he was also a success and made many friends. And he accomplished the wish of his heart. He met Miss Annabel Adams, and became more and more captivated by her charms.

At the end of a year the situation of Mr. Ralph Spencer was this: he had won the respect of the community, his shoe store was flourishing, and he and Annabel were engaged to be married in two weeks. Mr. Adams, the typical, plodding, country banker, approved of Spencer. Annabel's pride in him almost equaled her affection. He was as much at home in the family of Mr. Adams and that of Annabel's married sister as if he were already a member.

One day Jimmy sat down in his room and wrote this letter, which he mailed to the safe address of one of his old friends in St. Louis:

Dear Old Pal:

I want you to be at Sullivan's place in Little Rock, next Wednesday night at nine o'clock. I want you to wind up some little matters for me. And also, I want to make you a present of my kit of tools. I know you'll be glad to get them—you couldn't duplicate the lot for a thousand dollars. Say, Billy, I've quit the old business—a year ago. I've got a nice store. I'm making an honest living, and I'm going to marry the finest girl on earth two weeks from now. It's the only life, Billy—the straight one. I wouldn't touch a dollar of another man's money now for a million. After I get married, I'm going to sell out and go West, where there won't be so much danger of having old scores brought up against me. I tell you, Billy, she's an angel. She believes in me; and I wouldn't do another crooked thing for the whole world. Be sure to be at Sully's, for I must see you, I'll bring along the tools with me.

Your old friend,
Jimmy

On the Monday night after Jimmy wrote this letter, Ben Price jogged unobtrusively into Elmor in a livery buggy. He lounged about town in his quiet way until he found out what he wanted to know. From the drug store across the street from Spencer's shoe store, he got a good look at Ralph D. Spencer.

"Going to marry the banker's daughter are you, Jimmy?" said Ben to himself, softly. "Well, I don't know!"

The next morning Jimmy took breakfast at the Adamses. He was going to Little Rock that day to order his wedding suit and buy something nice for Annabel. That would be the first time he had left town since he came to Elmore. It had been more than a year now since those last professional "jobs," and he thought he could safely venture out.

After breakfast quite a family party went downtown together—Mr. Adams, Annabel, Jim, and Annabel's married sister with her two little girls, aged five and nine. They came by the hotel where Jimmy still boarded, and he ran up to his room and brought along his suitcase. Then they went on to the bank. There stood Jimmy's horse and buggy and Dolph Gibson, who was going to drive him over to the railroad station.

All went inside the high, carved oak railings into the banking-room—Jimmy included, for Mr. Adams's future son-in-law was welcome anywhere. The clerks were pleased to be greeted by the good-looking, agreeable young man who was going to marry Miss Annabel. Jimmy set his suitcase down. Annabel, whose heart was bubbling with happiness and lively youth, put on Jimmy's hat, and picked up the suitcase. "Wouldn't I make a nice drummer?" said Annabel. "My! Ralph, how heavy it is! Feels like it was full of gold bricks."

"Lot of nickel-plated shoe horns in there," said Jimmy coolly, "that I'm going to return. Thought I'd save express charges by taking them up. I'm getting awfully economical."

The Elmore Bank had just put in a new safe and vault. Mr. Adams was very proud of it, and insisted on an inspection by everyone. The vault was a small one, but it had a new, patented door. It fastened with three solid steel bolts thrown simultaneously with a single handle, and had a time lock. Mr. Adams beamingly explained its workings to Mr. Spencer, who showed a courteous but not too intelligent interest. The two children, May and Agatha, were delighted by the shining metal and funny clock and knobs.

While they were thus engaged Ben Price sauntered in and leaned on his elbow, looking casually inside between the railings. He told the teller that he didn't want anything; he was just waiting for a man he knew.

Suddenly there was a scream or two from the women, and a commotion. Unperceived by the elders, May, the nine-year-old girl, in a spirit of play, had shut Agatha in the vault. She had then shot the bolts and turned the knob of the combination as she had seen Mr. Adams do.

The old banker sprang to the handle and tugged at it for a moment. "The door can't be opened," he groaned. "The clock hasn't been wound nor the combination set."

Agatha's mother screamed again, hysterically.

"Hush!" said Mr. Adams, raising his trembling hand. "All be quiet for a moment. Agatha!" he called as loudly as he could. "Listen to me." During the following silence they could just hear the faint sound of a child wildly shrieking in the dark vault in a panic of terror.

"My precious darling!" wailed the mother. "She will die of fright! Open the door! Oh, break it open! Can't you men do something?"

"There isn't a man nearer than Little Rock who can open that door," said Mr. Adams, in a shaky voice. "My God! Spencer, what shall we do? That child—she can't stand it long in there. There isn't enough air, and besides, she'll go into convulsions from fright."

Agatha's mother, frantic now, beat the door of the vault with her hands. Somebody wildly suggested dynamite. Annabel turned to Jimmy, her large eyes full of anguish, but not yet despairing. To a woman nothing seems quite impossible to the powers of the man she worships.

"Can't you do something, Ralph—try, won't you?"

He looked at her with a queer, soft smile on his lips and in his keen eyes.

"Annabel," he said, "give me that rose you are wearing."

Hardly believing that she heard him aright, she unpinned the bud from the bosom of her dress, and placed it in his hand. Jimmy stuffed it into his vest pocket, threw off his coat and pulled up his shirtsleeves. With that act Ralph D. Spencer passed away and Jimmy Valentine took his place.

"Get away from the door, all of you," he commanded, shortly.

He set his suitcase on the table, and opened it out flat. From that time on, he seemed to be unconscious of the presence of anyone else. He laid out the shining, queer implements swiftly and orderly, whistling softly to himself as he always did when at work. In a deep silence and immovable, the others watched him as if under a spell.

In a minute Jimmy's pet drill was biting smoothly into the steel door. In ten minutes—breaking his own burglarious record—he threw back the bolts and opened the door.

Agatha, almost collapsed, but safe, was gathered into her mother's arms.

Jimmy Valentine put on his coat, and walked outside the railings toward the front door. As he went he thought he heard a far-away voice that he once knew call "Ralph!" but he never hesitated.

At the door a big man stood somewhat in his way.

"Hello, Ben!" said Jimmy, still with his strange smile. "Got around at last, have you? Well, let's go. I don't know that it makes much difference, now."

And then Ben Price acted rather strangely.

"Guess you're mistaken, Mr. Spencer," he said. "Don't believe I recognize you. Your buggy's waiting for you."

And Ben Price turned and strolled down the street.

Family Table

ELECE HOLLIS

Summers in Michigan, Dad rented rows in a community garden. The farmer tilled, Dad planted, another watered, we weeded and God gave the increase. Mama spent many days in a steamy kitchen putting up that increase in canning jars. We carried jars from the storeroom in the basement, washed them in hot soapy water, then later carried them filled, back down, arranging them in rows on the storeroom shelves.

I loved the garden, especially the corn rows, so long the ends seemed to meet and touch. The corn stalks were tall enough to make shady lanes to run down. I'm afraid Kent and I weren't much help. We played happily in the magical green aisles, chasing each other up and back until we tired. Then we sat in the delicious shade and played in the sandy dirt. Dad checked the corn often, and when he found it just right, we picked bushels to take home to feed to the Magic Seal pressure canner.

You may think that there were only two times when Jesus fed the multitude (Matthew 14:14 and Matthew 15:32), but there you would be wrong! Multitudes were fed at our house on a regular basis (often seeming like a miracle to us). On a summer evening a Volkswagen busload of cousins might turn in the drive. Mama would send one of us for a couple of jars of tomatoes and corn from the basement to add to the soup, along with a few potatoes and everyone would be fed!

A warm Sunday afternoon would bring a carload or two of church friends, lured to the country by the promise of a swim in the river, maybe followed by a slice of icy watermelon Dad had tied a rope to and lowered down into the river to cool; or maybe a bowl of sweet ice cream fresh from the cranker.

We saw pictures of the starving children in Ethiopia. We worried about them and prayed for them, although we could not know what starving was. We did our part by collecting for UNICEF every October. With our little milk cartons we went door to door asking the neighbors to give for the hungry. "The hungry" were not us. We had plenty to eat always.

Mama raised chickens one year. She hated chickens. We children thought the chickens were great. We liked to feed them and gather the eggs. Mama despised them. She thought they stank. They were a nuisance. They further would not oblige her by laying their eggs in the nesting boxes. Shortly following an episode in which little brother Fred, was chased and pecked by a mean old rooster, Kent and I were sent out to gather eggs. Finding only three in the nest boxes, we filled our basket with pearly whites from the woods.

Mama's cake batter was ruined by a horrible stinky rotten egg. That was the last straw. Mama made those feathers fly! She chased those hens down and she wrung necks until she'd exhausted herself. She and Dad spent all that evening cleaning chickens and Mama spent all the next day canning chicken, on the bone in half gallon Mason jars.

Many a hungry multitude was fed Texas style chicken and dumplings at our table that winter. Sickly friends were resuscitated with bowls of hearty chicken noodle soup from Mama's stores. On winter days when the snow was too deep for us to walk home from school for lunch, we carried hot chicken soup in our lunch box thermoses.

Often Mama rummaged up meals for strangers that Dad picked up and carried home. One night late in a snow storm, Dad came in with a family he had found in a broken down vehicle by the side of the road. The family had an infant, a little girl with a head grotesquely misshapen. She had encephalitis, water on the brain. They were hungry, cold, terrified, trying desperately to get the baby to a hospital. After warming them and feeding them, Dad took them on into the city. We never heard from them afterwards and often wondered if the baby lived.

Traveling evangelists and preachers often found a chair at our table as well. I especially recall one from Texas, with a lovely southern drawl, who spent an afternoon picnicking with us at the tree farm. Mama had fixed her specialty, fried chicken. We feasted on chicken, beans, bread and butter, potato salad, corn on the cob, all washed down with fresh cold milk. For dessert there were ice cream cones filled with chocolate pudding and decorated with sprinkles.

Kent and I polished off our puddings and then helped ourselves to a second one before running off to explore. The adults were busy talking about Texas, where Mama and Dad had lived when they first married. Kent and I went back and listened for a while, then ate a third cone. All was well until the preacher went to get his dessert. "Oh, no," he croaked, peering into the box, "The puddings are all gone! I was so looking forward to eating me one! Why, I could jeeeeest bawl!"

"I could jeeeeest bawl!" became our family's by-line for any disappointment in life. It helped us laugh through rough spots we faced now and then, and to keep our chins up.

My parents taught us that hospitality is more than elaborate dinner parties with fancy centerpieces and place settings or family holiday meals when the aunts, uncles and cousins crowded in, or even pretty candlelit teas with friends. Real hospitality is opening the door to a wounded life and comforting that heart with a generous hand. It is the giving up of your chair at the table to some lonely, road weary man down on his luck. It is opening your heart and your house and your hands to someone who will not or cannot reciprocate, purely for his benefit and despite your own needs.

When I picture family in my mind, love and laughter, caring and sharing, garden, kitchen and the dinner table are all a part of that picture. Every night at supper, Dad read aloud a chapter of the Bible before we ate. Many times he read his favorite, Psalm 128, about Mama, his fruitful vine and all of us, his little olive shoots growing strong and happy round about his table.

The Enemy's Hands

ERNEST GARFIELD

I was a cocky young man, barely nineteen, when I went off to war. Being small, I was as feisty as a banty rooster—had to be to survive in New Orleans in the forties. I had some muscled up arms from hard farm labor and a tanned back and plenty of dark brown hair that made my hat sit at a rakish angle. I rolled my own cigarettes.

Fresh from boot camp, we were loaded onto ships to cross the ocean. We were headed for the Big War. I was rough and ready to go. Before we reached France, the Armistice had been signed. The war was over.

I was assigned to guard prisoners in a POW camp. German prisoners, who had been part of the Nazi army, highly trained and hardened by the years they had served under Hitler's miserable Reich. Now they were prisoners being guarded by myself, a United States Army private, a naïve one, a teenager, hardly more than a boy.

I was nervous, to say the least, after all, these were the enemy and I certainly knew little about them. The world wasn't such a small place then. I thought I hid my anxiety well under my guise of fearlessness. I had come to fight and found the fight over. I had to muster some bluster, strut some stuff and show these unarmed men just how tough I was.

Calling the prisoners to attention, I faced them and proceeded to "amaze" them with the rifle drill I had perfected during boot camp. I held my face straight, yet as I went through my routine, I just couldn't keep the gleam out of my eye. Hey, I was really something!

Then I flubbed. I dropped my gun and it was instantly swept up by a burly German prisoner with the biggest, whitest hands I had ever seen. My face was whiter still.

I was petrified. I couldn't breath. Would he shoot me? Would he escape? My life replayed in slow motion before my mind's eye. The room full of prisoners was totally silent. Then a clap like thunder sounded. The soldier had clapped his heels together and with dexterity I could only dream of, he whipped and spun and worked that rifle through an awesome drill and without ever missing a beat, he opened the chamber and presented it in military style. This seasoned soldier had no doubt been trained in the Hitler Youth Organization from boyhood. He had been parading with a rifle before I was even dry behind the ears! Hitler himself would have been impressed with such an absolutely flawless performance.

His eyes met mine as he held my gun out to me. When I had taken it, he stepped back one pace and the heels clapped again in the deathly silent room. Not a word had been uttered. I was dumb struck. I couldn't have spoken, no way!

Finally, in the only voice I could drum up, a sort of squawk, I ordered the prisoners to stand, which I realized to my greater chagrin, they were already doing. They stared at me, wondering what I would do.

The gun felt hot. It felt almost molten and not near as big as it had been before, only somehow heavier. I did not feel so big either, nor so blustery. These were men, I realized. They were men like me, with homes and families and hopes and dreams. They had come to fight in a war they did not want to fight in. Their hands had known hardship much more than the hardships of my life, which had made me feisty and smart to cover my insecurities. Their hands were rough from work like mine. Their hands were trained and skilled even more so than mine.

That soldier had bested me, still he had shown mercy and presented me my dropped rifle soldier to soldier. His hands were finished now. His war was over. It made us almost brothers, almost comrades, almost friends.

Remember the Frandsens

Kathryn Forbes

The summer that I was twelve, I vacationed at my uncle's ranch in Santa Clara Valley, California. I was a reluctant visitor. That is, until I met Smithy.

Smithy, who lived on the next ranch, was the most forthright and the most completely adult boy I'd ever known. My aunt said it was because Smithy's parents died before he was eight, and a bachelor uncle had had to rear the boy as best he could. My uncle said that hard-working farm boys were usually old for their years, even at twelve.

Becoming friends with Smithy wasn't easy. I soon learned that the slightest lapse into things either fanciful or childish sent Smithy scurrying. He had an annoying habit of disappearing whenever he got bored or discomfited. My aunt said his real name was Lloyd, but he never admitted it; one called him Smithy, or went unanswered.

When the old Horlick farm was sold, by mail, to an eastern couple named Frandsen, I thought it exciting because I had heard that the new owners were stage people. Smithy remained non-committal, but on the day I chose to happen to walk up the Frandsen's driveway, Smithy was with me. And when, halfway up the walk, we bumped right into Mr. and Mrs. Frandsen and they greeted us with exclamations of joy and welcome, Smithy was too surprised to run away.

The newcomers were, I judged, nearly fifty. Mrs. Frandsen had a beautiful, soft face, and her lovely blond hair was just touched with gray. Mr. Frandsen was shorter than his wife, although he held himself exceedingly straight, and his little brown eyes twinkled with kindness.

We were their very first visitors, they said; we must come out of the hot sun and into the cool of the house. Neither Smithy nor I had ever met grownups like this before. We were not used to sitting in front rooms decorated with spears and masks and signed photographs of costumed ladies and gentlemen, nor to being served tea out of something called a samovar.

Most of all, we were not used to being treated as gay contemporaries. The Frandsens told us exciting anecdotes about New York, about their experiences when they had acted in road companies. We were allowed to glimpse their future plans, the dreams-that-were-going-to-come-true, now that they had retired and settled down.

George—of course we were to call them George and Lisa, were we not their first new friends?—was going to become a real farmer. He had all the Government bulletins. Most wonderful of all, the Frandsens were going to adopt a baby. "A baby girl," Lisa said, "with blue eyes."

George beamed. "For months, now, we have had our request in. When we came through San Francisco we filled out final forms."

"And always," Lisa said, "we'll tell her that we chose her." They showed us the books they had about raising babies. Now, as soon as the Agency people sent a lady down to inspect them, the baby would be theirs.

Smithy and I stayed on and on. Never had I felt so welcome, such a distinguished guest. I chattered, and no one said it was time for me to go home, or that my mother wanted me. When Lisa tried to get Smithy to talk, too, and asked his name, I—drunk with social success—blurted out that it was Lloyd Smith. Lisa said Lloyd was a fine name. I expected something to happen, but Smithy just rolled his eyes alarmingly, and looked, for a moment, like my uncle's colt.

When we finally stood up to go, George and Lisa said we were to come back often, often, and Lisa kissed my cheek.

I couldn't stay away from the Frandsens. They enchanted me. They called their stove Ophelia, because it was quite, quite mad. They named their bantam rooster Iago; their pig was Falstaff. When we sat on the cool side porch, George and Lisa told me whole plots out of plays, even acted them out. Sometimes I would catch a glimpse of Smithy, out in the orchard, and he would be listening, too.

When my uncle's farm dog, Old Ben, died of age, and no one but me was sad about it, I lugged the poor hound's body over to the Frandsens'. Halfway there, Smithy materialized, and took over my burden. He helped George dig a grave of honor at the foot of the Frandsens' pepper tree. After it was all over, Smithy listened quietly while George said the most beautiful words I had ever heard: "Fear no more the heat of the sun, or the furious winter's rages . . ."

As the days went on I despaired of making Lisa understand that Smithy was not a child. When she baked bread she sent him miniature loaves; when she made cake there was always a tiny one, baked in the lid of the baking powder tin, for Smithy. Obediently, I delivered them; silently, he pocketed them.

On the Saturday that the Agency lady came to inspect the Frandsens I went into the orchard, to be out of the way. I found Smithy there. We each picked a tree, leaned against it, and settled down to wait. I wasn't worried; anyone could see that the Frandsens were remarkable people.

"And the way they do everything," I said, "with—well, with ceremony. Smithy, aren't they wonderful?"

Smithy just grunted. I noticed, though, when we heard the Agency lady's car clatter away that he was on his feet as quickly as I. The moment we entered the house, we knew that something was terribly wrong.

Lisa was sitting quietly in a chair. She didn't look gay or young any more. George patted her shoulder, while he told us.

"We are too old. People past forty-five are not permitted to adopt small babies."

I was indignant. "But they must have known—the forms—"

George looked down. "In the theater, one takes off a year here, a year there. Truly, Lisa and I had forgotten—" He shrugged. "Today we told our true ages. The Agency lady is kind, but it is a new rule."

"I can understand," Lisa said bravely. "It is for the child's good. So that—so that a child shall not have old—parents." She began to cry.

I was suddenly aware of being a child, too, without experience or knowledge. I did not know what to say to my friends, how to comfort them. And Smithy was no help. He slipped away without a word.

When, a little later, we heard a thump on the porch, I had the wild hope that it might be the Agency lady coming back. But it was only Smithy. He had his Sunday suit on, and the knickers were too short, and he looked funny. He gave me a terrible frown, and set down three newspaper-wrapped packages and two fishing poles. Standing there in the open doorway, he said matter-of-factly, "People are always adopting children; why can't it be the other way around once in a while?" His voice began to climb. "So I choose you. I asked my uncle, and he doesn't care, because he wants to move to the city anyway. So if you—if you want—"

Lisa ran across the room and put her wet cheek against Smithy's face, and said, "Lloyd! Oh, Lloyd!" I was afraid she was going to try to kiss him, and I wished somebody would shut the door. I guess George understood, because he started shaking Smithy's hand manfully, and saying, "Well, now, welcome, welcome."

Smithy seemed to make some tremendous effort. "Isn't there some sort of ceremony?" he asked George. "Shouldn't you—carry me into the house, or something?"

"But that's a ceremony for—" I started to say, but couldn't finish.

I do not think that twelve-year-old girls are particularly aware of poignancy, but I do know that the scene, that day, touched me beyond tears. Vainly trying to swallow the hurting in my throat, I watched George Frandsen stoop and lift the tall, gangly boy, the long, blackstockinged legs awkwardly disposed. Gently, carefully, he carried Smithy over the threshold and into the house.

"Well, now," I heard George say, "well, now, son . . ."

Doc Brackett

DAMON RUNYON

Doc Brackett didn't have black whiskers.
Nonetheless, he was a fine man.
He doctored in Our Town for many years. He doctored more people than any other doctor in Our Town but made less money.

That was because Doc Brackett was always doctoring poor people, who had no money to pay.

He would get up in the middle of the coldest night and ride twenty miles to doctor a sick woman, or child, or to patch up some fellow who got hurt.

Everybody in Our Town knew Doc Brackett's office over Rice's clothing store. It was up a narrow flight of stairs. His office was always filled with people. A sign at the foot of the stairs said: DR. BRACKETT, OFFICE UPSTAIRS.

Doc Brackett was a bachelor. He was once supposed to marry Miss Elvira Cromwell, the daughter of old Junius Cromwell, the banker, but on the day the wedding was supposed to take place Doc Brackett got a call to go out into the country and doctor a Mexican child.

Miss Elvira got sore at him and called off the wedding. She said that a man who would think more of a Mexican child than of his wedding was no good. Many women in Our Town agreed with Miss Elvira Cromwell, but the parents of the Mexican child were very grateful to Doc Brackett when the child recovered.

For forty years, the lame, and the halt, and the blind of Our Town had climbed up and down the stairs to Doc Brackett's office.

He never turned away anybody.

But he lived to be seventy years old, and then one day he keeled over on the sofa in his office and died. By this time his black hair had turned white.

Doc Brackett had one of the biggest funerals ever seen in Our Town. Everybody went to pay their last respects when he was laid out in Gruber's undertaking parlors. He was buried in Riverview Cemetery.

There was talk of raising money to put a nice tombstone on Doc Brackett's grave as a memorial. The talk got as far as arguing about what should be carved on the stone about him. Some thought poetry would be very nice.

Doc Brackett hated poetry.

The matter dragged along and nothing whatever was done.

Then one day George Gruber, the undertaker, said that Doc Brackett's memorial was already over his grave, with an epitaph and all. George Gruber said the Mexican parents of the child Doc Brackett saved years ago had worried about him having no tombstone.

They had no money themselves, so they took the sign from the foot of the stairs at Doc Brackett's office and stuck it over his grave. It read: DR. BRACKETT, OFFICE UPSTAIRS.

We Were on That Raft— A Hundred Million of Us

MARGARET LEE RUNBECK

The Rickenbacker story wasn't the first one that happened. But it was the one that aroused many of us to noticing. Once our eyes were opened to them, we realized that there had been other stories, scattered timidly across the news, which told of men who prayed for rain and had it, who prayed for help and it came.

The Rickenbacker story gave a lot of people courage to tell theirs. Prayers came back into fashion for many people, when Captain Rickenbacker and his men said shamelessly that they had prayed. Some people began praying, experimentally, for the first time in their lives. Others came out into the light and admitted they always had prayed. And, what's more, that God had heard them praying.

Captain Rickenbacker and his men have all told of the rescue. They have covered every angle of it.

All but one. They have not told our part of that rescue, ours, the hundred million people who shared that adventure on a raft.

I do not need to tell you how it was, for you know it. It happened to you, just as it happened to me, and to all of us. When Eddie Rickenbacker was lost, we didn't give him up. We read it in our morning papers, and a stab of fear went through us, and then we said, 'No—he can't really be lost. Not Rickenbacker. He'll be back. Something will take care of him. You wait and see.'

Everybody felt that way. Mayor La Guardia asked the whole city of New York to pray for him, and I don't doubt that thousands of them did. Even the ones who didn't know how to pray had a kind of faith about him.

"He'll be back. You wait and see," they said.

We waited and we did see. Some of us almost gave up. But not the taxi-driver, nor the boy with the shoe-shine box, nor Joe who sells papers, nor Mrs. McGinty. Nor Mrs. Rickenbacker. Nor I.

We weren't very logical about it; but we knew that there was something about Rickenbacker that couldn't be lost at this moment. Not because he was tough or invulnerable, exactly. No, it was something different. Perhaps it was the conviction which all of us had that helped bring him back. Or does that make any sense?

Well, anyway—he came back. You remember the morning. You remember the front page of the Sunday newspaper. You called the news upstairs to the children when you brought in the newspaper; you said, "God." You don't often meet it in the newspaper. It gave you a funny feeling. And more than that. A strange excited feeling, as if something good had happened to all of us.

You read the words carefully. "And this part I would hesitate to tell, except that there were six witnesses who saw it with me," Captain Rickenbacker said. "A gull came out of nowhere, and lighted upon my head—I reached up my hand very gently—I killed him and then we divided him equally among us. We ate every bit, even the little bones. Never did anything taste so good. . . ."

There was something so moving in those simple words—a sort of biblical excitement about them—you were still standing in the middle of the floor reading them, and you felt your eyes prickling with a kind of tired tears . . .

You couldn't quite explain the tears. It was as if you'd terribly wanted something to be true which you had never really admitted, and now here it was on the front page of a newspaper. You remembered that dove which Noah had sent out to see if the flood had subsided enough for man to walk upon the earth again—here was the descendant of that dove, this gull which came out of nowhere and landed on a lost man's head in the middle of the Pacific. You hadn't read that story of Noah since you were a child; funny you should think of it now, standing here in the middle of the living-room floor reading a newspaper.

Sunday morning went on. Everybody spoke about it. Everybody had the same irrational feeling as if something good had happened to all of us, as if we had somehow been amplified by Rickenbacker and that gull, and those verses from Matthew read in the bobbing yellow rafts. In the middle of the afternoon, in the midst of the Philharmonic broadcast, suddenly the very air tingled. The music was broken off, and a clipped voice came from the loudspeaker saying that in a moment Captain Rickenbacker was going to speak. Then that curiously vibrant voice came on, not very sure of itself, terribly moving with earnestness, obviously stirred almost to the breaking of self-control.

Word for word he said what you had read that morning. You wanted more; you wanted it to go on from there.

If this could happen to those men, out on the Pacific, why couldn't it happen to all of us all the time? If it's true at all, it ought to be true everywhere, you said inside yourself. You wouldn't have said that out loud, of course. But you thought it to yourself.

Secretary Stemson said in the first meeting with the press: "He has come back. I think more of him came back than went away." More of us came back, too. More of you; you knew it.

Every little paper picked up the story; ministers preached sermons about it' there probably wasn't a person who didn't mention it to somebody. Everybody, from Eddie Cantor to Thomas Mann, made a public comment.

It wore off in a few days, of course. But those few days

showed everybody one thing. Man at this moment is pretty homesick for God; he'd like some news of Him, some kind of sign that He hasn't forgotten.

Then, after a few weeks, full-page advertisements appeared in the newspapers. Eddie Rickenbacker was going to tell the story again. We could hardly wait; we wanted more terribly.

But now something had happened to the story. He hadn't added anything to it. No. Something had been taken away from it. It was written better, much better. It was full of gripping details, and even diagrams of how the men had fitted into those three tiny rubber rafts. But when it came to the Lord's part, it suddenly got very self-conscious.

I wasn't there, of course, when Eddie Rickenbacker was writing his story. I haven't any real way of knowing, but I can imagine what happened. Perhaps it was something like this: Good, experienced, hard-headed editors said, "Listen, Rick, about that bird—of course there were lots of birds flying around all the time . . . "

"Yes, of course."

"They'd naturally light on something . . . "

"Yes. But this was different—we had prayed . . . "

"Sure. Well, look—let's sort of tone down that part a little— you were pretty emotional when you came back—anybody would have been, Rick . . . "

I can imagine Captain Rickenbacker protesting, and being embarrassed, and then finally just giving up. He has said he wasn't really a religious man; he was inexpert in finding those strange words to say what had seemed true. He had defended himself by making it clearly understood that he wasn't accustomed. I can imagine how he felt . . .

As he himself says in his *Life* magazine story: "Men place different values on experiences shared together. What stirred or depressed me may have seemed inconsequential to the others. While I sit in a Rockefeller Center office which I have all to myself, and where a push on a buzzer will summon nearly anything I need, much of what I went through on that ridiculously small raft now seems almost irrelevant. It is like trying to remember being dead."

On the contrary, Captain Rickenbacker, I think it must be like trying to remember being alive, after you have died again into the conventional banality of everydayness.

In that tragic paragraph, so wry and wistful, lies all human loneliness, the terrifying doubt that what we know and feel can ever really be shared by anyone at all. In a grotesque, frantic way we settle for anything just so we can agree between us that it is true.

For of all things men fear the most, there is no horror like the danger that we may be pushed out on a limb of aloneness, from which we see the thing differently from the rest of the race. Sometimes this human world seems like a fantastic, preposterous dream, but so long as we are certain we are all in the same dream, we do not need to worry too much about ourselves. It is only when we get outside it for a moment of clarity or madness that we are frightened.

We have told each other firsthand experiences about everything on earth. We have bolstered up and reinforced each other with recounted experiences. But the shape of the thing we fear the most we have not been able to form for each other. For of that one experience we have never had a first-hand account. Of death we have only the hearsay evidence of bystanders. Nobody has ever said to us, "Let me tell you about the day I died—it happened like this."

No, on second thought, there are two experiences we can't testify about. For no one has ever said, "Did I ever happen to tell you about when I was being born?" But it's too late for us to fear that one; we got through that somehow, and whatever anguish we suffered is forgotten. So we concentrate our fear on the other rumor.

People who want to talk about it are—well, queer and uncomfortable people. Even heroes who want to tell us how it did not happen. That is one of the first tragic cautions a hero must learn; not to talk too truly about it. Eddie Rickenbacker, and his men, learned it quickly.

When they first came back, those men knew what happened to them; I hope they still know unshakably.

When Colonel Hans Christian Adamson was rescued, he

wrote to his wife: "I have found a nearness to our Creator which I have never known before, and I am certain that this new feeling is going to affect both our lives in the future. While the drifting was a horrible experience, something wonderful has come of it."

Corporal John F. Bartek said: "I'm glad that plane fell. It took a lot of nonsense out of my life. I shall like the things I liked before, but there is something now inside me that won't permit me to forget that God stayed right by us out there."

We must help those men hold on to their story. We must not let rationalization nibble it away. It must not become merely a story of man's heroism, for it was much much more than that. It was a story of God's care.

Man's heroism we are accustomed to, this year. That is something we can get our teeth into. But that other thing . . . Well, we must keep holding to that, all of us hundred million people who have been on that raft with Rick.

You see, the reason it is so terribly important to us, why we read every word of it over and over, is that we know we're on a raft, each of us alone, when the last truth is told. We don't bother too much about it, but we know it. We know exactly what Captain Rickenbacker meant when he said, "Let the moment come when nothing is left but life, and you will find that you do not hesitate over the fate of material possessions." We have felt that, in extreme sickness and in grief, when we came inescapably close to verity. Over the bleak face of this earth rove thousands of refugees who have found that out in the last three years.

But here in America, most of the time we have been able to keep away from that edge of reality; we have amused ourselves and drugged ourselves and exhausted ourselves with our work and our possessions. But underneath we know, all right.

It is not always a desperate raft, of course; sometimes it has been gay and amusing and diverting, skipping over the expanse of nothingness all around us. But it is a raft, nevertheless, and we're not too sure where it's going, or where it came from, and we want with all our hearts to know that Something has us in His care.

And at the same time with wanting to believe it, we want also to disbelieve it. We are relatively safe and rational people living almost customary lives; we are delighted with our mentality because we have logical explanations for everything. If we can't explain it, then it probably didn't happen anyway.

This miracle that Captain Rickenbacker and his men brought back doesn't belong only to him. It belongs to all of us. All of us had it for a little while, even if we individually have lost it somewhere since that Sunday.

And yet, it may be that at the moment when each of us needs it again, it will come alive for us. "Out of nowhere," like the gull.

Like Summer's Cloud—
The Gossamer Dreams of Boyhood
Merle Crowell

All around the Boy in Maine were wonders of which he must find the meaning. The wonder of daybreak, for example. Often he stood at his attic bedroom window, or on the hill back of the barn, and watched dawn come striding over the eastern hills in its flowing crimson robes. As he waited, the first breeze would ruffle the grass, dewdrops would sparkle, and the trills of birds, those minstrels of the morning, would suddenly blend into a chorus. Sometimes the Boy would find himself trembling from ecstasy.

What was back of it all—those magic moments when the heart was lifted out of the rut of life? Who lit the funeral flares in the sky at the death of day? From what cradle of creation came the mystery of a May night with apple blossoms white in the moonlight? Who turned the hills to scarlet in October, wove the lacework of ice on the bare branches and twigs in winter?

Was it God? He would like to believe so. But somehow these miracles did not fit the God of eternal hell-fire, of infant and heathen damnation, whom they preached about in the white meetinghouse on the hill.

The Boy was profoundly puzzled.

He craved understanding and found little—for the ways of a boy's mind are hard to fathom. "What are you dreaming about?"

the Boy's father would ask.

"Oh, nothing."

He saw men work from dawn to night, plowing and planting. He saw them struggle against weeds and insects. Then would come drought. And hopes of the harvest would shrivel with it.

Life on a rocky New England farm was hard enough anyway. Why must men fight also against wanton fate?

He saw death steal down and carry off those whom the countryside could least afford to lose. And those whom few would miss lived on and on.

He saw the homes of the thrifty struck by lightning, well-kept herds hit by disease, careful folk the victims of accident.

If life was part of a purposeful plan, he could find no pattern for it.

And yet in the deepest shadow bloomed the twin flowers of faith and courage. Men whose fields had been laid waste squared their shoulders and looked hopefully ahead to another planting and another harvest. In homes brushed by the wings of the dark angel the battle of living went doggedly on. There was something invincible, indomitable, about the soul of man. Something that could not perish.

In the winter evenings, after the woodbox had been filled and the horses bedded and the cows milked, the Boy curled up in front of the fire with a book, to find things that were lacking in the world he knew. It stirred his imagination to learn what men and women were doing—and had done—far beyond those encircling hills. He dreamed of principalities and powers, of things present and things to come. Out there was a world he did not know. One day he would find out more about its mountains and deserts, rivers and plains. He would go to that great city where men were a milling herd striving for fame and fortune. Other farm boys had gone there before him. There must be room for one more.

The strings of his heart were strummed, too, by the cold fingers of the Maine winter. There was the endless sweep of snow punctuated by pines and firs, the snapping of nails in the roof as he lay in his attic bed at night, the thick white arabesques on the windowpanes when he crawled out of the warm hollow in the featherbed of a January morning. Blizzards might mean a snowbound household, but the howl of the wind along the eaves, the steady swish of the snow, drifts piling up till the windows were half hid, all talked to him of the mighty menace of nature. And when the skies were blue again, and men were breaking the roads with four or five teams of horses a-tandem, he felt a growing conviction that the wild will of the universe could never quite quell the human spirit.

The Boy was acutely sensitive to sights and sounds and smells. In summer, at haying time, the frightening flit of a ground sparrow as the horse rake came close; the fresh swaths in their green geometric patterns; the bulging muscles of the hired man as he tossed titanic forkfuls of hay into the rack; even the clank of ice in the tin pail as he brought water flavored with molasses and ginger to the men at work.

Autumn held for him a special spell. The round harvest moon rising over a field of shocked corn; the drift smoke of burning leaves; trees rustling in the wind; hills and valleys afire with color; in all these there was something eerie, as if ghosts of summer were riding the October air.

The Boy looked forward to Thanksgiving for weeks on end. While rolling pumpkins into a dump-cart, filling the cellar with a hoard of potatoes, and battening the barns against the inevitable onslaught of winter, he was forever anticipating that November day when the end of fall's work would be celebrated with feast and fun.

Yes, it was a good life. From the simplest things—a few toys at Christmas, a trip to the county fair, a husking with its yellow lanterns and kissing games and six kinds of frosted cake—he extracted a succulence that sometimes in later years he was to look back on with envy.

Does youth, with its tremendous trivialities, its gossamer dreams, its fantastic despairs, really transcend the more durable satisfaction of manhood? I suppose not. And yet youth has a special flavor that inevitability is drained dry as a boy or a girl grows up.

Richard Henry Stoddard captured that thought:

There are gains for all our losses,
There are balms for all our pain;
But when youth, the dream, departs,
It takes something from our hearts,
And it never comes again.

The Littlest Angel

CHARLES TAZEWELL

Once upon a time,—oh, many, many years ago as time is calculated by men—but which was only Yesterday in the Celestial Calendar of Heaven—there was, in Paradise, a most miserable, thoroughly unhappy, and utterly dejected cherub who was known throughout Heaven as The Littlest Angel.

He was exactly four years, six months, five days, seven hours and forty-two minutes of age when he presented himself to the venerable Gate-Keeper and waited for admittance to the Glorious Kingdom of God.

Standing defiantly, with his short brown legs wide apart, the Littlest Angel tried to pretend that he wasn't at all impressed by such Unearthly Splendor, and that he wasn't at all afraid. But his lower lip trembled, and a tear disgraced him by making a new furrow down his already tear-streaked face—coming to a precipitous halt at the very tip end of his small freckled nose.

But that wasn't all. While the kindly Gate-Keeper was entering the name in his great Book, the Littlest Angel, having left home as usual without a handkerchief, endeavored to hide the tell-tale evidence by snuffing. A most unangelic sound which so unnerved the good Gate-Keeper that he did something he had never done before in all Eternity. He blotted the page!

From that moment on, the Heavenly Peace was never quite the same, and the Littlest Angel soon became the despair of all the Heavenly Host. His shrill, ear-splitting whistle resounded at all hours through the Golden Streets. It startled the Patriarch Prophets and disturbed their meditations. Yes, and on top of that, he inevitably and vociferously sang off-key at the singing practice of the Heavenly Choir, spoiling its ethereal effect.

And, being so small that it seemed to take him just twice as long as anyone else to get to nightly prayers, the Littlest Angel always arrived late, and always knocked everyone's wings askew as he darted into his place.

Although these flaws in behavior might have been overlooked, the general appearance of the Littlest Angel was even more disreputable than his deportment. It was first whispered among the Seraphim and Cherubim, and then said aloud among the Angels and Archangels, that he didn't even look like an angel!

And they were all quite correct. He didn't. His halo was permanently tarnished where he held onto it with one hot little chubby hand when he ran, and he was always running. Furthermore, even when he stood very still, it never behaved like a halo should. It was always slipping down over his right eye.

Or over his left eye.

Or else, just for pure meanness, slipping off the back of his head and rolling away down some Golden Street just so he'd have to chase after it!

Yes, and it must be here recorded that his wings were neither useful nor ornamental. All paradise held its breath when the Littlest Angel perched himself like an unhappy fledgling sparrow on the very edge of a gilded cloud and prepared to take off. He would teeter this way—and that way—but, after much coaxing and a few false starts, he would shut both of his eyes, hold his freckled nose, count up to three hundred and three, and then hurl himself slowly into space!

However, owing to the regrettable fact that he always forgot to move his wings, the Littlest Angel always fell head over halo!

It was also reported, and never denied, that whenever he was nervous, which was most of the time, he bit his wing-tips!

Now, anyone can easily understand why the Littlest Angel would, soon or late, have to be disciplined. And so, on an Eternal Day of an Eternal Month in the Year Eternal, he was directed to present his small self before an Angel of the Peace.

The Littlest Angel combed his hair, dusted his wings and scrambled into an almost clean robe, and then, with a heavy heart, trudged his way to the place of judgment. He tried to postpone the dreaded ordeal by loitering along the Street of The

Guardian Angels, pausing a few timeless moments to minutely pursue the long list of new arrivals, although all Heaven knew he couldn't read a word. And he idled more than several immortal moments to carefully examine a display of aureate harps, although everyone in the Celestial City knew he couldn't tell a crotchet from a semi-quaver. But at length and at last he slowly approached a doorway which was surmounted by a pair of golden scales, signifying that Heavenly Justice was dispensed within. To the Littlest Angel's great surprise, he heard a merry voice, singing!

The Littlest Angel removed his halo and breathed upon it heavily, then polished it upon his robe, a procedure which added nothing to that garment's already untidy appearance, and then tip-toed in!

The Singer, who was know as the Understanding Angel, looked down at the small culprit, and the Littlest Angel instantly tried to make himself invisible by the ingenious process of with-drawing his head into the collar of his robe, very much like a snapping turtle.

At that, the Singer laughed, a jolly, heartwarming sound, and said, "Oh! So you're the one who's been making Heaven so unheavenly! Come here, Cherub, and tell me all about it!" The Littlest Angel ventured a furtive look from beneath his robe.

First one eye.

And then the other eye.

Suddenly, almost before he knew it, he was perched on the lap of the Understanding Angel, and was explaining how very difficult it was for a boy who suddenly finds himself transformed into an angel. Yes, and no matter what the Archangels said, he's only swung once. Well, twice. Oh, all right, then, he's swung three times on the Golden Gates. But that was just for something to do!

That was the whole trouble. There wasn't anything for a small angel to do. And he was very homesick. Oh, not that Paradise wasn't beautiful! But the Earth was beautiful, too! Wasn't it created by God, Himself? Why, there were trees to climb, and brooks to fish, and caves to play at pirate chief, the swimming hole, and sun, and rain, and dark, and dawn, and thick brown dust, so soft and warm beneath your feet!

The Understanding Angel smiled, and in his eyes was a long forgotten memory of another small boy long ago. Then he asked the Littlest Angel what would make him most happy in Paradise. The Cherub thought for a moment, and whispered in his ear.

"There's a box. I left it under my bed back home. If only I could have that?"

The Understanding Angel nodded his head. "You shall have it," he promised. And a fleet-winged heavenly messenger was instantly dispatched to bring the box to Paradise.

And then, in all those timeless days that followed, everyone wondered at the great change in the Littlest Angel, for, among all the cherubs in God's Kingdom, he was the most happy. His conduct was above the slightest reproach. His appearance was all that the most fastidious could wish for. And on excursions to Elysian Fields, it could be said, and truly said, that he flew like an angel!

Then it came to pass that Jesus, the Son of God, was born of Mary, of Bethlehem, of Judea. And as the glorious tidings spread through paradise, all the angels rejoiced and their voices were lifted to herald the Miracle of Miracles, the coming of the Christ Child.

The Angels and Archangels, the Seraphim and Cherubim, the Gate-Keeper, the Wingmaker, yes, even the Halosmith put aside their usual tasks to prepare their gifts for the Blessed Infant. All but the Littlest Angel. He sat himself down on the top-most step of the Golden Stairs and anxiously waited for inspiration.

What could he give that would be most acceptable to the Son of God? At one time, he dreamed of composing a lyric hymn of adoration. But the Littlest Angel was woefully wanting in musical talent.

Then he grew tremendously excited over writing a prayer! A prayer that would live forever in the hearts of men, because it would be the first prayer ever to be heard by the Christ Child. But the Littlest Angel was lamentably lacking in literate skill. "What, oh what, could a small angel give that would please the Holy Infant?"

The time of the Miracle was very close at hand when the

Littlest Angel at last decided on his gift. Then, on that Day of Days, he proudly brought it from its hiding place behind a cloud, and humbly, with downcast eyes, placed it before the Throne of God. It was only a small, rough, unsightly box, but inside were all those wonderful things that even a Child of God would treasure.

A small, rough, unsightly box, lying among all those other glorious gifts from all the Angels of Paradise! Gifts of such rare and radiant splendor and breathless beauty that Heaven and all the Universe were lighted by the mere reflection of their glory! And when the Littlest Angel saw this, he suddenly knew that his gift to God's Child was irreverent, and he devoutly wished he might reclaim his shabby gift. It was ugly. It was worthless. If only he could hide it away from the sight of God before it was even noticed!

But it was too late! The Hand of God moved slowly over all that bright array of shining gifts, then paused, then dropped, then came to rest on the lowly gift of the Littlest Angel!

The Littlest Angel trembled as the box was opened, and there, before the Eyes of God and all His Heavenly Host, was what he offered to the Christ Child.

And what was his gift to the Blessed Infant? Well, there was a butterfly with golden wings, captured one bright summer day on the high hills above Jerusalem, and a sky-blue egg from a bird's nest in the olive tree that stood to shade his mother's kitchen door. Yes, and two white stones, found on a muddy river bank, where he and his friends had played like small brown beavers, and, at the bottom of the box, a limp, tooth-marked leather strap, once worn as a collar by his mongrel dog, who had died as he had lived, in absolute love and infinite devotion.

The Littlest Angel wept hot, bitter tears, for now he knew that instead of honoring the Son of God, he had been most blasphemous.

Why had he ever thought the box was so wonderful?

Why had he dreamed that such utterly useless things would be loved by the Blessed Infant?

In frantic terror, he turned to run and hide from the Divine Wrath of the Heavenly Father, but he stumbled and fell, and with a horrified wail and clatter of halo, rolled in a ball of consummate misery to the very foot of the Heavenly Throne!

There was an ominous and dreadful silence in the Celestial City, a silence complete and undisturbed save for heart-broken sobbing of the Littlest Angel.

Then, suddenly, The Voice of God, like Divine Music, rose and swelled through Paradise!

And the Voice of God spoke, saying, "Of all the gifts of all the angels, I find that his small box pleases Me most. Its contents are of the Earth and of men, and My Son is born to be King of both. These are the things My Son, too, will know and love and cherish and then, regretful, will leave behind Him when His task is done. I accept this gift in the Name of the Child, Jesus, born of Mary this night in Bethlehem."

There was a breathless pause, and then the rough, unsightly box of the Littlest Angel began to glow with a bright, unearthly light, then the light became a lustrous flame, and the flame became a radiant brilliance that blinded the eyes of all the angels!

None but the Littlest Angel saw it rise from its place before the Throne of God. And he, and only he, watched it arch the firmament to stand and shed its clear, white, beckoning light over a Stable where a Child was Born.

There it shone on that Night of Miracles, and its light was reflected down the centuries deep in the heart of all mankind. Yet, earthly eyes, blinded, too, by its splendor, could never know that the lowly gift of the Littlest Angel was what all men would call forever "THE SHINING STAR OF BETHLEHEM!"

From Great Possessions

DAVID GRAYSON

I have just had one of the pleasant experiences of life. From time to time, these brisk winter days, I like to walk across the fields to Horace's farm. I take a new way each time and make nothing of the snow in the fields or the drifts along the fences.

"Why," asks Harriet, "do you insist on struggling through the snow when there's a good beaten road around?"

"Harriet," I said, "why should anyone take a beaten road when there are new and adventurous ways to travel?"

When I cross the fields, I never know at what moment I may come upon some strange or surprising experience, what new sights I may see, what new sounds I may hear, and I have the further great advantage of appearing unexpectedly at Horace's farm. Sometimes I enter by the cow lane, sometimes by way of the old road through the wood lot, or I appear casually, like a gust of wind, around the corner of the barn, or I let Horace discover me leaning with folded arms upon his cattle fence. I have come to love doing this, for unexpectedness in visitors, as in religion and politics, is disturbing to Horace; and as sand grits in oysters produce pearls, my unexpected appearances have more than once astonished new thoughts in Horace or yielded pearly bits of native humor.

Ever since I have known him, Horace has been rather high-and-mighty with me; but I know he enjoys my visits, for I give him always, I think, a pleasantly renewed sense of his own superiority. When he sees me, his eye lights up with the comfortable knowledge that he can plow so much better than I can, that his corn grows taller than mine, and his hens lay more eggs. He is a wonderfully practical man, is Horace; hard-headed, they call it here. And he never feels so superior, I think, as when he finds me sometimes of a Sunday or an evening walking across the fields where my land joins his, or sitting on a stone fence, or lying on my back in the pasture under a certain friendly thorn-apple tree. This he finds it difficult to understand and thinks it highly undisciplined, impractical, no doubt reprehensible.

One incident of the sort I shall never forget. It was on a June day only a year or so after I came here, and before Horace knew me as well as he does now. I had climbed the hill to look off across his own high-field pasture, where the white daisies, the purple fleabane, and the buttercups made a wild tangle of beauty among the tall herd's-grass. Light airs moved billowing across the field, bobolinks and meadow larks were singing, and all about were the old fences, each with its wild hedgerow of choke cherry, young elms, and black raspberry bushes, and beyond, across miles and miles of sunny green countryside, the mysterious blue of the ever-changing hills. It was a spot I loved then, and have loved more deeply every year since.

Horace found me sitting on the stone fence which there divides our possessions. I think he had been observing me with amusement for some time before I saw him, for when I looked around his face wore a comfortably superior, half-disdainful smile.

"David," said he, "what ye doin' here?"

"Harvesting my crops," I said.

He looked at me sharply to see if I was joking, but I was perfectly sober.

"Harvestin' yer crops?"

"Yes," I said, the fancy growing suddenly upon me, "and just now I've been taking a crop from the field you think you own."

I waved my hand to indicate his high-field pasture.

"Don't I own it?"

"No, Horace, I'm sorry to say, not all of it. To be frank with you, since I came here, I've quietly acquired an undivided interest in that land. I may as well tell you first as last. I'm like you, Horace; I'm reaching out in all directions."

I spoke in as serious a voice as I could command—the tone I use when I sell potatoes. Horace's smile wholly disappeared. A city feller like me was capable of anything!

"How's that?" he exclaimed sharply. "What do you mean? That field came down to me from my Grandfather Jamieson."

I continued to look at Horace with great calmness and gravity.

"Judging from what I now know of your title, Horace," said I, "neither your Grandfather Jamieson nor your father ever owned all of that field. And I've now acquired that part of it, in fee simple, that neither they nor you ever really had."

At this, Horace began to look seriously worried. The idea that anyone could get away from him anything that he possessed, especially without his knowledge, was terrible to him.

"What do you mean, Mr. Grayson?"

He had been calling me David, but he now returned sharply to Mister. In our country when we "Mister" a friend, something serious is about to happen. It's the signal for general mobilization.

I continued to look Horace rather coldly and severely in the eye.

"Yes," said I, "I've acquired a share in that field which I shall not soon surrender."

An unmistakable dogged look came into Horace's face, the look inherited from generations of land-owning, home-defending, fighting ancestors. Horace is New England of New England.

"Yes," I said, "I have already had two or three crops from that field."

"Huh!" said Horace. "I've cut the grass and I've cut the rowen every year since you bin here. What's more, I've got the money fer it in the bank."

He tapped his fingers on the top of the wall.

"Nevertheless, Horace," said I, "I've got my crops also from that field, and a steady income too."

"What crops?"

"Well, I've just now been fathering in one of them. What do you think of the value of the fleabane, and the daisies, and the yellow five-finger in that field?"

"Huh!" said Horace.

"Well, I've just been cropping them. And have you observed the wind in the grass—and those shadows along the southern wall? Aren't they valuable?"

"Huh!" said Horace.

"I've rarely seen anything more beautiful," I said, "than this field and the view across it. I'm taking that crop now, and later I shall gather in the rowen of goldenrod and aster, and the red and yellow of the maple trees—and store it all away in my bank—to live on next winter."

It was some time before either of us spoke again, but I could see from the corner of my eye that mighty things were going on inside of Horace. Suddenly he broke out into a big laugh and clapped his knee with his hand in a way he has.

"Is that all!" said Horace.

I think it only confirmed him in the light esteem in which he held me. Though I showed him unmeasured wealth in his own fields, ungathered crops of new enjoyment, he was unwilling to take them, but was content with hay. It is a strange thing to me, and a sad one, how many of our farmers (and be it said in a whisper, other people too) own their lands without ever really possessing them, and let the most precious crops of the good earth go to waste.

After that, for a long time, Horace loved to joke me about my crops and his. A joke with Horace is a durable possession.

"S'pose you think that's your field," he'd say.

"The best part of it," I'd return; "but you can have all I've taken, and there'll still be enough for both of us."

"You're a queer one!" he'd say, and then add sometimes dryly, "but there's one crop ye don't git, David," and he'd tap his pocket where he carries his fat, worn, leather pocketbook. "And as fer feelin's, it can't be beat."

So many people have the curious idea that the only thing the world desires enough to pay its hard money for is that which can be seen or eaten or worn. But there never was a greater mistake. While men will haggle to the penny over the price of hay, or fight for a cent more to the bushel of oats, they will turn out their very pockets for strange, intangible joys, hopes, thoughts, or for a moment of peace in a feverish world—the unknown Great Possessions.

So it was that one day, some months afterward, when we had been thus bantering each other with great good humor, I said to him, "Horace, how much did you get for your hay this year?"

"Off that one little piece," he replied, "I figger fifty-two dollars."

"Well, Horace," said I, "I have beaten you. I got more out of it this year than you did."

"Oh, I know what you mean—"

"No, Horace, you don't. This time I mean just what you do: money, cash, dollars."

"How's that, now?"

"Well, I wrote a little piece about your field, and the wind in the grass, and the hedges along the fences, and the weeds among the timothy, and the fragrance of it all in June and sold it last week—" I leaned over toward Horace and whispered behind my hand—in just the way he tells me the price he gets for his pigs.

"What!" he exclaimed.

Horace had long known that I was "a kind of literary feller," but his face was now a study in astonishment.

"What?"

Horace scratched his head, as he is accustomed to do when puzzled, with one finger just under the rim of his hat.

"Well, I vum!" said he.

Here I have been wandering all around Horace's barn—in the snow—getting at the story I really started to tell, which probably supports Horace's conviction that I am an impractical person. If I had the true business spirit, I should have gone by the beaten road from my house to Horace's, borrowed the singletree I went for, and hurried straight home. Life is so short when one is after dollars! I should not have wallowed through the snow, nor stopped at the top of the hill to look for a moment across the beautiful wintry earth—gray sky and bare wild trees and frosted farmsteads with homely smoke rising from the chimneys. I should merely have brought home a singletree—and missed the glory of life! As I reflect upon it now, I believe it took me no longer to go by the fields than by the road; and I've got the singletree as securely with me as though I had not looked upon the beauty of the eternal hills, nor reflected, as I tramped, upon the strange ways of man.

Oh, my friend, is it the settled rule of life that we are to accept nothing not expensive? It is not so settled for me. That which is freest, cheapest, seems somehow more valuable than anything I pay for; that which is given, better than that which is bought; that which passes between you and me in the glance of an eye, a touch of the hand, is better than minted money!

The Book that Converted Its Author

ELIZABETH RIDER MONTGOMERY

The balconies are crowded. Every eye is on the chariots in the great arena below as they speed faster and faster around the course. Will Ben-Hur win? Or will Messala triumph? People are shouting, screaming as the beautiful horses dash into the final stretch. But what has happened? A chariot is overturning. The driver is being dragged along the course! Surely he will be killed!

What a thrilling scene the chariot race in *Ben-Hur* is! In fact, the entire book is an exciting, absorbing story of life in the time of Christ. Though Ben-Hur is the hero, the figure of Christ is always in the background, never forgotten.

Yet *Ben-Hur: A Tale of the Christ* was not written by a religious man. The author, Lew Wallace, had been a soldier, a lawyer, a governor. When he began his famous book, he did not know what he believed about religion. He did not even know whether he believed in Christ. In fact, he began writing the book in an effort to learn for himself the truth about Jesus of Nazareth.

After his active years of service through the Civil War, General Lew Wallace returned to private life and his law practice in Crawfordsville, Indiana. For some time he was restless—the natural reaction from the excitement of war. But at last he settled down to an uneventful life.

Unaccountably, he found himself thinking about religion, although he had no religious convictions whatever. He was particularly haunted by the chapter in the Gospel of St. Matthew which relates the birth of Jesus and the visit of the Wise Men. Who were the Wise Men, he wondered? Where had they come from, and why? He decided to figure out his own conception of the Wise Men from the East.

And so, after much reading and study of the Bible, Wallace wrote an account of the meeting of the Magi in the desert, and their journey to Bethlehem to see the Christ-child. When it was finished, he left the manuscript on his desk, undecided what to do with it.

Some time later, on a night in 1876, Wallace was returning home after an evening with friends. He had been listening to a discussion of religion—of God, Jesus, heaven, and eternal life. Wallace had taken little or no part in the argument, for the very good reason that he knew nothing at all about the subject under discussion. Did he believe in God? He did not know. Was Jesus Christ divine? He did not know. Religion had had no place in his active life, and he was totally ignorant about technology.

As he walked home alone in the darkness that evening, Lew Wallace began to regret that ignorance. For the first time in his life he began to feel that religion might be a very important matter. He should believe something. But what? How did one find out what to believe? Read sermons? Read theology, on which no two men agreed? No, he would never come to any decision that way. The only thing to do was to read the Bible. As the Bible was the basis for all Christian theology, he would make it the basis for his own religious convictions.

But Wallace knew from experience that he would have to have some definite purpose in studying the Bible—something to keep him at it, to keep him interested. He was not a man to study just for the sake of studying. The search for religious convictions alone would not be enough. He needed something else.

For days Wallace mulled the matter over. Then one day an inspiration came. He went to his wife in great excitement.

"My dear, I'm going to write a book."

"That is splendid," she replied. "I'm glad you are going to start another book. You enjoyed so much your work on *The Fair God*. What will it be this time?"

"A tale of the Christ," Wallace answered. "I shall use what I wrote about the Wise Men as the beginning of the book, and I shall end with the crucifixion. In between—"

"Yes," prompted his wife. "In between—"

"Well, I hardly know yet. It will be a story which will show the religious and political condition of the world at the time of Christ."

"But will you have Jesus himself in your story?" asked his wife, troubled. "Won't that be dangerous? I'm afraid you will offend many readers who have their own conception of Christ and will not like to see Him pictured differently."

Lew Wallace frowned. "That is one of the greatest obstacles I shall have to hurdle," he agreed. "The only solution I can see at present is to have a human hero, who is the central figure in the story. The figure of Christ must be in the background. Yet He must dominate the book. Well, I shan't worry too much about that just yet. I shall be working on this project a long time, no doubt, and many of my difficulties may smooth themselves out before I come to them."

Wallace was right: he worked on his book a long time. More than seven years. Most of the time was taken up with research, rather than writing. He took infinite pains to verify every fact, to substantiate every statement.

And of course, to make his progress even slower, he had to make a living. Writing was merely spare-time work for him. He was in those years, to begin with, a lawyer, busy enough to suit any man. And then, in 1878, with his book far from finished, he was made governor of the territory of New Mexico. Then, indeed, Wallace knew what it was to be busy. Trying simultaneously to manage a legislature of jealous factions, to take care of an Indian war, and to sell some mines which had been located by the Spanish conquistadors, he found it increasingly difficult to finish his book. Sometimes he could not even start to write before midnight. To cap the climax, in the last months of his work on *Ben-Hur,* he knew that his life was in constant danger. "Billy the Kid" had sworn to kill him.

But Lew Wallace was not a man to let either the pressure of work or the fear of death keep him from finishing what he had started. Patiently, tirelessly he labored. And at last his book was completed and carefully copied in purple ink. His work was done. Not only that, he had discovered, himself, what he wanted: religious convictions. Lew Wallace, in writing his book of the Christ, had come to believe in Him.

In 1880, *Ben-Hur: A Tale of the Christ* was published by Harper and Brothers. At first it was not popular. Nearly two years passed before its sales started to grow. But at last it began to be appreciated, and before many more years went by it became one of the most popular books of the century.

A Handful of Clay

HENRY VAN DYKE

There was a handful of clay in the bank of a river. It was only common clay, coarse and heavy; but it had high thoughts of its own value, and wonderful dreams of the great place which it was to fill in the world when the time came for its virtues to be discovered.

Overhead, in the spring sunshine, the trees whispered together of the glory which descended upon them when the delicate blossoms and leaves began to expand, and the forest glowed with fair, clear colours, as if the dust of thousands of rubies and emeralds were hanging, in soft clouds, above the earth.

The flowers, surprised with the joy of beauty, bent their heads to one another, as the wind caressed them, and said: "Sisters, how lovely you have become. You make the day bright."

The river, glad of new strength and rejoicing in the unison of all its waters, murmured to the shores in music, telling of its release from icy fetters, its swift flight from the snow-clad mountains, and the mighty work to which it was hurrying—the wheels of many mills to be turned, and great ships to be floated to the sea.

Waiting blindly in its bed, the clay comforted itself with lofty hopes. "My time will come," it said. "I was not made to be hidden forever. Glory and beauty and honour are coming to me in due season."

One day the clay felt itself taken from the place where it had waited so long. A flat blade of iron passed beneath it, lifted it, and tossed it into a cart with other lumps of clay, and it was carried far away, as it seemed, over a rough and stony road. But it was not afraid, nor discouraged, for it said to itself: "This is necessary. The path to glory is always rugged. Now I am on my way to play a great part in the world."

But the hard journey was nothing compared with the tribulation and distress that came after it. The clay was put into a trough and mixed and beaten and stirred and trampled. It seemed almost unbearable. But there was consolation in the thought that something very fine and noble was certainly coming out of all this trouble. The clay felt sure that, if it could only wait long enough, a wonderful reward was in store for it.

Then it was put upon a swiftly turning wheel, and whirled around until it seemed as if it must fly into a thousand pieces. A strange power pressed it and moulded it, as it revolved, and through all the dizziness and pain it felt that it was taking a new form.

Then an unknown hand put it into an oven, and fires were kindled about it—fierce and penetrating—hotter than all the heats of summer that had ever brooded upon the bank of the river. But through it all, the clay held itself together and endured its trials, in the confidence of a great future. "Surely," it thought, "I am intended for something very splendid, since such pains are taken with me. Perhaps I am fashioned for the ornament of a temple, or a precious vase for the table of a king."

At last the baking was finished. The clay was taken from the furnace and set down upon a board, in the cool air, under the blue sky. The tribulation was past. The reward was at hand.

Close beside the board there was a pool of water, not very deep, nor very clear, but calm enough to reflect, with impartial truth, every image that fell upon it. There, for the first time, as it was lifted from the board, the clay saw its new shape, the reward of all its patience and pain, the consummation of its hopes—a common flower-pot, straight and stiff, red and ugly. And then it felt that it was not destined for a king's house, nor for a palace of art, because it was made without glory or beauty or honour; and it murmured against the unknown maker, saying, "Why hast thou made me thus?"

Many days it passed in sullen discontent. Then it was filled with earth, and something—it knew not what—but something rough and brown and dead-looking, was thrust into the middle of the earth and covered over. The clay rebelled at this new disgrace. "This is the worst of all that has happened to me, to be filled with dirt and rubbish. Surely I am a failure."

But presently it was set in a greenhouse, where the sunlight fell warm upon it, and water was sprinkled over it, and day by day as it waited, a change began to come to it. Something was stirring within it—a new hope. Still it was ignorant, and knew not what the new hope meant.

One day the clay was lifted again from its place, and carried into a great church. Its dream was coming true after all. It had a fine part to play in the world. Glorious music flowed over it. It was surrounded with flowers. Still it could not understand. So it whispered to another vessel of clay, like itself, close beside it, "Why have they set me here? Why do all the people look toward us?" And the other vessel answered, "Do you not know? You are carrying a royal sceptre of lilies. Their petals are white as snow, and the heart of them is like pure gold. The people look this way because the flower is the most wonderful in the world. And the root of it is in your heart."

Then the clay was content, and silently thanked its maker, because, though an earthen vessel, it held so great a treasure.

From the Moon and Sixpence

W. SOMERSET MAUGHAM

I have an idea that some men are born out of their due place. Accident has cast them amid certain surroundings, but they have always a nostalgia for a home they know not. They are strangers in their birthplace, and the leafy lanes they have known from childhood or the populous streets in which they have played, remain but a place of passage. They may spend their whole lives aliens among their kindred and remain aloof among the only scenes they have ever known. Perhaps it is this sense of strangeness that sends men far and wide in the search for something permanent, to which they may attach themselves. Perhaps some deep-rooted atavism urges the wanderer back to lands which his ancestors left in the dim beginnings of history. Sometimes a man hits upon a place to which he mysteriously feels that he belongs. Here is the home he sought, and he will settle amid scenes that he has never seen before, among men he has never known, as though they were familiar to him from his birth. Here at last he finds rest.

There is the story of a man I had known at St. Thomas's Hospital. He was a Jew named Abraham, a blond, rather stout young man, shy and very unassuming; but he had remarkable gifts. He entered the hospital with a scholarship, and during the five years of the curriculum gained every prize that was open to him. He was made house-physician and house-surgeon. His brilliance was allowed by all. Finally he was elected to a position on the staff, and his career was assured. So far as human things can be predicted, it was certain that he would rise to the greatest heights of his profession. Honours and wealth awaited him. Before he entered upon his new duties he wished to take a holiday, and, having no private means, he went as surgeon on a tramp steamer to the Levant. It did not generally carry a doctor, but one of the senior surgeons at the hospital knew a director of the line, and Abraham was taken as a favour.

In a few weeks the authorities received his resignation of the coveted position on the staff. It created profound astonishment, and wild rumours were current. Whenever a man does anything unexpected, his fellows ascribe it to the most discreditable motives. But there was a man ready to step into Abraham's shoes, and Abraham was forgotten. Nothing more was heard of him. He vanished.

It was perhaps ten years later that one morning on board ship, about to land at Alexandria, I was bidden to line up with the other passengers for the doctor's examination. The doctor was a stout man in shabby clothes, and when he took off his hat I noticed that he was very bald. I had an idea that I had seen him before. Suddenly I remembered.

"Abraham," I said.

He turned to me with a puzzled look, and then, recognizing me, seized my hand. After expressions of surprise on either side, hearing that I meant to spend the night in Alexandria, he asked me to dine with him at the English Club. When we met again I declared my astonishment at finding him there. It was a very modest position that he occupied, and there was about him an air of straitened circumstance. Then he told me his story. When he set out on his holiday in the Mediterranean he had every intention of returning to London and his appointment at St. Thomas's. One morning the tramp docked at Alexandria, and from the deck he looked at the city, white in the sunlight, and the crowd on the wharf; he saw the natives in their shabby gabardines, the blacks from the Soudan, the noisy throng of Greeks, and Italians, the grave Turks in tarbooshes, the sunshine and the blue sky; and something happened to him. He could not describe it. It was like a thunderclap, he said, and then, dissatisfied with this, he said it was like a revelation. Something seemed to twist his heart, and suddenly he felt an exultation, a sense of wonderful freedom. He felt himself at home, and he made up his mind there and then, in a minute, that he would live the rest of his life in Alexandria. He had a great difficulty in leaving the ship, and in twenty-four hours, with all his belongings, he was on shore.

"The Captain must have thought you as mad as a hatter," I smiled.

"I didn't care what anybody thought. It wasn't I that acted, but something stronger within me. I thought I would go to a little Greek hotel, while I looked about, and I felt I knew where to find one. And do you know, I walked straight there, and when I saw it, I recognized it at once."

"Had you been to Alexandria before?"

"No; I'd never been out of England in my life."

Presently he entered the Government service, and there he had been ever since.

"Have you never regretted it?"

"Never, not for a minute. I earn just enough to live upon, and I'm satisfied. I ask nothing more than to remain as I am till I die. I've had a wonderful life."

I left Alexandria next day, and I forgot about Abraham till a little while ago, when I was dining with another old friend in the profession, Alec Carmichael, who was in England on short leave. I ran across him in the street and congratulated him on the knighthood with which his eminent services during the war had been rewarded. We arranged to spend an evening together for old time's sake, and when I agreed to dine with him, he proposed that we could chat without interruption. He had a beautiful house on Queen Anne Street, and being a man of taste he had furnished it admirably. On the walls of the dining-room I saw a charming Bellotto, and there was a pair of Zoffanys that I envied. When his wife, a tall, lovely creature in cloth of gold, had left us, I remarked laughingly on the change in his present circumstances from those when we had both been medical students. We had looked upon it then as an extravagance to dine in a shabby Italian restaurant on the Westminster Bridge Road. Now Alec

Carmichael was on the staff of half a dozen hospitals. I should think he earned ten thousand a year, and his knighthood was but the first of the honours which must inevitably fall to his lot.

"I've done pretty well," he said, "but the strange thing is that I owe it all to one piece of luck."

"What do you mean by that?"

"Well, do you remember Abraham? He was the man who had the future. When we were students he beat me all along the line. He got the prizes and the scholarships that I went in for. I always played second fiddle to him. If he'd kept on he'd be in the position I'm in now. That man had a genius for surgery. No one had a look in with him. When he was appointed Registrar at Thomas's I hadn't a chance of getting on the staff. I should have had to become a G.P., and you know what likelihood there is for a G.P. ever to get out of the common rut. But Abraham fell out, and I got the job. That gave me my opportunity."

"I dare say that's true."

"It was just luck. I suppose there was some kink in Abraham. Poor devil, he's gone to the dogs altogether. He's got some twopenny-halfpenny job in the medical at Alexandria—sanitary officer or something like that. I'm told he lives with an ugly old Greek woman and has half a dozen scrofulous kids. The fact is, I suppose, that it's not enough to have brains. The thing that counts is character. Abraham hadn't got character."

Character? I should have thought it needed a good deal of character to throw up a career after half an hour's meditation, because you saw in another way of living a more intense significance. And it required still more character never to regret the sudden step. But I said nothing, and Alec Carmichael proceeded reflectively:

I wondered if Abraham really had made a hash of life. Is to do what you most want, to live under the conditions that please you, in peace with yourself, to make a hash of life; and is it success to be an eminent surgeon with ten thousand a year and a beautiful wife? I suppose it depends on what meaning you attach to life, the claim which you acknowledge to society, and the claim of the individual. But again I held my tongue, for who am I to argue with a knight?

A Day's Pleasure

HAMLIN GARLAND

When Markham came in from shoveling his last wagonload of corn into the crib, he found that his wife had put the children to bed, and was kneading a batch of dough with the dogged action of a tired and sullen woman.

He slipped his soggy boots off his feet, and having laid a piece of wood on top of the stove, put his heels on it comfortably. His chair squeaked as he leaned back on its hinder legs, but he paid no attention: he was used to it, exactly as he was used to his wife's lameness and ceaseless toil.

"That closes up my corn," he said after a silence. "I guess I'll go to town tomorrow to git my horses shod."

"I guess I'll git ready and go along," said his wife, in a sorry attempt to be firm and confident of tone.

"What do you want to go to town fer?" he grumbled.

"What does anybody want to go to town fer?" she burst out, facing him. "I ain't been out o' this house fer six months, while you go an' go!"

"Oh, it ain't six months. You went down that day I got the mower."

"When was that? The tenth of July, and you know it."

"Well, mebbe 'twas. I didn't think it was so long ago. I ain't no objection to your goin', only I'm goin' to take a load of wheat."

"Well, jest leave off a sack, an' that'll balance me an' the baby," she said spiritedly.

"All right," he replied good-naturedly, seeing she was roused.

"Only that wheat ought to be put up tonight if you're goin'. You won't have any time to hold sacks for me in the morning with them young ones to get off to school."

"Well, let's go do it then," she said, sullenly resolute.

"I hate to go out again; but I s'pose we'd better."

He yawned dismally and began pulling his boots on again, stamping his swollen feet into them with grunts of pain. She put on his coat and one of the boy's caps, and they went out to the granary. The night was cold and clear.

"Don't look so much like snow as it did last night," said Sam. "It may turn warm."

Laying out the sacks in the light of the lantern, they sorted out those which were whole, and Sam climbed into the bin with a tin pail in his hand, and the work began.

He was a sturdy fellow, and he worked desperately fast; the shining tin pail dived deep into the cold wheat and dragged heavily on the woman's tired hands as it came to the mouth of the sack, and she trembled with fatigue, but held on and dragged the sacks away when filled, and brought others, till at last Sam climbed out, puffing and wheezing, to tie them up.

"I guess I'll load 'em in the morning," he said, "You needn't wait fer me. I'll tie 'em up alone."

"Oh, I don't mind," she replied, feeling a little touched by his unexpectedly easy acquiescence to her request. When they went back to the house the moon had risen.

It had scarcely set when they were wakened by the crowing roosters. The man rolled stiffly out of bed and began rattling at the stove in the dark, cold kitchen.

His wife arose lamer and stiffer than usual, and began twisting her thin hair into a knot.

Sam did not stop to wash, but went out to the barn. The woman, however, hastily soused her face into the hard limestone water at the sink, and put the kettle on. Then she called the children. She knew it was early, and they would need several callings. She pushed breakfast forward, running over in her mind the things she must have: two spools of thread, six yards of cotton flannel, a can of coffee, and mittens for Kitty. These she must have—there were oceans of things she needed.

The children soon came scudding down out of the darkness of the upstairs to dress tumultuously at the kitchen stove. They humped and shivered, holding up their bare feet from the cold floor, like chickens in new fallen snow. They were irritable, and snarled and snapped and struck like cats and dogs. Mrs. Markham stood it for a while with mere commands to "hush up," but at last her patience gave out, and she charged down on the struggling mob and cuffed them right and left.

They ate their breakfast by lamplight, and when Sam went back to his work around the barnyard it was scarcely dawn. The children, left alone with their mother, began to tease her to let them go to town also.

"No, sir—nobody goes but baby. Your father's goin' to take a load of wheat."

She was weak with the worry of it all when she had sent the older children away to school and the kitchen work was finished. She went into the cold bedroom off the little sitting room and put on her best dress. It had never been a good fit, and now she was getting so thin it hung in wrinkled folds everywhere about the shoulders and waist. She lay down on the bed a moment to ease that dull pain in her back. She had a moment's distaste for going out at all. The thought of sleep was more alluring. Then the thought of the long, long day, and the sickening sameness of her life swept over her again, and she rose and prepared the baby for the journey.

It was but little after sunrise when Sam drove out into the road and started for Bellepaine. His wife sat perched upon the wheat sacks behind him, holding the baby in her lap, a cotton quilt under her, and a cotton horse blanket over her knees.

Sam was disposed to be very good-natured, and he talked back at her occasionally, though she could only understand him when he turned his face toward her. The baby stared out at the passing fence posts, and wiggled his hands out of his mittens at every opportunity. He was merry at least.

It grew warmer as they went on, and a strong south wind arose. The dust settled upon the woman's shawl and hat. Her hair loosened and blew unkemptly about her face. The road which led across the high, level prairie was quite smooth and dry, but still it jolted her, and the pain in her back increased. She had nothing to lean against, and the weight of the child grew greater till she was forced to place him on the sacks beside her, though she could not loose her hold for a moment.

The town drew in sight—a cluster of small frame houses and stores on the dry prairie beside a railway station. There were no trees yet which could be called shade trees. The pitilessly severe light of the sun flooded everything. A few teams were hitched about, and in the lee of the stores a few men could be seen seated comfortably, their broad hat-rims flopping up and down, their faces brown as leather.

Markham put his wife out at one of the grocery stores, and drove off down toward the elevators to sell his wheat.

The grocer greeted Mrs. Markham in a perfunctorily kind manner, and offered her a chair. She sat for a quarter of an hour almost without moving, leaning against the back of the high chair. At last the child began to get restless and troublesome, and she spent half an hour helping him amuse himself around the nail kegs.

At length she rose and went out on the walk, carrying the baby. She went into the dry-goods store and took a seat on one of the little revolving stools. A woman was buying some woolen goods for a dress. It was worth twenty-seven cents a yard, the clerk said, but he would knock off two cents if she took ten yards. It looked warm, and Mrs. Markham wished she could afford it for Mary.

A pretty young girl came in and laughed and chatted with the clerk, and bought a pair of gloves. She was the daughter of the grocer. Her happiness made the wife and mother sad. When Sam came back she asked him for some money.

"What you want to do with it?" he asked.

"I want to spend it," she said.

She was not to be trifled with, so he gave her a dollar.

"I need a dollar more."

"Well, I've got to go take up that note at the bank."

"Well, the children's got to have some new underclo'es," she said.

He handed her a two-dollar bill and then went out to pay his note.

She bought her cotton flannel and mittens and thread, and then sat leaning against the counter. It was noon, and she was hungry. She went out to the wagon, got the lunch she had brought, and took it into the grocery to eat it—where she could get a drink of water.

The grocer gave the baby a stick of candy and handed the

mother an apple.

"It'll kind o' go down with your doughnuts," he said.

After eating her lunch she got up and went out. She felt ashamed to sit there any longer. She entered another dry-goods store, but when the clerk came toward her saying, "Anything today, Mrs.—?" she answered, "No, I guess not," and turned away with a foolish face.

She walked up and down the street, desolately homeless. She did not know what to do with herself. She knew no one except the grocer. She grew bitter as she saw a couple of ladies pass, holding their demi-trains in the latest city fashion.

Another woman went by pushing a baby carriage, in which sat a child just about as big as her own. It was bouncing itself up and down on the long slender springs, and laughing and shouting. Its clean round face glowed from its pretty fringed hood. She looked down at the dusty clothes and grimy face of her own little one, and walked on savagely.

She went into the drug store where the soda fountain was, but it made her thirsty to sit there and she went out on the street again. She heard Sam laugh, and saw him in a group of men over by the blacksmith shop. He was having a good time and had forgotten her.

Her back ached so intolerably that she concluded to go in and rest once more in the grocer's chair. The baby was growing cross and fretful. She bought five cents' worth of candy to take home to the children, and gave the baby a little piece to keep him quiet. She wished Sam would come. It must be getting late. The grocer said it was not much after one. Time seemed terribly long. She felt that she ought to do something while she was in town. She ran over her purchases—yes, that was all she had planned to buy. She fell to figuring on the things she needed. It was terrible. It ran away up into twenty or thirty dollars at the least. Sam, as well as she, needed underwear for the cold winter, but they would have to wear the old ones, even if they were thin and ragged. She would not need a dress, she thought bitterly, because she never went anywhere. She rose and went out on the street once more, and wandered up and down, looking at everything in the hope of enjoying something.

A man from Boone Creek backed a load of apples up to the sidewalk, and as he stood waiting for the grocer he noticed Mrs. Markham and the baby, and gave the baby an apple. This was a pleasure. He had such a hearty way about him. He on his part saw an ordinary farmer's wife with dusty dress, unkempt hair, and tired face. He did not know exactly why she appealed to him, but he tried to cheer her up.

The grocer was familiar with these bedraggled and weary wives. He was accustomed to see them sit for hours in his big wooden chair, and nurse tired and fretful children. Their forlorn, aimless, pathetic wandering up and down the street was a daily occurrence, and had never possessed any special meaning to him.

In a cottage around the corner from the grocery store two men and a woman were finishing a dainty luncheon. The woman was dressed in cool, white garments, and she seemed to make the day one of perfect comfort.

The home of the Honorable Mr. Hall was by no means the costliest in the town, but his wife made it the most attractive. He was one of the leading lawyers of the county, and a man of culture and progressive views. He was entertaining a friend who had lectured the night before in the Congregational church.

They were by no means in serious discussion. The talk was rather frivolous. Hall had the ability to caricature men with a few gestures and attitudes, and was giving to his Eastern friend some descriptions of the old-fashioned Western lawyers he had met in his practice. He was very amusing, and his guest laughed heartily for a time.

But suddenly Hall became aware that Otis was not listening. Then he perceived that he was peering out of the window at some one, and that on his face a look of bitter sadness was falling.

Hall stopped. "What do you see, Otis?"

Otis replied, "I see a forlorn, weary woman."

Mrs. Hall rose and went to the window. Mrs. Markham was walking by the house, her baby in her arms. Savage anger and weeping were in her eyes and on her lips, and there was hopeless tragedy in her shambling walk and weak back.

In the silence Otis went on: "I saw the poor, dejected creature twice this morning. I couldn't forget her."

"Who is she?" asked Mrs. Hall, very softly.

"Her name is Markham; she's Sam Markham's wife," said Hall.

The young wife led the way into the sitting room, and the men took seats and lit their cigars. Hall was meditating on a diversion when Otis resumed suddenly:

"That women came to town today to get a change, to have a little play-spell, and she's wandering around like a starved and weary cat. I wonder if there is a woman in this town with sympathy enough and courage enough to go out and help that woman? The saloon-keepers, the politicians, and the grocers make it pleasant for the man—so pleasant that he forgets his wife. But the wife is left without a word."

Mrs. Hall's fork dropped, and on her pretty face was a look of pain. The man's harsh words had wounded her—and wakened her. She took up her hat and hurried out on the walk. The men looked at each other, and then the husband said:

"It's going to be a little sultry for the men around these diggings. Suppose we go out for a walk."

Delia felt a hand on her arm as she stood at the corner.

"You look tired, Mrs. Markham; won't you come in a little while? I'm Mrs. Hall."

Mrs. Markham turned with a scowl on her face and a biting word on her tongue, but something in the sweet, round little face of the other woman silenced her, and her brow smoothed out.

"Thank you kindly, but it's most time to go home. I'm looking fer Mr. Markham now."

"Oh, come in a little while, the baby is cross and tired out; please do."

Mrs. Markham yielded to the friendly voice, and together the two women reached the gate just as two men hurriedly turned the other corner.

"Let me relieve you," said Mrs. Hall.

The mother hesitated, "He's so dusty."

"Oh, that won't matter. Oh, what a big fellow he is! I haven't any of my own," said Mrs. Hall, and a look passed between the two women, and Delia was her willing guest from that moment.

They went into the little sitting room, so dainty and lovely to the farmer's wife, and as she sank into an easy chair she was faint and drowsy with the pleasure of it. She submitted to being bushed. She gave the baby into the hands of the Swedish girl, who washed its face and hands and sang it to sleep, while its mother sipped some tea. Through it all she lay back in her easychair, not speaking a word, while the ache passed out of her back, and her hot, swollen head ceased to throb.

But she saw everything—the piano, the pictures, the curtains, the wallpaper, the little tea stand. They were almost as grateful to her as the food and fragrant tea. Such housekeeping as this she had never seen. Her mother had worn her kitchen floor thin as paper in keeping a speckless house, and she had been in houses that were larger and costlier, but something of the charm of her hostess was in the arrangement of vases, chairs, or pictures. It was tasteful.

Mrs. Hall did not ask about her affairs. She talked to her about the sturdy little baby, and about the things upon which Delia's eyes dwelt. If she seemed interested in a vase she was told what it was and where it was made. She was shown all the pictures and books. Mrs. Hall seemed to read her visitor's mind. She kept as far from the farm and her guest's affairs as possible, and at last she opened the piano and sang to her—not slow-moving hymns, but catchy love songs full of sentiment—and then played some simple melodies, knowing that Mrs. Markham's eyes were studying her hands, her rings, and the flash of her fingers on the keys—seeing more than she heard—and through it all Mrs. Hall conveyed the impression that she, too, was having a good time.

The rattle of the wagon outside roused them both. Sam was at the gate for her. Mrs. Markham rose hastily. "Oh, it's almost sundown!" she gasped in astonishment as she looked out of the window.

"Oh, that won't kill anybody," replied her hostess. "Don't hurry. Carrie, take the baby out to the wagon for Mrs. Markham while I help her with her things."

"Oh, I've had such a good time," Mrs. Markham said as they went down the little walk.

"So have I," replied Mrs. Hall. She took the baby a moment

as her guest climbed in. "Oh, you big, fat fellow!" she cried as he gave him a squeeze. "You must bring your wife in oftener, Mr. Markham," she said, as she handed the baby up.

Sam was staring with amazement.

"Thank you, I will," he finally managed to say.

"Good night," said Mrs. Markham.

"Good night, dear," called Mrs. Hall, and the wagon began to rattle off.

The tenderness and sympathy in her voice brought the tears to Delia's eyes—not hot nor bitter tears, but tears that cooled her eyes and cleared her mind.

The wind had gone down, and the red sunlight fell mistily over the world of corn and stubble. The crickets were still chirping and the feeding cattle were drifting toward the farmyards. The day had been made beautiful by human sympathy.

Mother of Comptons

MILTON S. MAYER

Honorary degrees are supposed to signify achievement. Sometimes they signify the achievement of the recipient in science or the arts. Sometimes they signify (though seldom openly) the achievement of the college in wheedling a new dormitory from a prosperous citizen. A few years ago Ohio's historic Western College for Women bestowed a doctorate of laws for neither of these reasons. The recipient, whose bearing denied that a woman is old at 74, was awarded the LL.D. "for outstanding achieve-ment as wife and mother of Comptons."

Having received this recognition of her contribution to American life, the new doctor hurried back to the welcome obscurity of an old frame house on a quiet street in the little college town of Wooster, Ohio. Otelia Compton doesn't want to be famous, and she isn't. Four of the men to whom she is wife or mother occupy a whole page in "Who's Who in America," but the larger achievement of a middle western farm girl is unrecorded.

Those who extol the virtues of heredity may examine with profit the Compton family tree. For the ancestors of the first family of science were common farmers and unskilled mechanics, and the only one of them associated with scholarship was a carpenter who helped nail together the early buildings of Princeton. True, Elias Compton and Otelia Augspurger both taught school to help support the farms on which they were born, but so had farmers' sons and daughters before them. And there was no reason to predict that the union of two country school teachers would produce a page in "Who's Who."

Nor could the naked eye distinguish in the simple Compton household a special genius in the practice of domestic wisdom. Still, the genius must have been there, for of the four children born to Elias and Otelia Compton, Karl, the oldest, is a distinguished physicist, now [1938] president of the great institution, Massachusetts Institute of Technology; Mary, the second, is principal of a missionary school in India and wife of the president of Allahabad Christian College there; Wilson, the third, is a noted economist and general manager of the U.S. Lumber Manufacturers' Association; and Arthur, the "baby," is, at forty-five, one of the immortals of science—winner of the Nobel Prize in Physics.

How did it happen? The answer of the four famous Comptons is a nod in the direction of the old frame house in Wooster. In the "sitting room" at Wooster I found Elias Compton, beloved elder statesman of Ohio education, who died last May at the age of forty-five years. But I did not find the answer to my question in the sitting room, for the father of Comptons explained that he was just one of Otelia's boys and referred me to the kitchen, where the mother of Comptons, at the age of 79, manages the home that gave America one of its most eminent families.

It is characteristic of Otelia Compton's philosophy that she should deny she has a recipe for rearing great men and women. She will admit that her children are "worthy," but what the world calls great has no significance for her. When she heard the news that Arthur had won the world's highest award in science, her first words were: "I hope it doesn't turn his head." In the second place, she refuses to be an expert and has never before permitted herself to be quoted on the secret of successful motherhood. The only way I was able to pry her loose from her reticence was to get her into a good hot argument.

That was the weakness in her armor. For this doctor of laws actually has a set of laws, and to challenge them is to ask for a fight. There is nothing unfair about picking an intellectual quarrel with this woman of eighty years; she is more than equal to it. She reads as ardently as any scholar. She thinks as nimbly as any logician. And her youthfulness is such that when, one day this summer, she forgot to take off her wrist-watch before her daily swim, her children kidded her about getting old.

She may disclaim her expertness, but her record is against her. There are her four children, with their total of thirty-one college and university degrees and their memberships in thirty-nine learned societies. They didn't just grow. In addition, there are the hundreds of boys and girls whose lives Otelia Compton shaped during the thirty-five years she spent directing the Presbyterian Church's two homes for the children of its missionaries. Cornered in her kitchen, the mother of Comptons simply had to admit that she knows something about motherhood.

Her recipe is so old it is new, so orthodox it is radical, so commonplace that we have forgotten it and it startles us. "We used the Bible and common sense," she told me. I replied that "the Bible and common sense" was inadequate, since the Bible has been misused by knaves and common sense is an attribute every fool imputes to himself. She looked at me hard through her gold-rimmed glasses. Slowly her gray eyes softened. She smiled, and told me to go ahead and tell her what I wanted to know.

The first thing I wanted to know was, "How important is heredity?"

"That depends on what you mean by heredity."

"Well," I said, "let's say 'blue blood.'"

That was easy for the descendant of Alsatian farmers. "If you mean the principle that worth is handed down in the blood-stream, I don't think much of it. Lincoln's 'heredity' was nil. The dissolute kings of history and the worthless sons and daughters of some of the 'best families' in our own country are pretty good evidence that blood can run awfully thin. No, I've seen too many extraordinary men and women who were children of the common people to put much stock in heredity.

"Don't misunderstand me. There is a kind of heredity that is all-important. That is the heredity of training. A child isn't likely to learn good habits from his parents unless they learned them from their parents. Call that environment if you want to, or environmental heredity. But it is something that is handed down from generation to generation."

In connection with misplaced faith in heredity, the mother of Comptons has something to say about the notion held by so many today that their children "haven't got a chance." It is a notion, she feels, which is becoming entirely too prevalent. "This denial of the American reality of equal opportunity," she said, "suggests a return to the medieval psychology of a permanently degraded peasant class. Once parents have decided their children haven't got a chance, they are not likely to give them one. And the children, in turn, become imbued with this paralyzing attitude of futility."

Certainly the four young Comptons would never have had a chance had their parents regarded economic hardship as insuperable. Elias Compton was earning $1,400 a year as a professor while his wife was rearing four children and maintaining the status a college community demands of faculty households. The children all had their chores, but household duties were never allowed to interfere either with school work or the recreation that develops healthy bodies and sportsmanship.

If heredity is not the answer, I wanted to know, what is?

"The home."

"That's a pleasant platitude," she replied sharply. "The tragedy of American life is that the home is becoming incidental at a time when it is needed as never before. Parents forget that neither school nor the world can reform the finished product of a bad home. They forget that their children are their first responsibility.

"Today servants are hired to take care of children. In my day, no matter how many servants a mother could afford she took care of her children herself.

"The first thing parents must remember is that their children are not likely to be any better than they are themselves. Mothers and fathers who wrangle and dissipate need not be surprised if their observant young ones take after them. The next thing is that parents must obtain the confidence of their children in all things if they do not want to make strangers of them and have them go to the boy on the street corner for advice. Number three is that parents must explain to the child every action that affects him, even at the early age when parents believe, usually mistakenly, that the child is incapable of understanding. Only thus will the child mature with the sense that justice has been done him and the impulse to be just himself.

"The mother or father who laughs at a youngster's 'foolish' ideas forgets that those ideas are not foolish to the child. When Arthur was 10 years old he wrote an essay taking issue with other experts on why some elephants were three-toed and others five-toed. He brought it to me to read, and I had a hard time keeping from laughing. But I knew how seriously he took his ideas, so I sat down and worked on them with him."

Arthur—he of the Nobel Prize—was listening to our conversation, and here he interrupted. "Mother," he said, "if you had laughed at me that day, I think you would have killed my interest in research."

"The reason why many parents laugh at their children," Mrs. Compton went on, "is that they have no interest in the child's affairs. The mother and father can not retain their influence over their children if their children's life is foreign to them. And it isn't enough to encourage the child; the parents must participate in his interests. They must work with him, and if his interest turns out to be something about which they know nothing it is their business to educate themselves. If they don't, the child will discover their ignorance and lose his respect for them."

When Karl Compton was twelve, he wrote a "book" on Indian fighting. Mary was absorbed with linguistics. Wilson's devotion to the spitball made him the greatest college pitcher in the Middle West. Arthur, too, was a notable athlete, but his first love was astronomy. The combination of Indian fighting, linguistics, the spitball and astronomy might have driven a lesser woman to despair, but Otelia Compton mastered them all as she did their other diversions. For instance, the summer the Compton family caught 1,120 pounds of fish, mother landed her share.

All the toys the young Comptons had could have been bought for a few dollars, but when the four of them were still under ten years of age their mother packed them up, together with a father who had almost died from pneumonia, and took them to the wilds of northern Michigan, where mother and children hewed a clearing and pitched a tent. There these urban-bred children learned simplicity and hard work. There they found that the things which tempt children need not be forbidden them when those things are fishing and woodcraft and the stars. There they imbibed, as the mother of Comptons would have every city child imbibe, of the unity and mystery of nature.

The boys all worked summers and in college, gaining priceless experience; and they all had their own bank accounts, "not," their mother explains, "because we wanted them to glorify money but because we wanted them to learn that money, however much or however little, should never be wasted." Would she put hard work first in her lexicon? Mrs. Compton thought a moment, "Yes," she said, "I would. That is, hard work in the right direction. The child who has acquired the habits of work of the right kind does not need anything else."

And what is the "right kind" of hard work?

"The kind of work that is good in itself."

I baited the trap. "What's wrong with working for money?"

The mother of Comptons exploded. "Everything! To teach a child that money-making for the sake of money is worthy is to teach him that the only thing worth while is what the world calls success. That kind of success has nothing to do either with usefulness or happiness. The man who lives for money never gets enough, and he thinks that that is why he isn't happy. The real reason is that he has had the wrong goal of life set before him."

What did she mean by parents and schools "teaching" that money is happiness?

"I mean all this talk about 'careers' and 'practical' training. Children should be taught how to think, and thinking isn't always practical. Children should be encouraged to develop their natural bents and not forced to choose a 'career.' When our children were still in high school, a friend of ours asked Elias what they were going to be. His answer was, 'I haven't asked them.' Some of our neighbors thought we were silly when we bought Arthur a little telescope and let him sit up all night studying the stars. It wasn't 'practical.'" Yet it was his "impractical" love of the stars that brought him the Nobel Prize and something over $20,000; and in order that he might pursue his cosmic ray research, the University of Chicago equipped a $100,000 laboratory for him.

I thought of the four Comptons and the success that has resulted from their early training, and I wondered if "impractical" parents weren't perhaps the most practical. What could be more tangible than the satisfaction and the honors that have come to them because of their far-flung labors?

Where Love Is, God Is

LEO TOLSTOY

In a little town in Russia there lived a cobbler, Martin Avedvitch by name. He had a tiny room in a basement, the one window of which looked out on to the street. Through it one could see only the feet of those who passed by, but Martin recognized the people by their boots. He had lived long in the place and had many acquaintances. There was hardly a pair of boots in the neighborhood that had not been once or twice through his hands, so he often saw his own handiwork through the window. Some he had re-soled, some patched, some stitched up, and to some he had even put fresh uppers. He had plenty to do, for he worked well, used good material, did not charge too much, and could be relied on. If he could do a job by the day required, he undertook it; if not, he told the truth and gave no false promises. So he was well known and never short of work.

Martin had always been a good man, but in his old age he began to think more about his soul and to draw nearer to God.

From that time Martin's whole life changed. His life became

peaceful and joyful. He sat down to his task in the morning, and when he had finished his day's work, he took the lamp down from the wall, stood it on the table, fetched his Bible from the shelf, opened it, and sat down to read. The more he read the better he understood, and the clearer and happier he felt in his mind.

It happened once that Martin sat up late, absorbed in his book. He was reading Luke's Gospel, and in the sixth chapter he came upon the verses: "To him that smiteth thee on the one cheek offer also the other; and from him that taketh away thy cloak withhold not thy coat also. Give to every man that asketh thee; and of him that taketh away thy goods ask them not again. And as ye would that men should do to you, do ye also to them likewise."

He thought about this, and was about to go to bed, but was loath to leave his book. So he went on reading the seventh chapter about the centurion, the widow's son, and the answer to John's disciple—and he came to the part where a rich Pharisee invited the Lord to his house. And he read how the woman who was a sinner anointed his feet and washed them with her tears, and how he justified her. Coming to the forty-fourth verse, he read: "And turning to the woman, he said unto Simon, 'Seest thou this woman? I entered into thine house, thou gavest me no water for my feet, but she hath wetted my feet with her tears, and wiped them with her hair. Thou gavest me no kiss, but she, since the time I came in, hath not ceased to kiss my feet. My head with oil thou didst not anoint, but she hath anointed my feet with ointment.'"

He read these verses and thought: "He gave no water for his feet, gave no kiss, his head with oil he did not anoint." And Martin took off his spectacles once more, laid them on his book, and pondered.

"He must have been like me, that Pharisee. He too thought only of himself—how to get a cup of tea, how to keep warm and comfortable, never a thought of his guest. He took care of himself, but for his guest he cared nothing at all. Yet who was the guest? The Lord himself! If he came to me, should I behave like that?"

Then Martin laid his head upon both his arms and, before he was aware of it, he fell asleep.

"Martin!" He suddenly heard a voice, as if someone had breathed the word above his ear.

He started from his sleep. "Who's there?" he asked.

He turned around and looked at the door; no one was there. He called again. Then he heard quite distinctly: "Martin, Martin! Look out into the street tomorrow, for I shall come."

Martin roused himself, rose from his chair and rubbed his eyes, but did not know whether he had heard these words in a dream or awake. He put out the lamp and lay down to sleep.

The next morning he rose before daylight, and after saying his prayers, he lit the fire and prepared his cabbage soup and buckwheat porridge. Then he lit the samovar, put on his apron, and sat down by the window to his work. He looked out into the street more than he worked, and whenever anyone passed in unfamiliar boots, he would stoop and look up, so as to see not only the feet but the face of the passerby as well.

A house-porter passed in new felt boots, then a water-carrier. Presently an old soldier of Nicholas's reign came near the window, spade in hand. Martin knew him by his boots, which were shabby old felt once, galoshed with leather. The old man was called Stepanitch. A neighboring tradesman kept him in his house for charity, and his duty was to help the house-porter. He began to clear away the snow before Martin's window. Martin glanced at him and then went on with his work.

After he had made a dozen stitches he felt drawn to look out of the window again. He saw that Stepanitch had leaned his spade against the wall, and was either resting himself or trying to get warm. The man was old and broken down, and had evidently not enough strength even to clear away the snow.

"What if I called him in and gave him some tea?" thought Martin. "The samovar is just on the boil."

He stuck his awl in its place, and rose, and putting the samovar on the table, made tea. Then he tapped the window with his fingers. Stepanitch turned and came to the window. Martin beckoned to him to come in, and went himself to open the door.

"Come in," he said, "and warm yourself a bit. I'm sure you

must be cold."

"May God bless you!" Stepanitch answered. "My bones do ache, to be sure." He came in, first shaking off the snow, and lest he should leave marks on the floor, he began wiping his feet. But as he did so he tottered and nearly fell.

"Don't trouble to wipe your feet," said Martin. "I'll wipe up the floor—it's all in the day's work. Come, friend, sit down and have some tea."

Filling two tumblers, he passed one to his visitor, and pouring his own tea out into the saucer, began to blow on it.

Stepanitch emptied his glass and, turning it upside down, put the remains of his piece of sugar on the top. He began to express his thanks, but it was plain that he would be glad of some more.

"Have another glass," said Martin, refilling the visitor's tumbler and his own. But while he drank his tea, Martin kept looking out into the street.

"Are you expecting anyone?" asked the visitor.

"Am I expecting anyone? Well, now, I'm ashamed to tell you. It isn't that I really expect anyone, but I heard something last night which I can't get out of my mind. Whether it was a vision, or only a fancy, I can't tell. You see, friend, last night I was reading the Gospel, about Christ the Lord, how he suffered, and how he walked on earth. You have heard tell of it, I dare say."

"I have heard tell of it," answered Stepanitch. "But I'm an ignorant man and not able to read."

"Well, you see, I was reading how he walked on earth. I came to that part, you know, where he went to a Pharisee who did not receive him well. Well, friend, as I read about it, I thought how that man did not receive Christ the Lord with proper honor. Suppose such a thing could happen to such a man as myself, I thought, what would I not do to receive him! But that man gave him no reception at all. Well, friend, as I was thinking of this, I began to doze, and as I dozed I heard someone call me by name. I got up, and thought I heard someone whispering, 'Expect me. I will come tomorrow.' This happened twice over. And to tell you the truth, it sank so into my mind that, though I am ashamed of it myself, I keep on expecting him, the dear Lord!"

Stepanitch shook his head in silence, finished his tumbler, and laid it on its side, but Martin stood it up again and refilled it for him.

"Thank you, Martin Avedvitch," he said. "You have given me food and comfort both for soul and body."

"You're very welcome. Come again another time. I am glad to have a guest," said Martin.

Stepanitch went away, and Martin poured out the last of the tea and drank it up. Then he put away the tea things and sat down to his work, stitching the back seam of a boot. And as he stitched he kept looking out of the window, and thinking about what he had read in the Bible. And his head was full of Christ's sayings.

Two soldiers went by: one in Government boots, the other in boots of his own; then the master of a neighboring house, in shining galoshes; then a baker carrying a basket. All these passed on.

Then a woman came up in worsted stockings and peasant-made shoes. She passed the window, but stopped by the wall. Martin glanced up at her through the window, and saw that she was a stranger, poorly dressed, and with a baby in her arms. She stopped by the wall with her back to the wind, trying to wrap the baby up though she had hardly anything to wrap it in. The woman had only summer clothes on, and even they were shabby and worn. Through the window Martin heard the baby crying, and the woman trying to soothe it, but unable to do so. Martin rose, and going out of the door and up the steps he called to her. "My dear, I say, my dear!"

The woman heard, and turned around. "Why do you stand out there with the baby in the cold? Come inside. You can wrap him up better in a warm place. Come this way!"

The woman was surprised to see an old man in an apron, with spectacles on his nose, calling to her, but she followed him in.

They went down the steps, entered the little room, and the old man led her to the bed.

"There, sit down, my dear, near the stove. Warm yourself, and feed the baby."

"Haven't any milk. I have eaten nothing myself since early morning," said the woman, but still she took the baby to her breast.

Martin shook his head. He brought out a basin and some bread. Then he opened the oven door and poured some cabbage soup into the basin. He took out the porridge pot also, but the porridge was not yet ready, so he spread a cloth on the table and served only the soup and bread.

"Sit down and eat, my dear, and I'll mind the baby. Why, bless me, I've had children of my own; I know how to manage them."

The woman crossed herself, and sitting down at the table began to eat, while Martin put the baby on the bed and sat down by it.

Martin sighed. "Haven't you any warmer clothing?" he asked. "How could I get warm clothing?" said she. "Why, I pawned my last shawl for sixpence yesterday." Then the woman came and took the child, and Martin got up.

He went and looked among some things that were hanging on the wall, and brought back an old cloak.

"Here," he said, "though it's a worn-out old thing, it will do to wrap him up in."

The woman looked at the cloak, then at the old man, and taking it, burst into tears. Martin turned away, and groping under the bed brought out a small trunk. He fumbled about in it, and again sat down opposite the woman. And the woman said, "The Lord bless you, friend."

"Take this for Christ's sake," said Martin, and gave her sixpence to get her shawl out of pawn. The woman crossed herself, and Martin did the same, and then he saw her out.

After a while Martin saw an apple-woman stop just in front of his window. On her back she had a sack full of chips, which she was taking home. No doubt she had gathered them at someplace where building was going on.

The sack evidently hurt her, and she wanted to shift it from one shoulder to the other, so she put it down on the footpath and, placing her basket on a post, began to shake down the chips in the sack.

While she was doing this, a boy in a tattered cap ran up, snatched an apple out of the basket, and tried to slip away. But the old woman noticed it, and turning, caught the boy by his sleeve. He began to struggle, trying to free himself, but the old woman held on with both hands, knocked his cap off his head, and seized hold of his hair. The boy screamed and the old woman scolded.

Martin dropped his awl, not waiting to stick it in its place, and rushed out of the door. Stumbling up the steps and dropping his spectacles in his hurry, he ran out into the street. The old woman was pulling the boy's hair and scolding him, and threatening to take him to the police. The lad was struggling and protesting, saying, "I did not take it. What are you beating me for? Let me go!"

Martin separated them. He took the boy by the hand and said, "Let him go, Granny. Forgive him for Christ's sake."

"I'll pay him out, so that he won't forget it for a year! I'll take the rascal to the police!"

Martin began entreating the old woman. "Let him go, Granny. He won't do it again."

The old woman let go, and the boy wished to run away, but Martin stopped him.

"Ask the Granny's forgiveness!" said he. "And don't do it another time. I saw you take the apple."

The boy began to cry and to beg pardon.

"That's right. And now here's an apple for you," and Martin took an apple from the basket and gave it to the boy, saying, "I will pay you, Granny."

"You will spoil them that way, the young rascals," said the old woman. "He ought to be whipped so that he should remember it for a week."

"Oh, Granny, Granny," said Martin, "that's our way—but it's not God's way. If he should be whipped for stealing an apple, what should be done to us for our sins?"

The old woman was silent.

And Martin told her the parable of the lord who forgave his servant a large debt, and how the servant went out and seized his debtor by the throat. The old woman listened to it all, and the boy, too, stood by and listened.

"God bids us forgive," said Martin, "or else we shall not be forgiven. Forgive everyone, and a thoughtless youngster most of all."

The old woman wagged her head and sighed.

"It's true enough," said she, "but they are getting terribly spoiled."

"Then we old ones must show them better ways," Martin replied.

"That's just what I say," said the old woman. "I have had seven of them myself, and only one daughter is left." And the old woman began to tell how and where she was living with her daughter, and how many grandchildren she had.

"There, now," she said, "I have but little strength left, yet I work hard for the sake of my grandchildren; and nice children they are too. No one comes out to meet me but the children. Little Annie, now, won't leave me for anyone. It's 'Grandmother, dear grandmother, darling grandmother.'" And the old woman completely softened at the thought.

"Of course, it was only his childishness," said she, referring to the boy.

As the old woman was about to hoist her sack on her back, the lad sprang forward to her, saying, "Let me carry it for you, Granny. I'm going that way."

The old woman nodded her head, and put the sack on the boy's back, and they went down the street together, the old woman quite forgetting to ask Martin to pay for the apple. Martin stood and watched them as they went along talking to each other.

When they were out of sight, Martin went back to the house. Having found his spectacles unbroken on the steps, he picked up his awl and sat down again to work. He worked a little, but soon could not see to pass the bristle through the holes in the leather, and presently, he noticed the lamplighter passing on his way to light the street lamps.

"Seems it's time to light up," thought he. So he trimmed his lamp, hung it up, and sat down again to work. He finished off one boot and, turning it about, examined it. It was all right. Then he gathered his tools together, swept up the cuttings, put away the bristles and the thread and the awls, and, taking down the lamp, placed it on the table.

Then he took the Gospels from the shelf. He meant to open them at the place he had marked the day before with a bit of morocco, but the book opened at another place.

As Martin opened it, his yesterday's dream came back to his mind, and no sooner had he thought of it than he seemed to hear footsteps, as though someone were moving behind him. Martin turned round, and it seemed to him as if people were standing in the dark corner, but he could not make out who they were.

And a voice whispered in his ear: "Martin, Martin, don't you know me?"

"Who is it?" muttered Martin. "It is I," said the voice.

And out of the dark corner stepped Stepanitch, who smiled and vanishing like a cloud was seen no more.

"It is I," said the voice again. And out of the darkness stepped the woman with the baby in her arms, and the woman smiled and the baby laughed, and they too vanished.

"It is I," said the voice once more. And the old woman and the boy with the apple stepped out and both smiled, and then they too vanished.

And Martin's soul grew glad. He crossed himself, put on his spectacles, and began reading the Gospel just where it had opened. And at the top of the page he read: "I was hungry, and ye gave me meat. I was thirsty, and ye gave me drink. I was a stranger, and ye took me in."

And at the bottom of the page he read: "In as much as ye did it unto one of these my brethren, even these least, ye did it unto me."

And Martin understood that his dream had come true, and that the Savior had really come to him that day, and he had welcomed him.

Notes

1. A.W. Tozer, *Man: The Dwelling Place of God* (Camp Hill, Penn.: Christian Publications, 1966, 1977). www.christianpublications.com Used by permission.

2. Taken from *My Utmost for His Highest* by Oswald Chambers. Copyright © 1935 by Dodd Mead & Co., renewed © 1963 by the Oswald Chambers Publications Assn. Ltd., and is used by permission of Discovery House Publishers, Box 3566, Grand Rapids, MI 49501. All rights reserved.

3. Watchman Nee, The Normal Christian Life, Chapter 4. "The Path of Progress: Reckoning," Copyright © Angus Kinnear, 1961. Used by permission of Kingsway Publications, Eastbourne, England.

Index

Also available from Honor Books

Mothers of Influence:
Inspiring Stories of Women Who Made a Difference in Their Children and Their World

God's Treasury of Virtues:
An Inspirational Collections of Stories, Quotes, Hymns, Scriptures, and Poems

Graduation Moments:
Wisdom and Inspiration from the Best Commencement Speakers Ever

Treasury of Love and Romance:
A Classic Collection of Stories, Quotes, Ballads, Verses, and Poems

If you have enjoyed this book, or if it has impacted your life, we would like to hear from you.

Please contact us at:
Honor Books
An Imprint of Cook Communications Ministries
4050 Lee Vance View
Colorado Springs, CO 80918
www.cookministries.com